Practical AI for Cybersecurity

Practical AI for Cybersecurity

Ravi Das

CRC Press
Taylor & Francis Group
Boca Raton London New York

CRC Press is an imprint of the
Taylor & Francis Group, an **informa** business

AN AUERBACH BOOK

First edition published 2021
by CRC Press
6000 Broken Sound Parkway NW, Suite 300
Boca Raton, FL 33487-2742

and by CRC Press
2 Park Square, Milton Park, Abingdon, Oxon OX14 4RN

Library of Congress Cataloging-in-Publication Data
A catalog record has been requested for this book

ISBN: 978-0-367-70859-7 (hbk)
ISBN: 978-0-367-43715-2 (pbk)
ISBN: 978-1-003-00523-0 (ebk)

This is book is dedicated to my Lord and Savior, Jesus Christ. It is also dedicated in loving memory to Dr. Gopal Das and Mrs. Kunda Das, and also to my family in Australia, Mr. Kunal Hinduja and his wife, Mrs. Sony Hinduja, and their two wonderful children.

Contents

Acknowledgments

I would like to thank John Wyzalek, my editor, for his help and guidance in the preparation of this book. Many special thanks go out to Randy Groves, for his contributions to this book as well.

Notes on Contributors

Ravi Das is a business development specialist for The AST Cybersecurity Group, Inc., a leading Cybersecurity content firm located in the Greater Chicago area. Ravi holds a Master of Science degree in Agribusiness Economics (Thesis in International Trade), and a Master of Business Administration degree in Management Information Systems.

He has authored six books, with two more upcoming ones on COVID-19 and its impacts on Cybersecurity and Cybersecurity Risk and its impact on Cybersecurity Insurance Policies.

Randy Groves is the SVP of Engineering at SparkCognition, the world-leader in industrial artificial intelligence solutions. Before SparkCognition, he was the chief technology officer of Teradici Corporation where he was responsible for defining the overall technology strategy and technology partnerships which led to the adoption of the industry-leading, PCoIP protocol for VMware Virtual Desktop Infrastructure, Amazon WorkSpaces Desktop-as-a-Service, and Teradici Cloud Access Software. He also served as vice president of Engineering at LifeSize Communications, Inc. (acquired by Logitech) and led the team that released the first high-definition video conferencing products into the mainstream video conferencing market. Before joining LifeSize, he served as the chief technology officer of Dell Inc.'s product group responsible for the architecture and technology direction for all of Dell's product offerings. Prior to that, he served as general manager of Dell Enterprise Systems Group and led the worldwide development and marketing of Dell's server, storage and systems management software products. He also spent 21 years with IBM where he held many product development roles for IBM's Intel- and RISC-based servers, as well as roles in corporate strategy and RISC microprocessor development and architecture.

He is the author of numerous technical papers, disclosures and patents, as well as the recipient of several corporate and industry awards. He holds a Masters of Electrical Engineering from the University of Texas at Austin, a Masters in Management of Technology from Massachusetts Institute of Technology, and a Bachelors of Electrical Engineering and Business from Kansas State University.

Chapter 1

Artificial Intelligence

There is no doubt that the world today is a lot different than it was fifty or even thirty years ago, from the standpoint of technology. Just imagine when we landed the first man on the moon back in 1969. All of the computers that were used at NASA were all mainframe computers, developed primarily by IBM and other related computer companies. These computers were very large and massive—in fact, they could even occupy an entire room.

Even the computers that were used on the Saturn V rocket and in the Command and Lunar Excursion Modules were also of the mainframe type. Back then, even having just 5 MB of RAM memory in a small computer was a big thing. By today's standards, the iPhone is lightyears away from this kind of computing technology, and in just this one device, we perhaps have enough computing power to send the same Saturn V rocket to the moon and back at least 100 times.

But just think about it, all that was needed back then was just this size of memory. The concepts of the Cloud, virtualization, etc. were barely even heard of. The computers that were designed back then, for example, had just one specific purpose: to process the input and output instructions (also known as "I/O") so that the spacecrafts could have a safe journey to the moon, land on it, and return safely back to Earth once again.

Because of these limited needs (though considered to be rather gargantuan at the time), all that was needed was just that small amount of memory. But by today's standards, given all of the applications that we have today, we need at least 1,000 times that much just to run the simplest of Cloud-based applications. But also back then, there was one concept that was not even heard of quite yet: Cybersecurity.

In fact, even the term of "Cyber" was not even heard of. Most of the security issues back then revolved around physical security. Take, for example, NASA again. The main concern was only letting the authorized and legitimate employees into Mission Control. Who would have thought that back then there was even the slightest possibility that a Cyberattacker could literally take over control of the computers and even potentially steer the Saturn V rocket away from its planned trajectory.

But today, given all of the recent advancements in technology, this doomsday scenario is now a reality. For example, a Cyberattacker could very easily gain access to the electronic gadgetry that is associated with a modern jetliner, automobile, or even ship. By getting access to this from a covert backdoor, the Cyberattacker could potentially take over the controls of any these modes of vessels and literally take it to a destination that it was not intended to.

So as a result, the concept of Cybersecurity has now come front and center, especially given the crisis that the world has been in with the Coronavirus, or COVID-19. But when we think of this term, really, what does it mean exactly? When one thinks of it, many thoughts and images come to mind. For instance, the thoughts of servers, workstations, and wireless devices (which include those of notebooks, tablets, and Smartphones such as that of the Android- and iOS devices) come into view.

Also, one may even think of the Internet and all of the hundreds of thousands of miles of cabling that have been deployed so that we can access the websites of our choice in just a mere second or so. But keep in mind that this just one aspect of Cybersecurity. Another critical aspect that often gets forgotten about is that of the physical security that is involved. As described previously with our NASA example, this involves primarily protecting the physical premises of a business or corporation. This includes protecting both the exterior and interior premises. For instance, this could not only be gaining primary access to premises itself, but also the interior sections as well, such as the server rooms and places where the confidential corporate information and data are held at. It is very important to keep in mind that all of this, both physical and digital, is at grave risk from being attacked.

No one individual or business entity is free from this, all parties are at risk from being hit by a Cyberattack. The key thing is how to mitigate that risk from spreading even further once you have discovered that you indeed have become a victim. So, now that we have addressed what the scope of Cybersecurity really is, how is it specifically defined?

It can be defined as follows:

> Also referred to as information security, cybersecurity refers to the practice of ensuring the integrity, confidentiality, and availability (ICA) of information. Cybersecurity is comprised of an evolving set of tools, risk management approaches, technologies, training, and best practices designed to protect networks, devices, programs, and data from attacks or unauthorized access.
>
> **(Forcepoint, n.d.)**

Granted that this a very broad definition of it, in an effort to narrow it down some more, Cybersecurity involves the following components:

- Network security (protecting the entire network and subnets of a business);
- Application security (protecting mission critical applications, especially those that are Web-based);
- Endpoint security (protecting the origination and destination points of a network connection);
- Data security (protecting the mission critical datasets, especially those that relate to the Personal Identifiable Information (PII))
- Identity management (making sure that only legitimate individuals can gain logical and/or physical access);
- Database and infrastructure security (protecting those servers that house the PII);
- Cloud security (protecting the Infrastructure as a Service (IaaS), Software as a Service (SaaS), and the Platform as a Service (PaaS) components of a Cloud-based platform);
- Mobile security (protecting all aspects of wireless devices and Smartphones, both from the hardware and operating system and mobile standpoints);
- Disaster recovery/business continuity planning (coming up with the appropriate plans so that a business can bring mission critical applications up to operational level and so that they can keep continuing that in the wake of a security breach);
- End-user education (keeping both employees and individuals trained as to how they can mitigate the risk of becoming the net victim).

Now that we have explored the importance, definition, and the components of Cybersecurity, it is now important to take a look at the evolution of it, which is illustrated in the next section.

The Chronological Evolution of Cybersecurity

Just as much as technology has quickly evolved and developed, so too has the world of Cybersecurity. As mentioned, about 50 years, during the height of the Apollo space program, the term "Cyber" probably was barely even conceived of. But in today's times, and especially in this decade, that particular term now is almost a part of our everyday lives.

In this section, we now provide an outline of just how Cybersecurity actually evolved.

The Morris Worm (1988):

*This was created by Robert Morris, a grad student at Cornell.

*It brought down 10% of the 70,000 computers that were connected to the Internet on a worldwide basis.

*It caused at least $96 Million in total damages.

*This actually served as the prototype for the Distributed Denial of Service (DDoS) attacks that we see today.

The Melissa Virus (March 1999):

*This was named after a Florida based stripper, and it infected .DOC files which were transmitted to the address books in Microsoft Outlook.

*This virus caused Microsoft, Lockheed Martin, and Intel to shut down the entire operations for a substantial period of time.

*This caused $80 Million in damages, and infected well over 1,000,000 computers on a global basis.

*The inventor of the virus, David L. Smith, spent some 20 months in prison.

The United States Department The United Statespartment of Defnse (DoD) (August 1999):

*Jonathan James, a 15 year old hacker, broke into the IT/Network Infrastructure at the Defense Threat Reduction Agency.

*He was the first juvenile to be to be a converted a major Cybercrime.

*NASA had to close down their entire base of operations for at least three weeks.

*Not only were passwords stolen, but this Cyberattacker also stole software applications worth at least $1.7 Million which supported the International Space Station.

Mafiaboy (February 2002):

*Another juvenile hacker, Michael Calce (aka "Mafiaboy"), launched a special threat variant known as "Project Rivolta".

*This was a series of Denial of Service (DoS) attacks that brought down the websites of major United States corporations.

*Examples of this include Yahoo, eBay, CNN, E-Trade, and Amazon based servers.

*This prompted the White House to have their first ever Cybersecurity summit.

*The financial damage exceeded well over $1.2 Billion.

Target (November 2013):

*This was deemed to be one of the largest retail Cyberattacks in recent history, and it hit right during the 2013 Holiday Season.

*Because of this Cyberattacks, the net profits of Target dropped as much as 46%.

*Over 40 Million credit card numbers were stolen.

*The malware installed into the Point of Sale (PoS) terminals at all of the Target stores.

*This was sold on the Dark Web for a huge profit.

*This served as the model for subsequent retail based Cyberattacks.

Sony Pictures (November 2014):

*The Social Security and credit card numbers were leaked to the public.

*Confidential payroll information and data were also released.

*This Cyberattack prompted the Co Chair of Sony pictures, Amy Pascal, to step down from her position.

Anthem (January 2015):

*This was deemed to be the largest Cyberattack to hit a major health organization.

*The Personal Identifiable Information (PII) of over 80,000,000 members were stolen which included Social Security numbers, Email addresses, and employment information.

The First Ransomworm (2017):

*The Wanna Cry was deemed to be the first of the Ransomware threat variants, and it targeted computers which ran the Windows OS.

*The only way that the victim could get their computer to work again is if they paid a ransom to the Cyberattacker, in the form of a Virtual Currency. One such example of this is the Bitcoin.

*In just one day, the Wanna Cry threat variant infected well over 230,000 computers in over 50 countries.

*A newer version of the threat variant was the "NotPetya". This infected well over 12,500 computers on a global basis. The impacted industries included energy firms, banks, and government agencies.

The Largest Credit Card Cyberattack (2017):

*The credit card agency, known as Equifax, total failed to install the latest software patches and upgrades to their Apache Struts Server.

*The Cyberattackers were able to gain access over 210,000 consumer credit cards, which impacted over 143 Million Americans.

Facebook, MyHeritage, Mariott Hotels, and British Airways (2018):

*Facebook was hit with a major Cyberattack with the analytics firm Cambridge Analytica. The Personal Identifiable Information (PII) that was stolen resulted in impacting over 87 Million users.

*With MyHeritage, over 92 Million users were impacted. Luckily, no credit card or banking information was stolen, DNA tests, or passwords.

*With Marriott Hotels, over 500 Million users were impacted. Although this breach occurred in 2018, it the underlying Malware was actually deployed in 2014, and was handed down a whopping $123 Million fine.

*With British Airways, over 500,000 credit card transactions were affected. The stolen Personal Identifiable Information (PII) included names, Email addresses, telephone numbers, addresses, and credit card numbers. The company faced a gargantuan $230 Million fine as imposed by the GDPR, or 1.5% of its total revenue.

The Singapore Health Sector (2019):

*The Singapore's Health Sciences Authority (HSA) outsourced some of their functionality to a third party vendor known as the Secur Solutions Group. The Personal Identifiable Information (PII) of 808,000 donors were revealed online, and items that were hijacked include the names, ID card numbers, gender, dates of the last three donations, and in some instances, blood type, height, and weight of the donors.

*Singapore's Ministry of Health's National Public Health Unit was impacted when the HIV status of 14,200 people were revealed online.

So as you can see, this is a chronological timeline of all of the major Cybersecurity events that have led us up to the point where we are today. Even in the world of Cybersecurity, there have also been major technological advancements that have been made in order to thwart the Cyberattacker and to keep up with the ever-changing dynamics of the Cyber Threat Landscape.

One such area in this regard is known as "Artificial Intelligence," or "AI" for short. This is further reviewed in the next section, and is the primary focal point of this entire book.

An Introduction to Artificial Intelligence

The concept of Artificial Intelligence is not a new one; rather it goes back a long time—even to the 1960s. While there were some applications for it being developed at the time, it has not really picked up the huge momentum that it has now until recently, especially as it relates to Cybersecurity. In fact, interest in AI did not even pique in this industry until late 2019. As of now, along with the other techno jargon that is out there, AI is amongst one of the biggest buzzwords today.

But it is not just in Cybersecurity in and of itself that AI is getting all of the interest in. There are many others as well, especially as it relates to the manufacturing and supply chain as well as even the logistics industries. You may be wondering at this point, just what is so special about Artificial Intelligence? Well, the key thing is that this is a field that can help bring task automation to a much more optimal and efficient level than any human ever could.

For example, in the aforementioned industries (except for Cybersecurity), various robotic processes can be developed from AI tools in order to speed up certain processes. This includes doing those repetitive tasks in the automobile production line, or even in the warehouses of the supply chain and logistics industries. This is an area known as "Robotic Process Automation," or "RPA" for short, and will be examined in more detail later in this book.

But as it relates to Cybersecurity, one of the main areas where Artificial Intelligence is playing a key role is in task automation, as just discussed. For example, both Penetration Testing and Threat Hunting are very time consuming, laborious, and mentally grueling tasks. There are a lot of smaller steps in both of these processes that have to take place, and once again, many of them are repetitive. This is where the tools of AI can come into play.

As a result, the team members on both the Penetration Testing and Threat Hunting sides are thus freed up to focus on much more important tasks, which include finding both the hidden and unhidden holes and weaknesses in their client's IT and Network Infrastructure and providing the appropriate courses of action that need to be taken in order to cover up these gaps and weaknesses.

Another great area in Cybersecurity where Artificial Intelligence tools are being used is that of filtering for false positives. For example, the IT security teams of many businesses and corporations, large or small, are being totally flooded with warnings and alerts as a result of the many security tools they make use of, especially when it comes to Firewalls, Network Intrusion Devices, and Routers. At the present time, they have to manually filter through each one so that they can be triaged appropriately.

But because of the time it takes to this, many of the real alerts and warnings that come through often remain unnoticed, thus increasing that business entities' Cyberrisk by at least 1,000 times. But by using the tools as they relate to Artificial Intelligence, all of these so-called false positive are filtered out, thus leaving only the real and legitimate ones that have to be examined and triaged. As a result of this, the IT security teams can react to these particular threats in a much quicker fashion, and most importantly, maintain that proactive mindset in order to thwart off these threat variants.

It should also be noted that many businesses and corporations are now starting to realize that having too many security tools to beef up their respective lines of defenses is not good at all—in fact, it only increases the attack surface for the Cyberattacker. So now, many of these business entities are starting to see the value of implementing various risk analysis tools to see where all of these security technologies can be strategically placed.

So rather than taking the mindset that more is better, it is now shifting that quality of deployment is much more crucial and important. So rather than deploying ten Firewalls, it is far more strategic to deploy perhaps just three where they are needed the most. Also, by taking this kind of mindset, the business or corporation will achieve a far greater Return On Investment (ROI), which means that the CIO and/ or CISO, will be in a much better position to get more for their security budgets.

But, you may even be asking at this point, just what exactly is Artificial Intelligence? A formal definition of it is here:

> Artificial intelligence (AI) makes it possible for machines to learn from experience, adjust to new inputs and perform human-like tasks. Most

AI examples that you hear about today—from chess-playing computers to self-driving cars—rely heavily on deep learning and natural language processing. Using these technologies, computers can be trained to accomplish specific tasks by processing large amounts of data and recognizing patterns in the data.

(SAS(a), n.d.)

As one can see from the above definition, the main objective of Artificial Intelligence is to have the ability to learn and project into the future by learning from past behaviors. In this regard, past behavior typically means making use of large datasets that arise and stem from various data feeds that are fed into the various AI technologies that are being used, learning those trends, and having the ability to perform the task at hand and look into the future.

In this regard, another great boon that Artificial Intelligence brings to Cybersecurity is its ability to predict into the future, and assess what the newer potential threat variants could look like as well. We will be examining the sheer importance of data for Artificial Intelligence later in this chapter. But at this point, it is very important to keep in mind that Artificial Intelligence is just the main field, and there are many other sub-fields that fall just below it; the most common ones are as follows:

- Machine Learning;
- Neural Networks;
- Computer Vision.

A formal definition for each of the above is provided in the next section.

The Sub-Fields of Artificial Intelligence

Machine Learning

The first sub-field we will take a brief look into is what is known as "Machine Learning," or "ML" for short. A specific definition for it is as follows:

Machine-learning algorithms use statistics to find patterns in massive amounts of data. And data, here, encompasses a lot of things—numbers, words, images, clicks, what have you. If it can be digitally stored, it can be fed into a machine-learning algorithm.

Machine learning is the process that powers many of the services we use today—recommendation systems like those on Netflix, YouTube, and Spotify; search engines like Google and Baidu; social-media feeds like Facebook and Twitter; voice assistants like Siri and Alexa. The list goes on.

(MIT Technology Review, n.d.)

The sub-field of Machine Learning is actually very expansive, diverse, and even quite complex. But to put it in very broad terms, as the above definition describes, it uses much more statistical techniques rather than mathematical ones in order to mine and comb through huge amounts of datasets to find those unhidden trends. This can then be fed into the Artificial Intelligence tool, for example, to predict the future Cyber Threat Landscape. But it also has many other applications, as exemplified by the second part of the definition.

Neural Networks

The second sub-field next to be examined is that of the Neural Networks (also known as NNs). A specific definition for it is as follows:

> Neural networks are a set of algorithms, modeled loosely after the human brain, that are designed to recognize patterns. They interpret sensory data through a kind of machine perception, labeling or clustering raw input. The patterns they recognize are numerical, contained in vectors, into which all real-world data, be it images, sound, text or time series, must be translated.
>
> Neural networks help us cluster and classify. You can think of them as a clustering and classification layer on top of the data you store and manage. They help to group unlabeled data according to similarities among the example inputs, and they classify data when they have a labeled dataset to train on. (Neural networks can also extract features that are fed to other algorithms for clustering and classification; so you can think of deep neural networks as components of larger machine-learning applications involving algorithms for reinforcement learning, classification and regression).
>
> **(Pathmind, n.d.)**

In a manner similar to that of Machine Learning, Neural Networks are also designed to look at massive datasets in order to recognize both hidden and unhidden patterns. But the primary difference here is that with Neural Networks, they are designed to try to replicate the thinking process of the human brain, by closely examining neuronic activity of the brains.

The human brain consists of hundreds of millions of neurons, and it is hypothesized that they are the catalyst for the rationale behind the decision-making process that occurs within the brain. Another key difference is that Neural Networks can also be used to organize, filter through, and present those datasets that are the most relevant. Back to our previous example of filtering for false positives, this is a prime example of where Neural Networks are used. The concept of the neuron will be later examined in more detail in this book.

Computer Vision

The third sub-field to be examined is that of Computer Vision. A specific definition for it is as follows:

> Computer vision is the process of using machines to understand and ana-lyze imagery (both photos and videos). While these types of algorithms have been around in various forms since the 1960s, recent advances in Machine Learning, as well as leaps forward in data storage, com-puting capabilities, and cheap high-quality input devices have driven major improvements in how well our software can explore this kind of content.
>
> Computer vision is the broad parent name for any computations involving visual content—that means images, videos, icons, and any-thing else with pixels involved. But within this parent idea, there are a few specific tasks that are core building blocks:
>
> In object classification, you train a model on a dataset of specific objects, and the model classifies new objects as belonging to one or more of your training categories.
>
> For object identification, your model will recognize a specific instance of an object—for example, parsing two faces in an image and tagging one as Tom Cruise and one as Katie Holmes.
>
> **(Algorithmia, n.d.)**

As one can see from the above definition, Computer Vision is used primarily for examining visual types and kinds of datasets, analyzing them, and feeding them into the Artificial Intelligence tool. As it relates to Cybersecurity, this is most pertinent when it comes to protecting the physical assets of a business or a corporation, not so much the digital ones.

For example, CCTV cameras are used to help confirm the identity of those individuals (like the employees) that are either trying to gain primary entrance access or secondary access inside the business or corporation. Facial Recognition is very often used here, to track and filter for any sort of malicious or anomalous behavior.

This is often viewed as a second tier to the CCTV camera, but in addition to this, a Computer Vision tool can also be deployed with the Facial Recognition technology in order to provide for much more robust samples to be collected, and to be able to react to a security breach in a much quicker and more efficient manner.

These are the main areas that will covered in this book, and an overview is provided into the next section.

A Brief Overview of This Book

As mentioned, and as one can even tell from the title of this first chapter, the entire premise for this book is built around Artificial Intelligence. True, there are many books out there that are focused on this subject matter, but many of them are very theoretical in nature, and perhaps do not offer as much value to businesses and corporations. Rather, they are geared much more for the academic and government markets, such as for research scientists, university professors, defense contractors, and the like. Not many of them have actually dealt with the application side of Artificial Intelligence. This is what separates this book, quite literally, from the others that are out there.

For example, there is a theoretical component to each chapter. This is necessary because in order to understand the application side of Artificial Intelligence, one needs to have a firm background in the theory of it as well. This actually encompasses about the first half of each chapter. But the second half of each chapter will be devoted to the practical side of Artificial Intelligence—which is namely the applications.

What is unique about this book is that the applications that are discussed and reviewed are those that have actually been or are in the process of being deployed in various types and kinds of Cybersecurity applications. These are written by the Subject Matter Experts (SMEs) themselves. To the best of our knowledge, there is no other book that does this. As you go through these chapters, you will find it very enriching to read about these particular applications.

Finally, the very last chapter is devoted to the best practices for Artificial Intelligence. In other words, not only have we covered both the theoretical and application angles, but we also offer a Best Practices guide (or, if you will, a checklist) in both the creation and deployment of Artificial Intelligence applications.

Therefore, this book can really serve two types of audiences: 1) the academic and government sector as discussed before; and, 2) the CIO's, CISO's, IT Security Managers, and even the Project Managers that want to deploy Artificial Intelligence applications.

Therefore, the structure and layout of this book is as follows:

Chapter 1: An Introduction to Artificial Intelligence
Chapter 2: An Overview into Machine Learning
Chapter 3: The Importance of Neural Networks
Chapter 4: Examining a Growing Sub-Specialty of Artificial Intelligence—
   Computer Vision
Chapter 5: Final Conclusions

To start the theoretical component of this first chapter, we first provide an examination into Artificial Intelligence and how it came to be such an important component of Cybersecurity today. Secondly, this is followed by looking at the importance of data—after all, as it has been reviewed earlier, this is the fuel that literally drives the engines of the Artificial Intelligence applications.

The History of Artificial Intelligence

To start off with, probably the first well-known figure in the field of Artificial Intelligence is that of Alan Turing. He was a deemed to be a pioneer in the field of computer science, and in fact, is very often referred to as the "Father of Artificial Intelligence." Way back in 1936, he wrote a major scientific paper entitled "On Computable Numbers." In this famous piece of work, he actually lays down the concepts for what a computer is and what its primary purposes are to be. It is important to keep in mind that computers hardly existed during this time frame, and in fact the first "breed" of computers would not come out until much later in the next decade.

The basic idea for what his idea of a computer is was based upon the premise that it has to be intelligent in some sort of manner or fashion. But at this point in time, it was very difficult to come up with an actual measure of what "intelligence" really is. Thus, he came up with the concept that became ultimately known as the "Turing Test."

In this scenario, there is a game with three players involved in it. One of the participants is a human being, and another is a computer. The third participant is the moderator, or evaluator. In this scenario, the moderator would ask a series of open-ended questions to both of them, in an effort to determine which of the two participants is actually a human being. If a determination could not be made by asking these open-ended questions, it would then be assumed that the computer would be deemed as the "intelligent" entity.

The Turing Test is illustrated below:

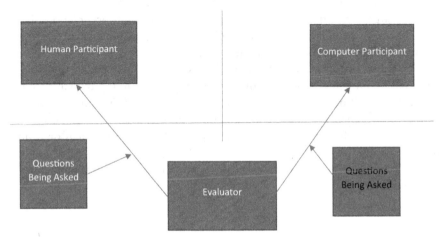

In this model, it is not necessary that the computer actually has to know something specific, possess a large amount of information and data, or even be correct in its answers to the open-ended questions. But rather, there should be solid indications that the computer can, in some way or another, communicate with the Evaluator on its own, without any human intervention involved.

Believe it or not, the Turing Test has certainly stood the test of time by still being difficult to crack, even in this new decade of the twenty-first century. For example, there have been many contests and competitions to see if computers can hold up to the Turing Test, and some of the most noteworthy ones have been the "Loebner Prize" and the "Turing Test Competition."

A turning point occurred in a competition held in May 2018 at the I/O Conference that was held by Google. The CEO of Google at the time, Sundar Pichai, gave a direct demonstration of one of their newest applications, which was known as the "Google Assistant." This application was used to place a direct call to a local hairdresser in order to establish and set up an appointment. Somebody did pick up on the other line, but this scenario failed the Turing Test.

Why? Because the question that was asked was a closed-ended one and not an open-ended question.

The next major breakthrough to come after the Turing Test came with the creation and development of a scientific paper entitled the "Minds, Brains, and Programs." This was written by the scientist known as John Searle, and was published in 1980. In this research paper, he formulated another model which closely paralleled the Turing Test, which became known as the "Chinese Room Argument."

Here is the basic premise of it: Suppose there is an individual named "Tracey." She does not know or even comprehend or understand the Chinese language, but she has two manuals in hand with step-by-step rules in how to interpret and communicate in the Chinese language. Just outside of this room is another individual by the name of "Suzanne." Suzanne does understand the Chinese language, and gives help to Tracey by helping her to decipher the many characters.

After a period of time, Suzanne will then get a reasonably accurate translation from Tracey. As such, it is plausible to think that Suzanne assumes safely that Tracey can understand, to varying degrees, the Chinese language.

The thrust of this argument is that if Tracey cannot understand the Chinese language by implementing the proper rules for understanding the Chinese language despite all of the aids she has (the two manuals and Suzanne, just outside of the room), then a computer cannot learn by this methodology because no single computer has any more knowledge than what any other man or woman possesses.

The paper John Searle wrote also laid down the two types of Artificial Intelligence that could potentially exist:

1) <u>Strong AI</u>:

   This is when a computer truly understands and is fully cognizant of what is transpiring around it. This could even involve the computer having some sort of emotions and creativity attached to it. This area of Artificial Intelligence is also technically known as "Artificial General Intelligence," or "AGI" for short.

2) <u>Weak AI</u>:

   This is a form of Artificial Intelligence that is deemed to be not so strong in nature, and is given a very narrowed focus or set of tasks to work on. The prime examples of this include the Virtual Personal Assistants (VPAs) of Siri and Alexa (which belong to Apple and Amazon, respectively).

The advent of the Turing Test also led to the other development of some other noteworthy models, which include the following:

1) <u>The Kurzweil-Kapor Test</u>:

   This model was created and developed by Ray Kurzweil and Mitch Kapor. In this test, it was required that a computer carry out some sort of conversation with three judges. If two of them deem the conversational to be "intelligent" in nature, then the computer was also deemed to be intelligent. But the exact permutations of what actually defines an "intelligent conversation" were not given.

2) <u>The Coffee Test</u>:

   This model was developed by Apple founder Steve Wozniak, and it is actually quite simple: A robot must be able to enter into a home, find where the kitchen is located, and make/brew a cup of coffee.

The next major breakthrough to come in Artificial Intelligence was a scientific paper entitled "A Logical Calculus of the Ideas Immanent In Nervous Activity." This was co-written by Warren McCulloch and Walter Pitts in 1943. The major premise of this paper was that logical deductions could explain the powers of the human brain. This paper was subsequently published in the *Bulletin of Mathematical Biophysics*.

In this paper, McCulloch and Pitts posit that the core functions of the human brain, in particular the neurons and synaptic activities that take place, can be fully explained by mathematical logical operators (for example, And, Not, etc.).

In an effort to build off this, Norbert Wiener created and published a scientific book entitled *Cybernetics: Or Control and Communication In The Animal and The Machine*. This particular book covered such topics as Newtonian Mechanics, Statistics, Thermodynamics, etc. This book introduced a new type of theory called "Chaos Theory." He also equated the human brain to that of a computer in that it should be able to play a game of chess, and it should be able to learn at even higher planes as it played more games.

The next major period of time for Artificial Intelligence was known as "The Origin Story," and it is reviewed in more detail in the next sub section.

The Origin Story

The next major stepping stone in the world of Artificial Intelligence came when an individual by the name of John McCarthy organized and hosted a ten-week research program at Dartmouth University. It was entitled the "Study of Artificial Intelligence," and this was the first time that this term had ever been used. The exact nature of this project is as follows:

> The study is to proceed on the basis of the conjecture that every aspect of learning or any other feature of intelligence can in principle be so precisely described that a machine can be made to simulate it. An attempt will thus be made to find out how to make machines use language, form abstractions and concepts, solve kinds of problems now reserved for humans, and improve themselves. We think that a significant advance can be made in one or more of these problems if a carefully selected group of scientists work on it together for a summer.
>
> **(Taulli, 2019)**

During this particular retreat, a computer program called the "Logic Theorist" was demonstrated, which was actually developed at the RAND Corporation. The focus of this was to solve complex mathematical theorems from the publication known as the "Principia Mathematica." In order to create this programming language, an IBM 701 mainframe computer was used, which used primarily machine language for the processing of information and data.

But in order to further optimize the speed of the "Logic Theorist," a new processing language was used, and this became known as the "Information Processing Language," or "IPL" for short. But the IBM 701 mainframe did not have enough memory or processing power for the IPL, so this led to the creation of yet another development: Dynamic Memory Allocation. As a result, the "Logic Theorist" has been deemed to be the first Artificial Intelligence programming language to ever be created.

After this, John McCarthy went onto create other aspects for Artificial Intelligence in the 1950s. Some of these included the following:

- The LISP Programming Language:
  - This made the use of nonnumerical data possible (such as qualitative data points);
  - The development of programming functionalities such as Recursion, Dynamic Typing, and Garbage Collection were created and deployed;

■ Time sharing mainframe computers:
These were created, which was actually the forerunner to the first Internet, called the "APRANET";
■ The Computer Controlled Car:
This was a scientific paper he published that described how a person could literally type directions using a keyboard and a specialized television camera would then help to navigate the vehicle in question. In a way, this was a primitive version of the GPS systems that are available today.

From this point onwards, the era for Artificial Intelligence became known as the "Golden Age for AI," with key developments taking place. This is reviewed in more detail in the next subsection.

The Golden Age for Artificial Intelligence

During this time period, much of the innovation that took place for Artificial Intelligence came from the academic sector. The primary funding source for all AI-based projects came from the Advanced Research Projects Agency, also known as "ARPA" for short. Some of the key developments that took place are as follows:

1) The Symbolic Automatic INTegrator:
Also known as "SAINT," this program was developed by James Slagle, a researcher at MIT, in 1961. This was created to help solve complex calculus problems and equations. Other types of computer programs were created from this, which were known as "SIN" and "MACSYMA," which solved much more advanced mathematical problems with particular usage of linear algebra and differential equations. SAINT was actually deemed to be what became known as the first "Expert System."
2) ANALOGY:
This was yet another computer program that was developed by an MIT professor known as Thomas Evans in 1963. It was specifically designed to solve analogy-based problems that are presented in IQ tests.
3) STUDENT:
This type of computer program was developed by another researcher at MIT, Daniel Bobrow, in 1964. This was the first to use what is known as "Natural Language Processing," and is a topic that will be reviewed in more detail later in this book.
4) ELIZA:
This is also another Artificial Intelligence program which was developed in 1965 by Joseph Weizenbaum, a professor at MIT. This was actually the precursor to the Chatbot, which is in heavy demand today. In this particular application, an end user could type in various questions, and the computer

in turn would provide some sort of response. The application here was for psychology—the program acted much like a virtual psychoanalyst.

5) Computer Vision:

In 1966, an MIT researcher, Marvin Minsky led the way to what is known as Computer Vision, which is a subsequent chapter in this book. He linked a basic camera to a computer and wrote a special program to describe in some detail what it saw. It detected basic visual patterns.

6) Mac Hack:

This was also another Artificial Intelligence program that was developed Richard Greenblatt, another professor at MIT, in 1968.

7) Hearsay I:

This was considered to be one of the most advanced Artificial Intelligence programs during this time. It was developed by Raj Reddy in 1968, and was used to create the first prototype of Speech Recognition Systems.

During this Golden Age Period, there were two major theories of Artificial Intelligence that also came about and they are as follows:

■ The need for symbolic systems: This would make heavy usage of computer logic, such as "If-Then-Else" statements.
■ The need for Artificial Intelligence Systems to behave more like the human brain: This was the first known attempt to map the neurons in the brain and their corresponding activities. This theory was developed by Frank Rosenblatt, but he renamed the neurons as "perceptrons."

Back in 1957, Rosenblatt created the first Artificial Intelligence program to do this, and it was called the "Mark I Perceptron." The computer that ran this particular program was fitted two cameras to differentiate two separate images, whose scale was 20 by 20 pixels. This program would also make use of random statistical weightings to go through this step-by-step, iterative process:

1) Create and insert an input, but come up with an output that was perceptron-based.
2) The input and the output should match, and if they do not, then the following steps should be taken:
   – If the output (the perceptron) was "I" (instead of being 0), the statistical weight for "I" should be decreased.
   – In the reverse of the above, if the output (the perceptron) was "0" (instead of being I), the statistical weight for "I" should be increased by an equal manner.
3) The first two steps should be repeated in a continued, iterative process until "I" = 0, or vice versa.

This program also served as the protégé for Neural Networks (which is also a subsequent chapter in this book), but as successful as it was deemed to be, it had also had its fair share of criticisms. One of the major flaws of it that was pointed out was that it had one layer of processing.

The next major phase to happen in Artificial Intelligence was the development of Expert Systems, which is reviewed in more detail in the next subsection.

The Evolution of Expert Systems

During this era, there were many other events that took place in the field of Artificial Intelligence. One of these was the development of the back propagation technique. This is a technique which is widely used in statistical weights for the inputs that go into a Neural Network system. As mentioned earlier, there is a chapter in this book that is devoted to this topic, both from the theoretical and the application standpoints.

Another key development was the creation of what is known as the "Recurrent Neural Network," or "RNN" for short. This technique permits the connections in the Artificial Intelligence system to move seamlessly through both the input and the output layers. Another key catalyst was the evolution of the Personal Computer and their minicomputer counterparts, which in turn led to the development of what are known as "Expert Systems," which made heavy usage of symbolic logic.

The following diagram illustrates the key components of what is involved in an Expert System:

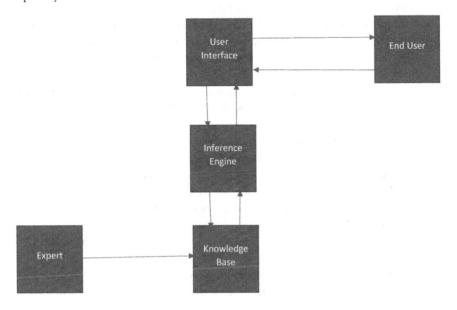

In this regard, one of the best examples of an Expert System was that of the "eXpert CONfigurer," also known as the "XCON" for short. This was developed by John McDermott at the Carnegie Mellon University. The main purpose of this was to further optimize the choice of computer components, and it had about 2,500 rules (both mathematical and statistical) that were incorporated into it. In a way, this was the forerunner to the Virtual Personal Assistants (VPAs) of Siri and Cortana, which allow you to make choices.

The development of the XCON further proliferated the growth of Expert Systems. Another successful implementation of an Expert System was the development of the "Deep Blue" by IBM in 1996. In fact, its most successful application came when it played a game of chess against Grandmaster Garry Kasparov. In this regard, Deep Blue could process well over 200 million positions in just one second.

But despite all of this, there were a number of serious shortcomings with Expert Systems, which are as follows:

- They could not be applied to other applications; in other words, they could only be used for just one primary purpose, and thus, they had a very narrow focus.
- As the Expert Systems became larger, it became much more difficult and complicated to not only manage them but to keep feeding them because these were all mainframe-based technologies. As a result, this led to more errors occurring in the outputs.
- The testing of these Expert Systems proved to be a much more laborious and time-consuming process than first expected.
- Unlike the Artificial Intelligence tools of today, Expert Systems could not learn on their own over a certain period of time. Instead, their core logic models had to be updated manually, which led to much more expense and labor.

Finally, the 1980s saw the evolution of yet another new era in Artificial Intelligence, known as "Deep Learning." It can be specifically defined as follows:

Deep learning is a type of machine learning that trains a computer to perform human-like tasks, such as recognizing speech, identifying images, or making predictions. Instead of organizing data to run through predefined equations, deep learning sets up basic parameters about the data and trains the computer to learn on its own by recognizing patterns using many layers of processing.

(SAS(b), n.d.)

In simpler terms, this kind of system does not need already established mathematical or statistical algorithms in order to learn from the data that is fed into it. All it needs are certain permutations and from there, it can literally learn on its own—and even make projections into the future.

There were also two major developments at this time with regards to Deep Learning:

- In 1980, Kunihiko Fukushima developed an Artificial Intelligence called the "Neocognitron." This was the precursor to the birth of what are known as "Convolutional Neural Networks," or "CNNs" for short. This was based upon the processes that are found in the visual cortex of various kinds of animals.
- In 1982, John Hopfield developed another Artificial Intelligence system called "Hopfield Networks." This laid down the groundwork for what are known as "Recurrent Neural Networks," or "RNNs" for short.

Both CNNs and RNNs will be covered in the chapter on Neural Networks.

The next section of this book will now deal with data and datasets, which are essentially the fuel that drives Artificial Intelligence algorithms and applications of all types and kinds.

The Importance of Data in Artificial Intelligence

So far in this chapter, we have examined in great detail what Artificial Intelligence is and what its subcomponents are, as well as provided a very strong foundation in terms of the theoretical and practical applications of it, which has led to the power-house that it is today in Cybersecurity. In this part of the chapter, we now focus upon the key ingredient that drives the engines of Artificial Intelligence today—the data that is fed into it, and the feeds from where it comes.

We all have obviously have heard of the term "data" before. This is something that has been taught to us ever since we started elementary school. But what really is data? What is the scientific definition for it? It can be defined as follows:

> In computing, data is information that has been translated into a form that is efficient for movement or processing. Relative to today's computers and transmission media, data is information converted into binary digital form.
>
> **(TechTarget, n.d.)**

So, as this can be applied to Artificial Intelligence, the underlying tool will take all of the data that is fed into it (both numerical and non-numerical), convert it into a format that it can understand and process, and from there provide the required output. In a sense, it is just like garbage in/garbage out, but on a much more sophisticated level.

This section will cover the aspect of data and what it means for Artificial Intelligence from the following perspectives:

- The fundamentals of data basics;
- The types of data that are available;
- Big Data;
- Understanding preparation of data;
- Other relevant data concepts that are important to Artificial Intelligence.

The Fundamentals of Data Basics

Let's face it, everywhere we go, we are exposed to data to some degree or another. Given the advent of the Smartphone, digitalization, wireless technology, social media, the Internet of Things (IoT), etc. we are being exposed to it every day in ways that we are not even cognizant of. For example, when we type in a text message or reply to an email, that is actually considered to be data, though more of a qualitative kind. Even videos that you can access on YouTube or podcasts can be considered data as well.

It is important to keep in mind that data does not have to be just the numerical kind. If you think about it, anything that generates content, whether it is written, in the form audio or video, or even visuals, are all considered to be data. But in the word of Information Technology, and even to that of a lesser extent in Artificial Intelligence, data is much more precisely defined, and more often than not symbolically represented, especially when the source code compiles the datasets that it has been given.

In this regard, the data that is most often used by computers are those of the binary digits. It can possess the value of either 0 or 1, and in fact, this is the smallest piece of data that a computer will process. The computers of today can process at least 1,000 times data sizes more than that, primarily because of the large amounts of memory that they have and their very powerful processing capabilities.

In this regard, the binary digit is very often referred to merely as a "Bit." Any data sizes larger than this are referred to as a "Byte." This is illustrated in the table below:

Unit	Value
Megabyte	1,000 Kilobytes
Gigabyte	1,000 Megabytes
Terabyte	1,000 Gigabytes
Petabyte	1,000 Terabytes
Exabyte	1,000 Petabytes
Zettabyte	1,000 Exabytes
Yottabyte	1,000 Zetabytes

The Types of Data that are Available

In general, there are four types of data that can be used by an Artificial Intelligence system. They are as follows:

1) <u>Structured Data</u>:
   These are datasets that have some type or kind of preformatting to them. In other words, the dataset can reside in a fixed field within a record or file from within the database that is being used. Examples of this typically include values such as names, dates, addresses, credit card numbers, stock prices, etc. Probably some of the best examples of structured data are those of Excel files, and data that is stored in an SQL database. Typically, this type of data accounts for only 20 percent of the datasets that are consumed by an Artificial Intelligence application or tool. This is also referred to as "Quantitative Data."

2) <u>Unstructured Data</u>:
   These are the datasets that have no specific, predefined formatting to them. In other words, there is no way that they will fit nicely into an Excel spreadsheet or even an SQL database. In other words, this is all of the data out there that has boundaries that are not clearly defined. It is important to keep in mind that although it may not have the external presence of an organized dataset, it does have some sort of internal organization and/or formatting to it. This is also referred to as "Qualitative Data," and the typical examples of this include the following:

   ■ Text files: Word processing, spreadsheets, presentations, email, logs.
   ■ Email: Email has some internal structure thanks to its metadata, and we sometimes refer to it as semi-structured. However, its message field is unstructured and traditional analytics tools cannot parse it.
   ■ Social Media: Data from Facebook, Twitter, LinkedIn.
   ■ Website: YouTube, Instagram, photo sharing sites.
   ■ Mobile data: Text messages, locations.
   ■ Communications: Chat, IM, phone recordings, collaboration software.
   ■ Media: MP3, digital photos, audio and video files.
   ■ Business applications: MS Office documents, productivity applications (Geeks for Geeks(b), n.d.).

   These kinds of datasets account for about 70 percent of the data that is consumed by an Artificial Intelligence tool.

3) <u>Semi-Structured Data</u>:
   As its name implies, there is no rigid format into how this data is typically organized, but either externally or internally, there is some kind of organization to it. It can be further modified so that it can fit into the columns and fields of a database, but very often, this will require some sort of human intervention in order to make sure that it is processed in a proper way. Some

of the typical examples of these kinds of datasets include the "Extensible Markup Language," also known as "XML" for short. Just like HTML, XML is considered to be a markup language that consists of various rules in order to identify and/or confirm certain elements in a document. Another example of Semi-Structured Data is that of the "JavaScript Object Notation," also known as "JSO" for short. This is a way in which information can be transferred from a Web application to any number of Application Protocol Interfaces (also known as "APIs" for short), and from there, to the server upon which the source code of the web application resides upon. This process can also happen in the reverse process as well. These kinds of datasets account for about 10 percent of the data that is consumed by an Artificial Intelligence tool.

4) <u>Time Series Data</u>:

As its name also implies, these kinds of datasets consist of data points that have some sort of time value attached to them. At times, this can also be referred to as "Journey" data, because during a trip, there are data points that can be access throughout the time from leaving the point of origination to finally arriving at the point of destination. Some typical examples of this include the price range of a certain stock or commodity as it is traded on an intraday period, the first time that a prospect visits the website of a merchant and the various web pages they click on or materials that they download until they log off the website, etc.

Now that we have defined what the four most common datasets are, you may even be wondering at this point, just what are some examples of them? They include the following:

<u>For Structured Datasets</u>:

- SQL Databases;
- Spreadsheets such as Excel;
- OLTP Systems;
- Online forms;
- Sensors such as GPS or RFID tags;
- Network and Web server logs;
- Medical devices (Geeks for Geeks(a), n.d.).

<u>For Unstructured Sets</u>:

- Social media;
- Location & Geo Data;
- Machined Generator & Sensor-based;
- Digital streams;
- Text documents;

- Logs;
  - Transactions
  - Micro-blogging

For Semi-Structured Datasets:

- Emails;
- XML and other markup languages;
- Binary Executables;
- TCP/IP packets;
- Zipped Files;
- Integration of data from different sources;
- Web pages (Oracle, n.d.).

For Time Series Datasets:

- Statista;
- Data-Planet Statistical Datasets;
- Euromonitor Passport;
- OECD Statistics;
- United Nations Statistical Databases;
- World Bank Data;
- U.S. Census Bureau: International Data Base;
- Bloomberg;
- Capital IQ;
- Datastream;
- Global Financial Data;
- International Financial Statistics Online;
- MarketLine Advantage;
- Morningstar Direct.

As it was mentioned earlier, it is the Unstructured Datasets that account for a majority of the datasets that are fed into an Artificial Intelligence application, and there is a beauty about them. They are so powerful that they can take just about any kind or type of dataset that is presented to them, literally digest it into a format it can understand, process it, and provide the output or outputs that are required. In other words, there are no limiting factors with regards to this, and as a result, they can give just about any kind of prediction or answer that is asked of them.

Big Data

As also previously reviewed, the size and the number of datasets are growing at an exponential clip on a daily basis, given all of the technological advancements that are currently taking place. There is a specific term for this, and it is called "Big Data." The technical definition of it is as follows:

> Big data is larger, more complex data sets, especially from new data sources. These data sets are so voluminous that traditional data processing software just can't manage them. But these massive volumes of data can be used to address business problems that wouldn't have been able to be tackled before.
>
> **(Datamation, n.d.)**

In a way, this can also be likened to another concept known as "Data Warehousing."

There are three main characteristics that are associated with "Big Data," and they are as follows:

1) <u>Volume</u>:
   This refers to sheer size and scale of the datasets. Very often, they will be in the form of Unstructured Data. The dataset size can go as high as into the Terabytes.
2) <u>Variety</u>:
   This describes the diversity of all of the datasets that reside in the Big Data. This includes the Structured Data, the Unstructured Data, the Semi-Structured Data, and the Time Series Data. This also describes the sources where all of these datasets come from.
3) <u>Velocity</u>:
   This refers to the rapid speed at which the datasets in the Big Data are actually being created.
4) <u>Value</u>:
   This refers to just how useful the Big Data is. In other words, if it is fed into an Artificial Intelligence system, how close will it come to giving the desired or expected output?
5) <u>Variability</u>:
   This describes how fast the datasets in the Big Data will change over a certain period of time. For example, Structured Data, Time Series Data, and Semi-Structured Data will not change that much, but Unstructured Data will. This is simply due its dynamic nature at hand.
6) <u>Visualization</u>:
   This is how visual aids are used in the datasets that are in the Big Data. For example, these could graphs, dashboards, etc.

Understanding Preparation of Data

As it has been mentioned before, it is data that drives the Artificial Intelligence application to do what it does. In other words, data is like the fuel these applications need to run. Although the applications are quite robust in providing the output that is asked of them, this is still viewed as a "Garbage In and Garbage Out" process. Meaning, the quality of outputs that you are going to get is only going to be as good as the data that is put into the application.

Therefore, you must take great effort to make sure that the datasets that you are feeding into your Artificial Intelligence systems are very robust and that they will meet the needs you are expecting in terms of what you want the desired outputs to be. The first step in this process is known as "Data Understanding":

1) Data Understanding:
   In this regard, you need to carefully assess where the sources of your data and their respective feeds are coming from. Depending upon what your exact circumstances and needs are, they will typically come from the following sources:

   ■ In-House Data:
   As the name implies, these are the data points that are actually coming into your business or corporation. For example, it could be data that originates from your corporate intranet, or even your external website, as customers and prospects download materials from your site or even fill out the contact form. Also, it could be the case that you may have datasets already in your organization that you can use.

   ■ Open Source Data:
   These are the kinds of data that are freely available from the Internet, especially when you are using Google to find various data sources. For example, the Federal Government is a great resource for this, as well as many private enterprises (obviously, you will have to pay for this as a subscription, but initially, they will more than likely offer a free trial at first to test drive their respective datasets. This would be a great opportunity to see if what they are offering will be compatible with your Artificial Intelligence system, and if it will potentially yield the desired outputs. These kinds of datasets will very likely use a specialized Application Protocol Interface (API) in order to download the data. Other than the advantage of being free, another key advantage of using Open Source Data is that it already comes in a formatted manner that can be uploaded and fed into your Artificial Intelligence system.

   ■ Third Party Data:
   These are the kind of datasets that are available exclusively from an outside vendor. Examples of these can be seen in the last subsection of this chapter. The primary advantage of obtaining data from these sources is that you can be guaranteed, to a certain degree, that it has been validated. But the disadvantage of this is that they can be quite expensive, and if you ever need to update your datasets, you will have to go back to the same vendor and pay yet another premium price for it.

According to recent research, about 70 percent of the Artificial Intelligence systems that are in use today make use of In House Data, 20 percent of them use Open Source Data, and the remaining 10 percent comes from outside vendors. In order to fully understand the robustness of the datasets you are about to procure, the following must first be answered:

■ Are the datasets complete for your needs and requirements? Is there any missing data?
■ How was the data originally collected?
■ How was the data initially processed?
■ Have there been any significant changes made to it that you need to be aware of? .
■ Are there any Quality Control (QC) issues with the datasets?

2) The Preparation of the Data:
   This part is often referred to as "Data Cleansing," and it requires the following actions that you must take before you can feed the data into your Artificial Intelligence system:
   ■ Deduplication:
     It is absolutely imperative to make sure that your data does not contain duplicate sets. If this is the case, and it goes unnoticed, it could greatly affect and skew the outputs that are produced.
   ■ Outliers:
     These are the data points that lie to the extremes of the rest of the datasets. Perhaps they could be useful for some purpose, but you need to make sure first that they are needed for your particular application. If not, then they must be removed.
   ■ Consistency:
     In this situation, you must make sure that all of the variables have clear definitions to them, and that you know what they mean. There should be no overlap in these meanings with the other variables.
   ■ Validation Rules:
     This is where you try to find the technical limitations of the datasets that you intend to use. Doing this manually can be very time consuming and laborious, so there many software applications that are available that can help you determine these specific kinds of limitations. Of course, you will first need to decide on and enter in the relevant permutations, and these can be referred to as the "thresholds."
   ■ Binning:
     When you procure your datasets, it may also be the case that you may not need each and every one to feed into your Artificial Intelligence system. As

a result, you should look at each category and decide which ones are the most relevant for the outputs that you are trying to garner.

■ <u>Staleness</u>:
This is probably one of the most important factors to consider. Just how timely and relevant are the datasets that you are using? For an Artificial Intelligence application, it is absolutely crucial that you get data that is updated in real time if your desired output is to predict something in the future.

■ <u>Merging</u>:
It could be the case that two columns in your dataset could contain very similar pieces of information. If this is the case, you may want to consider bringing these two columns together by merging them. By doing so, you are actually using the processing capabilities of your Artificial Intelligence much more efficiently.

■ <u>One Hot Encoding</u>:
To a certain degree, it may be possible to represent qualitative data as quantitative data, once again, depending upon your needs and requirements.

■ <u>Conversions</u>:
This is more of an aspect of formatting the units as to how you want your outputs to look like. For example, if all of your datasets are in a decimal system, but your output calls for the values to be in the metric system, then using this technique will be important.

■ <u>Finding Missing Data</u>:
When you are closely examining your datasets, it could quite often be the case that there may some pieces that are missing. In this regard, there are two types of missing data:

*Randomly missing data: Here, you can calculate a median or even an average as a replacement value. By doing this, it should only skew the output to a negligible degree.
*Sequentially missing data: This is when the data is missing in a successive fashion, in an iterative manner. Taking the median or average will not work because there is too much that is not available in order to form a scientific estimate. You could try to extrapolate the preceding data and the subsequent data to make a hypothesized guess, but this is more of a risky proposition to take. Or you could simply delete those fields in which the sequential data is missing. But in either case, the chances are much greater that the output will much more skewed and not nearly as reliable.

- Correcting Data Misalignments:

  It is important to note that before you merge any fields together in your datasets, that the respective data points "align" with the other datasets that you have. To account and correct for this, consider the following actions that you can take:

  *If possible, try to calculate and ascertain any missing data that you may have in your data sets (as previously reviewed);
  *Find any other missing data in all of the other datasets that you have and intend to use;
  *Try to combine the datasets so that you have columns which can provide for consistent fields;
  *If need be, modify or further enhance the desired outcome that the output produces in order to accommodate for any changes that have been made to correct data misalignment.

Other Relevant Data Concepts that are Important to Artificial Intelligence

Finally, in this subsection we examine some other data concepts that are very pertinent to Artificial Intelligence systems, and are as follows:

1) Diagnostic Analytics:
   This is the careful examination of the datasets to see why a certain trend has happened the way it did. An example of this is discovering any hidden trends which may not have been noticed before. This is very often done in Data Warehousing or Big Data projects.
2) Extraction, Transformation, and Load (ETL):
   This is a specialized type of data integration, and is typically used in, once again, Data Warehousing applications.
3) Feature:
   This is a column of data.
4) Instance:
   This is a row of data.
5) Metadata:
   This the data that is available about the datasets.
6) Online Analytical Processing (OLAP):
   This is a technique which allows you to examine the datasets from types of databases into one harmonized view.
7) Categorical Data:
   This kind of data does not have a numerical value per se, but has a textual meaning that is associated with it.

8) Ordinal Data:
This is a mixture of both Categorical Data and Numerical Data.

9) Predictive Analytics:
This is where the Artificial Intelligence system attempts to make a certain prediction about the future (this is displayed as an output), based upon the datasets that are fed into it.

10) Prescriptive Analytics:
This is where the concepts of Big Data (as previously examined) are used to help make better decisions based upon the output that is yielded.

11) Scalar Variables:
These are the types of variables that hold and consist of only single values.

12) Transactional Data:
These are the kinds of datasets that represent data to actual transactions that have occurred in the course of daily business activities.

So far, we have provided an extensive overview of just how important data and datasets are to an Artificial Intelligence system. The remainder of this book will examine Machine Learning, Neural Networks, and Computer Vision in much greater detail.

Resources

Algorithmia: "Introduction to Computer Vision: What It Is and How It Works;" n.d. <algorithmia.com/blog/introduction-to-computer-vision>

Alpaydin E: Introduction to Machine Learning, 4th Edition, Massachusetts: The MIT Press; 2020.

Datamation: "Structured vs. Unstructured Data;" n.d. <www.datamation.com/big-data/structured-vs-unstructured-data.html>

Forcepoint: "What is Cybersecurity?" n.d. <www.forcepoint.com/cyber-edu/cybersecurity>

Geeks for Geeks(a): "What is Semi-Structured Data?" n.d. <www.geeksforgeeks.org/what-is-semi-structured-data/>

Geeks for Geeks(b): "What is Structured Data?" n.d. <www.geeksforgeeks.org/what-is-structured-data/>

Graph, M: *Machine Learning*, 2019.

MIT Technology Review: "What is Machine Learning?" n.d.

Oracle: "What is Big Data?" n.d. <www.oracle.com/big-data/guide/what-is-big-data.html>

Pathmind: "A Beginner's Guide to Neural Networks and Deep Learning;" n.d. <pathmind.com/wiki/neural-network>

SAS(a): "Artificial Intelligence: What It Is and Why It Matters;" n.d. <www.sas.com/en_us/insights/analytics/what-is-artificial-intelligence.html>

SAS(b): "Deep Learning: What It Is and Why It Matters;" n.d. <www.sas.com/en_us/insights/analytics/deep-learning.html>

Taulli, T: *Artificial Intelligence Basics: A Non-Technical Introduction,* New York: Apress; 2019.

TechTarget. "Data;" n.d. <searchdatamanagement.techtarget.com/definition/data>

Chapter 2

Machine Learning

In our last chapter (Chapter 1), we reviewed what Artificial Intelligence was by providing an overview. Specifically, the following topics were covered:

- An introduction to Cybersecurity;
- The various aspects of Cybersecurity;
- A chronological timeline into the evolution of Cybersecurity;
- An introduction to Artificial Intelligence;
- A definition of Artificial Intelligence;
- The various components of Artificial Intelligence and their technical definitions (this includes the likes of Machine Learning, Computer Vision, and Neural Networks);
- An overview into the book;
- The history of Artificial Intelligence;
- The importance of data and its role with Artificial Intelligence systems and applications;
- The applications of Artificial Intelligence.

In this chapter, we examine the very first subcomponent of Artificial Intelligence, which is that of Machine Learning, also known as "ML" for short. We will do a deep dive first in the theoretical aspects of Machine Learning, and then this will be followed by the various applications, just like in the last chapter. But before we start getting into all of the theoretical aspects of Machine Learning, we will first provide a high level overview of what it is all about.

The High Level Overview

Although Machine Learning has been around for a long time (some estimates have it as long as a couple of decades), there are a number of key applications in which Machine Learning is used. Some examples of these are as follows:

1) <u>Predictive Maintenance</u>:
   This kind of application is typically used in supply chain, manufacturing, distribution, and logistics sectors. For example, this is where the concept of Quality Control comes into key play. In manufacturing, you want to be able to predict how many batches of products that are going to be produced could actually become defective. Obviously, you want this number to be as low as possible. Theoretically, you do not want any type or kind of product to be defective, but in the real world, this is almost impossible to achieve. With Machine Learning, you can set up the different permutations in both the mathematical and statistical algorithms with different permutations as to what is deemed to be a defective product or not.

2) <u>Employee Recruiting</u>:
   There is one common denominator in the recruitment industry, and that is the plethora of resumes that recruiters from all kinds of industries get. Consider some of these statistics:
   - Just recently, Career Builder, one of the most widely used job search portals reported:
     * 2.3 million jobs were posted;
     * 680 unique profiles of job seekers were collected;
     * 310 million resumes were collected;
     * 2.5 million background checks were conducted with the Career Builder platform.

   (SOURCE: 1).

   Just imagine how long it would take a team of recruiters to have to go through all of the above. But with Machine Learning, it can all be done in a matter of minutes, by examining it for certain keywords in order to find the desired candidates. Also, rather than having the recruiter post each and every job entry manually onto Career Builder, the appropriate Machine Learning tool can be used to completely automate this process, thus freeing up the time of the recruiter to interview with the right candidates for the job.

3) <u>Customer Experience</u>:
   In the American society of today, we want to have everything right here and right now, at the snap of a finger. Not only that, but on top of this we also expect to have impeccable customer service delivered at the same time. And when none of this happens, well, we have the luxury to go to a competitor to see if they can do any better. In this regard, many businesses

and corporations have started to make use of Virtual Agents. These are the little chat boxes typically found on the lower right part of your web browser. With this, you can actually communicate with somebody in order to get your questions answered or shopping issues resolved. The nice thing about these is that they are also on demand, on a 24/7/365 basis. However, in order to provide a seamless experience to the customer or prospect, many business entities are now making use of what are known as "Chat Bots." These are a much more sophisticated version of the Virtual Agent because they make use of Machine Learning algorithms. By doing this, the Chat Bot can find much more specific answers to your queries by conducting more "intelligent" searches in the information repositories of the business or corporation. Also, many call centers are making use of Machine Learning as well. In this particular fashion, when a customer calls in, their call history, profile, and entire conversations are pulled up in a matter of seconds for the call center agent, so that they can much easier anticipate your questions and provide you with the best level of service possible.

4) <u>Finance</u>:

In this market segment, there is one thing that all people, especially the traders, want to do, and that is to have the ability to predict the financial markets, as well as what they will do in the future, so that they can hedge their bets and make profitable trades. Although this can be done via a manual process, it can be a very laborious and time-consuming process to achieve. Of course, we all know that the markets can move in a matter of mere seconds with uncertain volatility, as we have seen recently with the Coronavirus. In fact, exactly timing and predicting the financial markets with 100 percent accuracy is an almost impossible feat to accomplish. But this is where the role of Machine Learning can come into play. For example, it can take all of the data that is fed into it, and within a matter of seconds make more accurate predictions as to what the market could potentially do, giving the traders valuable time to make the split-second decisions that are needed to produce quality trades. This is especially useful for what is known as "Intra Day Trading," where the financial traders try to time the market as they are open on a minute-by-minute basis.

The Machine Learning Process

When you are applying Machine Learning to a particular question that you want answered or to predict a certain outcome, it is very important to follow a distinct process in order to accomplish these tasks. In other words, you want to build an effective model that can serve well for other purposes and objectives for a subsequent time down the road. In other words, you want to train this model in a particular fashion, so that it can provide a very high degree of both accuracy and reliability.

This process is depicted below:

Data Order

In this step, you want to make sure that the data is as unorganized and unsorted as possible. Although this sounds quite contrary, if the datasets are by any means sorted or organized in any way shape or form, the Machine Learning Algorithms that are utilized may detect this as a pattern, which you do not want to happen in this particular instance.

Picking the Algorithm

In this phase, you will want to select the appropriate Machine Learning algorithms for your model. This will be heavily examined in this part of the chapter.

Training the Model

The datasets that you have will be fed into the Machine Learning system, in order for it to learn first. In other words, various associations and relationships will be created and examined so that the desired outputs can be formulated. For example, one of the simplest algorithms that can be used in Machine Learning is the Linear Regression one, which is represented mathematically as follows:

$$Y = M*X + B$$

Where:
  M = the slope on a graph;
  B = the Y intercept on the graph.

Model Evaluation

In this step, you will make use of a representative sample of data from the datasets, which are technically known as the "Test Data." By feeding this initially into the Machine Learning system, you can gauge just how accurate your desired outputs will be in a test environment before you release your datasets into the production environment.

Fine Tune the Model

In this last phase, you will adjust the permutations that you have established in the Machine Learning system so that it can reasonably come up with desired outputs that you are looking for.

In the next subsection, we examine the major classifications and types of Machine Learning Algorithms that are commonly used today.

The Machine Learning Algorithm Classifications

There are four major categorizations of the Machine Learning Algorithms, and they are as follows:

1) Supervised Learning:
   These types of algorithms make use of what are known as "labeled data." This simply means that each dataset has a certain label that is associated with them. In this instance, one of the key things to keep in mind is that you need to have a large amount of datasets in order to produce the dataset you are looking for when you are using algorithms based on this category. But if the datasets do not come already labeled, it could be very time-consuming to create and

assign a label for each and every one of them. This is the primary downside of using Machine Learning algorithms from this particular category.

2) <u>Unsupervised Learning</u>:

These kinds of algorithms work with data that is typically not labeled. Because of the time constraints it would take to create and assign the labels for each category (as just previously mentioned), you will have to make use of what are known as "Deep Learning Algorithms" in order to detect any unseen data trends that lie from within all of your datasets. In this regard, one of the most typical approaches that is used in this category is that of "Clustering." With this, you are merely taking all of the unlabeled datasets and using the various algorithms that are available from within this particular category to put these datasets into various groups, which have common denominators or affiliations with them. To help out with this, there are a number of ways to do this, which are the following:

■ <u>The Euclidean Metric</u>:

This is a straight line between two independent datasets.

■ <u>The Cosine Similarity Metric</u>:

In this instance, a trigonometric function known as the "Cosine" is used to measure any given angles between the datasets. The goal here is to find any closeness or similarities between at least two or more independent datasets based upon their geometric orientation.

■ <u>The Manhattan Metric</u>:

This technique involves taking the summation of at least two or more absolute value distances from the datasets that you have.

■ <u>The Association</u>:

The basic thrust here is that if a specific instance occurs in one of your datasets, then it will also likely occur in the datasets that have some sort of relationship with the initial dataset that has been used.

■ <u>The Anomaly Detection</u>:

With this methodology, you are statistically identifying those outliers or other anomalous patterns that may exist within your datasets. This technique has found great usage in Cybersecurity, especially when it relates to filtering out for false positives from the log files that are collected from the Firewalls, Network Intrusion Devices, and Routers, as well as any behavior that may be deemed suspicious or malicious in nature.

■ <u>The Autoencoders</u>:

With this particular technique, the datasets that you have on hand will be formatted and put into a compressed type of format, and from that, it will be reconstructed once again. The idea behind this is to detect and find any sort of new patterns or unhidden trends that may exist from within your datasets.

3) The Reinforcement Learning:

In this instance, you are learning and harnessing the power of your datasets through a trial and error process, as the name of this category implies.

4) The Semi-Supervised Learning:
   This methodology is actually a mixture of both Supervised Learning and Unsupervised Learning. However, this technique is only used when you have a small amount of datasets that are actually labeled. Within this, there is a sub-technique which is called "Pseudo-Labeling." In this regard, you literally translate all of the unsupervised datasets into a supervised state of nature.

The Machine Learning Algorithms

There are many types and kinds of both mathematical and statistical algorithms that are used in Machine Learning. In this subsection, we examine some of the more common ones, and we will do a deeper dive into them later in this chapter. Here are the algorithms:

1) The Naïve Bayes Classifier:
   The reason why this particular algorithm is called "naïve" is because the underlying assumption is that the variables in each of the datasets that you have are actually all independent from one another. In other words, the statistical occurrence from one variable in one dataset will have nothing to do whatsoever with the variables in the remaining datasets. But there is a counterargument to this which states that this association will prove to be statistically incorrect if any of the datasets have actually changed in terms of their corresponding values. It should be noted that there are also specific alterations or variations to this particular algorithm, and they are as follows:
   ■ The Bermoulli:
     This is only used if you have binary values in your datasets.
   ■ The Multinomial:
     This technique is only used if the values in your datasets are discrete, in other words, if they contain mathematical absolute values.
   ■ The Gaussian:
     This methodology is used only if your datasets line up to a statistically normal distribution.
   It should be noted that this overall technique is heavily used for analyzing in granular detail those datasets that have a text value assigned to them. In Cybersecurity, this technique proves to be extremely useful when it comes to identifying and confirming phishing emails by examining the key features and patterns in the body of the email message, the sender address, and the content in the subject line.
2) The K-Nearest Neighbor:
   This specific methodology is used for classifying any dataset or datasets that you have. The basic theoretical construct of the values that are closely related or associated with one another in your datasets will statistically be good predictors for a Machine Learning model. In order to use this model, you first

need to compute the numerical distance between the closest values. If these values are quantitative, you could then use the Euclidean Distance formula. But if your datasets have some sort of qualitative value, you could then use what is known as the "Overlap Metric." Next, you will then have to ascertain the total number of values that are closely aligned with one another. While having more of these kinds of values in your datasets could mean a much more efficient and robust Machine Learning Model, this also translates into using much more processing resources of your Machine Learning System. To help accommodate for this, you can always assign higher value statistical weights to those particular values that are closely affiliated with one another.

3) The Linear Regression:

This kind of methodology is strictly statistical. This means that it tries to examine and ascertain the relationship between preestablished variables that reside from within your datasets. With this, a line is typically plotted, and can be further smoothed out using a technique called "Least Squares."

4) The Decision Tree:

This methodology actually provides an alternative to the other techniques described thus far. In fact, the Decision Tree works far better and much more efficiently with non-numerical data, such as those that deal with text values. The main starting point of the decision is at the node, which typically starts at the top of any given chart. From this point onwards, there will be a series of decision branches that come stemming out, thus giving it its name. The following example depicts a very simple example of a Decision Tree:

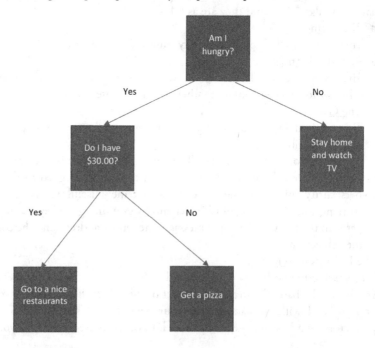

The above is of course, a very simple Decision Tree to illustrate the point. But when it comes to Machine Learning, Decision Trees can become very long, detailed, and much more complex. One of the key advantages of using a Decision Tree is that they can actually work very well with very large datasets and provide a degree of transparency during the Machine Leaning Model building process.

But, on the flip side, a Decision Tree can also have its serious disadvantages as well. For example, if just one branch of it fails, it will have a negative, cascading effect on the other branches of the Decision Tree.

5) The Ensemble Model:

As its name implies, this particular technique means using more than just one model, it uses a combination of what has been reviewed so far.

6) The K-Means Clustering:

This methodology is very useful for extremely large datasets—it groups together the unlabeled datasets into various other types of groups. The first step in this process is to select a group of clusters, which is denoted with the value of "k." For illustration purposes, the diagrams below represent two different clusters:

Once you have decided upon these clusters, the next step will be to calculate what is known as the "Centroid." This is technically the midpoint of the two clusters, illustrated below:

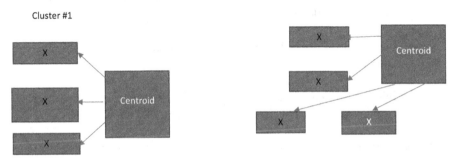

Finally, this specific algorithm will then calculate the average distance of the two Centroids, and will keep doing so in an iterative fashion until the two Centroids reach the point of convergence—that is, when the boundaries of the two clusters will actually meet with each other. It should be noted that this technique suffers from two different drawbacks:

- It does not work well with non-spherical datasets;
- There could be some clusters with many data points in them, and some with hardly any at all. In this particular instance, this technique will not pick up on the latter.

Key Statistical Concepts

Apart from the mathematical side of the algorithms, Machine Learning also makes heavy usage of the principles of statistics, and some of the most important ones that are used are described in this subsection:

1) The Standard Deviation:
   This measures the average distance from the statistical aspect of any dataset.
2) The Normal Distribution:
   This is the "bell-shaped curve" that we have heard so often about. In more technical terms, it represents the sum of the statistical properties in the variables of the all the datasets that you are going to use for the Machine Learning system.
3) The Bayes Theorem:
   This theorem provides detailed, statistical information about your datasets.
4) The Correlation:
   This is where the statistical correlations or commonalities (or even associations) are found amongst all of the datasets. Here are the guiding principles behind it:
   - Greater than 0:
     This occurs when a variable increases by an increment of one. Consequently, the other variables will also increase by at least of a value of one.
   - 0:
     There is no statistical correlation between any of the variables in the datasets.
   - Less than 0:
     This occurs when a variable increases by an increment of one. Consequently, the other variables will also *decrease* by at least of a value of one.

So far, we have provided a high level overview of the theoretical aspects of Machine Learning. In the next section of this book, we will now do the "Deep Dive."

The Deep Dive into the Theoretical Aspects of Machine Learning

Understanding Probability

If you haven't noticed already, one of the key drivers behind any Machine Learning is the quality and the robustness of the data sets that you have for the system that you are using. In fact, it is probably safe to say that the data is roughly 80 percent of the battle to get your Machine Learning system up and running and to produce the outputs that you need for your project. So in this regard, you will probably rely upon the concepts of statistics much more so than pure and discrete mathematics, as your data sets will be heavily reliant upon this.

In the field of statistics, the concepts of probability are used quite often. Probability, in much more specific terms, is the science of trying to confirm the uncertainty of an event, or even a chain of events. The value "E" is most commonly used to represent a particular event, and the value of P€ will represent the level of probability that will occur for it. If this does not really happen, this is called the "Trail." In fact, many of the algorithms that are used for Machine Learning come from the principles of probability and the naïve Bayesian models.

It should be noted at this point that there are three specific categories for the purposes of further defining probability, and they are as follows:

1) The Theoretical Probability:
   This can be defined as the number of ways that a specific event can occur, which is mathematically divided by the total number of possible outcomes that can actually happen. This concept is very often used for Machine Learning systems in order to make better predictions for the future, such as predicting what the subsequent Cyberthreat Landscape will look like down the road.

2) The Empirical Probability:
   This describes the specific number of times that an event will occur, which is then mathematically divided by the total number of incidents that are also likely to occur.

3) The Class Membership:
   In this instance, when a particular dataset is assigned and given a label, this is known technically as "Classification Predictive Modeling." In this case, the probability that a certain observation will actually happen, such as assigning a particular dataset to each class, can be predicted. This makes it easier to lay down the actual objectives for what the Machine Learning system will accomplish before you select the algorithms that you will need.

It should be noted that the above-mentioned classifications of probability can also be converted into what are known as "Crisp Class Labels." In order to conduct this specific procedure, you need to choose the dataset that has the largest levels of probability, as well as those that can be scaled through a specific calibration process.

Keep in mind that at least 90 percent of the Machine Learning models are actually formulated by using a specific sequencing of various iterative algorithms. One of the most commonly used techniques to accomplish this task is the known as the "Expectation Maximization Algorithm" which is most suited for clustering the unsupervised data sets. In other words, it specifically minimizes the difference between a predicted probability distribution and a predicted probability distribution.

As it will be further reviewed in the next subsection, Bayesian Optimization is used for what is known as "Hyperparameter Optimization." This technique helps to discover the total number of possible outcomes that can happen for all of your datasets that you are making use of in your Machine Learning system. Also, probabilistic measures can be used to evaluate the robustness of these algorithms. One such other technique that can be used in this case is known as "Receiver Operating Characteristic Curves," or "ROC" for short.

For example, these curves can be used to further examine the tradeoffs of these specific algorithms.

The Bayesian Theorem

At the heart of formulating any kind or type of Machine Learning algorithm is what is known as the "Bayesian Probability Theory." In this regard, the degree of uncertainty, or risk, of collecting your datasets before you start the optimization process is known as the "Prior Probability," and the examining of this level of risk after the dataset optimization process has been completed is known as the "Posterior Probability." This is also known in looser terms as the "Bayes Theorem."

This simply states that the relationship between the probability of a hypothesis before getting any kind of statistical evidence (which is represented as P[H]) and after can be driven into the Machine Learning system by making use of the following mathematical computation:

$$\Pr(H|E) = \Pr(E|H) * \Pr(H) / \Pr(E)$$

In the world of Machine Learning, there are two fields of statistics that are the most relevant, and they are as follows:

1) Descriptive Statistics:
   This is the sub-branch of statistics that further calculates any useful properties of your datasets that are needed for your Machine Learning system. This actually involves a simple set, such as figuring out the mean, median, and mode values amongst all of your datasets. Here:
   ■ The Mean: This is the average value of the dataset;
   ■ The Mode: This is the most frequent value that occurs in your datasets;

■ The Median: This is the middle value which physically separates the higher half of the values in your dataset from the lower half of the values in your dataset.

2) <u>Inferential Statistics</u>:

This grouping of statistics is implemented into the various methods that actually support the various quantifying properties of the datasets that you are using for your Machine Learning system. These specific techniques are used to help quantify the statistical likelihood of any given dataset that is used in creating the assumptions for the Machine Learning model formulation process.

The Probability Distributions for Machine Learning

In Machine Learning, the statistical relationship between the various events of what is known as "Continuous Random Variable" and its associated probabilities is known as the "Continuous Probability Distribution." These specific distribution sets are in fact a key component of the operations that are performed by the Machine Learning models in terms of optimizing the numerical input and output variables.

Also, the statistical probability of an event that is equal to or less than a particular defined value is technically known as the "Cumulative Distribution Function," or "CDF" for short. The inverse, or reverse, of this function is called the "Percentage Point Function," or "PPF" for short. In other words, the Probability Density Function calculates the statistical probability of a certain, continuous outcome, and the Cumulative Density Function calculates the statistical probability that a value that is less or equal to a certain outcome will actually transpire in the datasets that you are using in your Machine Learning system.

The Normal Distribution

The Normal Distribution is also known as the "Gaussian Distribution." The premise for this is that there is a statistical probability of a real time event occurring in your Machine Learning system from your given datasets. This distribution also consists of what is known as a "Continuous Random Variable," and this possesses a Normal Distribution that is evenly divided amongst your datasets.

Further, the Normal Distribution is defined by making use of two distinct and established parameters which are the Mean (denoted as "mu") and the Variance (which is denoted as Sigma ^2). Also, the Standard Deviation is typically the average spread from the mean and is denoted as "Sigma" as well. The Normal Distribution can be represented mathematically as follows:

$$F(X) = 1/aSQRT\ PI\ {}^{\wedge}e - (u - x)^{\wedge}2/2O^{\wedge}2.$$

It should be also noted that this mathematical formula can be used in the various Machine Learning Algorithms in order to calculate both distance and gradient descent measures, which also include the "K-Means" and the "K-Nearest Neighbors." At times, it will be necessary to rescale the above-mentioned formula until the appropriate statistical distribution is actually reached. In order to perform the rescaling process, the "Z-Score Normalization" and the "Min-Max Transformation" are used.

Finally, in terms of the Machine Learning Algorithms, the independent variables that are used in your datasets are also known as "Features." The dependent variables are also known as the "Outputs."

Supervised Learning

Earlier in this chapter, Supervised Learning was reviewed. Although just a high level overview of it was provided, in this subsection, we now go into a much deeper exploration of it. It should be noted that many of the Machine Learning algorithms actually fall under this specific category. In general, Supervised Learning works by using a targeted independent variable (it can also even be a series of dependent variables). From this point onwards, a specific mathematical function can then be created which can associate, or map, the inputs from the datasets to what the desired or expected outputs should be.

This is an iterative process that keeps going until an optimal level of accuracy is reached, and the desired output has an expected outcome with it as well. The following are typical examples of some of the statistical techniques that are used in this iterative process:

1) Linear Regression:

This is probably the best approach to be used in order to statistically estimate any real or absolute values that are based upon the continuous variables that are present in the Machine Learning model. With this technique, a linear relationship (as its name implies) is actually established and placed amongst both the independent variable and the dependent variables that are present in the Machine Learning model. Technically, this is known as the "Regression Line," and the mathematical formula for this is as follows:

$$Y = a * X + b.$$

With this kind of modeling technique, the statistical relationships are actually created and filtered via numerous Linear Predictor Functions. From here, the parameters of these particular functions are then estimated from the datasets that are used in the Machine Learning system. Although Linear Regression is widely used in Machine Learning, there are also a number of specific other uses for it as well, which are as follows:

■ Determining the strength of the predictors, which can be a very subjective task to accomplish;

- Trend Forecasting, in that it can be used to estimate the level of the impact of any changes that may transpire from within the datasets;
- Predicting or forecasting a specific event into the future. For example, as it relates to Cybersecurity, it can be used to help predict what a new threat vector variant could potentially look like.
- In the case that there are multiple independent variables that are being used (typically, there is just one, as denoted by the value of "Y" in the above equation), then other techniques have to be used as well, which include those of Forward Selection, Step Wise Elimination, and Backward Elimination.

2) Logistic Regression:

This statistical technique is used for determining the levels of probability of both an outcome success and an outcome failure. Thus, the dependent variables that are present must be in binary format, which is either a 0 or a 1. This kind of technique can be mathematically represented as follows:

$$Odds = p/(1-p)$$

$$Ln(odds) = ln[p/(1-p)]$$

$$Logit(p) = ln\ ln[p/(1-p)].$$

It should be noted also that this technique also makes use of what are known as "Binomial Distributions." In other words, a Link Function must be selected for the specific distribution that is at hand. Unlike the previously mentioned technique, there is no linear relationship that is required. Further, this kind of technique is mostly used for the purposes of problem classification for the Machine Learning system.

3) Stepwise Regression:

As mentioned previously, this kind of technique works best when there are multiple independent variables that are present. In this regard, these independent variables can be further optimized with the following tools:

- The AIC Metric;
- The T-Test;
- The R Squared, as well as the Adjusted R Squared.

One of the main benefits of this technique is that Covariant Variables can be added one at a time, but permutations for doing this have to be established first. One of the key differences between Stepwise Regression and the Forward Regression is that the former can actually remove any kind of statistical predictors, but the with the latter, a "Significant Predictor" can add any other extra statistical variables that are needed in the development of the Machine Learning model. Also, Backward Elimination starts this process with all of the statistical predictors present in the Machine Learning model, and from there removes every least significant variable that occurs throughout this entire iterative cycle.

4) <u>Polynomial Regression</u>:
If it were to be the case that the power of an independent variable happens to be greater than one (this can be mathematically represented as "$Y^1 > 1$"), this then becomes what is known as the "Polynomial Regression Equation." This can be mathematically represented as follows:

$$Y = a+b*Y^2.$$

5) <u>Ridge Regression</u>:
This technique is specifically used when the datasets that are used for the Machine Learning system undergo a transformation which is known as "Multicollinearity." This typically occurs when the independent variables are highly correlated, or associated, amongst one another, and from there, the Least Squares calculations remain at a neutral or unchanged point.

To counter for the Multicollinearity effect, a certain degree of statistical bias is added in order to help reduce any Standard Errors or other types of statistical deviations that may occur in the Machine Learning model. The effects of Multicollinearity can be mathematically represented as follows:

$$Y = a+y\ a+ b1x1+ b2x2+, b3x3,\ etc.$$

Also in this technique, the "Regularization Method" can be used to make sure that the values of the coefficients that are present in the above formula will never reach zero during the time that the Machine Learning system is in use.

6) <u>Least Absolute Shrinkage & The Selector Operator Regression (aka the "Lasso Regression")</u>:
This specific technique possesses the ability to reduce any of the statistical variability that is present in the Machine Learning model, by reducing the amount of variability that is present. This can be deemed also as an optimization or a "regularization" technique in that only one single statistical option is picked from an aggregate group of predictors. This technique also can make future predictions even much more accurate in nature.

The fundamental question that often gets asked at this point is what type of Regression Technique should be used for the Machine Learning model? The basic rule of thumb is that if the outputs should be continuous (or linear) in nature, then Linear Regression should be used. However, if the output is multiple options in nature, such as being binary, then either the Binary or the Logistic Regression models should be used.

But, there are other factors that need to be taken into consideration, which include the following:

- The type of the independent and the dependent variables that are being used;
- The characteristics of the datasets that are being used as well as their mathematical dimensionality.

The Decision Tree

An overview of the Decision Tree was provided earlier in this chapter, and in this subsection, we do a deeper dive into it. This technique is actually considered to be a part of Supervised Learning. The ultimate goal of the Decision Tree is to create a Machine Learning model which has the potential to predict a certain value of a target variable by learning the decision's rules, or permutations, that have been initially deployed into the datasets, in order to make a more effective learning environment for the Machine Learning system.

It should be noted that Decision Trees can also be called "Classification and Regression Trees," or "CART" for short. In this particular situation, the ability to predict the value of a target variable is created by what are known as "If/Then Statements." Some of the attributes of a Decision Tree include the following:

1) The Attribute:
   This is a numerical quantity that describes the value of an instance.
2) The Instance:
   These are the attributes that further define the input space and are also referred to as the "Vector of Features."
3) The Sample:
   This is the set of inputs that are associated with or combined with a specific label. This then becomes known as the "Training Set."
4) The Concept:
   This is a mathematical function that associates or maps a specific input to a specific output.
5) The Target Concept:
   This can be deemed to be the output that has provided the desired results or outcome.
6) The Hypothesis Class:
   This is a set or category of possible outcomes.
7) The Testing Set:
   This is a sub-technique that is used to further optimize the performance of the "Candidate Concept."
8) The Candidate Concept:
   This is also referred to as the "Target Concept."

An graphical example of a Decision Tree was provided earlier in this chapter. It should be noted that this technique also makes further usage of Boolean functions, AND OR XOR mathematical operators, as well as Boolean gates.

The specific steps for creating any kind of Machine Learning-based Decision Tree are as follows:

- Obtain the datasets that will be needed and from there compute the statistical uncertainty for each of them;
- Establish a list of questions that have to be asked at every specific node of the Decision Tree;
- After the questions have been formulated, create the "True" and "False" rows that are needed;
- Compute the information that has been established from the partitioning that took place in the previous step;
- Next, update the questions that are being asked from the results of the process that have been garnered in the last step;
- Finally, divide, and if need be, sub-divide the nodes and keep repeating this iterative process until you have completed the objective of the Decision Tree and it can be used for the Machine Learning system.

It should also be noted that in Machine Learning, the Python Programming Language is used quite extensively. This will be examined in much greater detail, but the below provides an example of how it can be used in creating a Decision Tree as well:

```
Import numpy as np
Import pandas as pd
From sklearn.metrics import confusion_matrix
From sklearn.cross -validation import train_test_split
From sklearn.tree import DecisionTreeClassifier
From sklearn.metrics import accuracy_score
From sklearn.metrics import classification_report

# Function importing data set
Def importdata ();
        Balance_data = pd.read_csv(
#Printing the dataswet shape
Print ("data set Length:",len(balance_data)
Print ("data set Shape: ", balance_data.shape)

#Printing the data set observations
Print "[data set: ", balance _data.head()]
Return balance_data
```

```
#Function to split the data set
Def splitdata set(balance_data):

#Separating the target variable
X = balance_data.values [:, 1:5]
Y = balance_data.values[:, 0]
#Splitting the dataset into train and test
X_train, X-test, y_train, y_test, = train_test_split(
X, Y, test_size = 0.3, random_state = 100)

Return X, Y, X _train; X_test; y_train, Y_test
#Function to perform training with giniIndex.
Def train_using_gini(X_train. X_test, y_train);

#Creating the classifier object
Of_gini = DecisionTreeClassifer(criterion = "gin",

Random_state = 100,max_depth=3,
Min_samples_leaf=5)

#Performing training
Cif_gini.fit(X_train, y_train)
Retrn cif_gini
#Function to perform training with entropy.
Def tarin_using_entropy(X_train, X_test, y_train);

#Decision tree with entropy
Clf_entropy_= DecisionTreeClassifier(
        Criterion = "entropy", random_state#
100,
Max_depth= 3, min _samples_leaf =5)
#Performing training
Clf_enrtropy.fit(X_train, y_train)
Return clf_entropy

#Function to make predictions
Def prediction(X_test, clf_object):
#Prediction on test with giniIndex
Y_pred = clf_object.predict(X_test)
Print("Predicted values:")
Return y_pred

#Function to compute accuracy
Def cal_accuracy(y_test, y_pred):
```

```
          Print("Confusion Matrix: ";
                    Confusion_matrix(y_test, y_pred)
    Print ("Accuracy :"
    Accuracy_score(y_test, y_pred)*100)
    Print ("Report : ",
    Classification_report(y_test, y_pred)

    #Driver code
    Def():

    #Building Phase
    Data = importdata()
    X, Y, X_train, X_test, y_train, y_test = splitdata set(data)
    Clf_gini = train_using_gini(X_train, X_test, y_train)
    Clf_entropy = train_using_entropy(X_train, X_test, y_train)

    #Operational Phase
    Print("Results Using Gini Index:")
    #Prediction using gini
    Y_pred_gini = prediction(X_test, clf_gini)
    Cal_accuracy(y_test, y_pred_gini)

    Print("Results Using Entropy:")
          #Prediction using entropy
    Y_pred_entropy = prediction(X_test, clf_entropy)
          Cal_accuracy(y_test, y_pred_entropy)

    #Calling amin function
    If_name_=="_main_:"
          Main()
```

(Sharma, n.d.)
(SOURCE: 2).

The Problem of Overfitting the Decision Tree

Once the Decision Tree has been completed, one of major drawbacks of it is that is very susceptible to what is known as "Overfitting." This simply means that there are more datasets than what is needed for the Machine Learning system; therefore, further optimization is thus needed in order to gain the desired outputs. In order to prevent this phenomenon from happening, you need to carefully study those branches on the Decision Tree that are deemed to be not as important.

In these instances, these specific branches, or nodes, then need to be removed. This process is also called "Post Pruning," or simply "Pruning." In this particular instance, there are two more specific techniques, which are as follows:

1) The Minimum Error:
   In this instance, the Decision Tree is pruned back to the point where the Cross Validation Error is at its minimum point.
2) The Smallest Tree:
   In this case, the Decision Tree is reduced even more than the established value for the Minimum Error. As a result, this process will create a Decision Tree with a Cross Validation Error that is within at least one Standard Deviation away from the Minimum Error.

But, it is always very important to check for Overfitting as you build the Decision Tree. In this case, you can use what is known as the "Early Stopping Heuristic."

The Random Forest

Random Forests are a combination of many Decision Trees, probably even in the range at a minimum of hundreds or even thousands of them. Each of the individual trees are trained and simulated in a slightly different fashion from each other. Once the Random Forest has been completed and optimized, the final outputs are computed by the Machine Learning system in a process known as "Predictive Averaging."

With Random Forests, the datasets are split into much smaller subsets that are based upon their specific features at hand, and which also reside only under one particular Label Type. They also have certain statistical splits by a statistical measure calculated at each from within the Decision Tree.

Bagging

This is also known as "Bootstrap Aggregation." This is a specific approach that is used to combine the predictions from the various Machine Learning systems that you are using and put them together for the sole purposes of accomplishing more accurate Mode Predictions than any other individual that is presently being used. Because of this, the Decision Tree can be statistically very sensitive to the specific datasets that they have been trained and optimized for.

Bagging can also be considered to be a further subset in the sense that it is typically applied to those Machine Learning algorithms that are deemed to be of "High

Variance" in nature. The Decision Trees that are created from Bootstrap Aggregation can also be highly sensitive in nature once again to the datasets that are being used for the tasks that they have been trained to do. The primary reason for this is that any small or incremental changes can drastically alter the composition and makeup of the Decision Tree structure.

With the Bagging technique, the datasets are not actually further subdivided; instead, each node of the Decision Tree is associated with a specific sample of the dataset in question. A random size is typically assigned. This stands in sharp contrast to a more normalized Decision Tree in which the randomness typically happens when that specific node is further subdivided, and from there, a greater degree of statistical separation can thus be achieved.

A question that typically gets asked at this point is, which is better: the Random Forest, or making use of multiple Decision Trees that are not interlinked or otherwise connected with one another? In most cases, the choice of the former is a much better one, because better Pooling Techniques, as well as various other types of Machine Learning algorithms can be used as well, and bonded all together into one cohesive unit.

The Naïve Bayes Method

This is a well-known technique that is typically used for Predictive Modeling scenarios by the Machine Learning system. It should be noted that with Machine Learning, the computations are done on a specific dataset in which the best statistical hypothesis must be figured out in order to yield the desired outputs. The Naïve Bayes Method can be mathematically represented as follows:

$$P(h|d) = [P(d|h) * P(h))/P(d)]$$

Where:

P(h|d) = is the statistical probability of a given hypothesis (known as "h") which is computed onto a particular dataset (which is known as "d").

P(d|h) = is the probability of dataset "d," assuming the hypothesis "h" is actually statistically correct.

P(d) = is the probability of a dataset absent of any kind of hypothesis ("h") or any form of dataset "d").

In this regard, if all of the above are also correct, then one can conclude that the hypothesis "h" is also correct. What is known as a "Posterior Probability" is further associated with this concept as well.

The above methodology can also be used to compute the "Posterior Probability" for any given number of statistical hypothesis. Of course, the one that has the highest level of probability will be selected for the Machine Learning System because it is deemed the most successful and most robust in nature. But, if the situation arises where all levels of statistical hypotheses are equal in value, then this can be mathematically represented as follows:

$$MAP(h) = max[(P(d|h)).$$

It is also worth mentioning that this methodology consists of yet another algorithm which is known as the "Naïve Bayes Classification." This technique is typically used to determine and ascertain if a certain statistical value is either Categorical or Binary by design. The Class Probabilities and their associated conditional sets are also known as the "representations" of the Naïve Bayes Model. Also, Class Probabilities are the statistical odds of each class that is present in the datasets; the Conditional Probabilities are ascertained form the given input values for each Value Class from the datasets that are used in the Machine Learning system.

Another common question that typically gets asked at this point is, how does the Naïve Bayes Theorem actually work, at least on a high level? Well, one needs to first compute the Posterior Probability (which is denoted as $P(c|x)$ from the $P©$, the $P(X)$, and the $PX|C$. In other words, the foundations for this algorithm can be mathematically represented as follows:

$$P(c|x) = P(x|c)P©/P(x)$$

Where:

$P(c|x)$ = the Posterior Probability;
$P(x|c)$ = the Statistical Likelihood;
$P©$ = the Class Prior Probability;
$P(x)$ = the Predictor Prior Probability.

Given the above mathematical representation, the specific class that has the highest levels of statistical Posterior Probability will likely be the candidate to be used in computing the final output from the Machine Learning system.

The advantages of the Naïve Bayes Method are as follows:

■ It is one of the most widely used algorithms in Machine Learning to date;
■ It gives very robust results for all sorts of Multi-Class predictions;
■ It requires much less training versus some of the other methods just reviewed;
■ It is best suited for Real Time Prediction purposes, especially for Cybersecurity purposes when it comes to filtering for false positives;
■ It can predict the statistical probability of various Multiple Classes of the targeted variables;
■ It can be used for text classification purposes (this is typically where the datasets are not quantitative in nature, but rather qualitative;

■ With the filtering approaches that it has, it can very easily find hidden trends much more quickly than the other previously reviewed methods.

The disadvantages of the Naïve Bayes Method are as follows:

■ It is not efficient for predicting the class of a test data set;
■ If any Transformation Methods are used, it cannot convert the datasets into a Standard Normal Distribution curve;
■ It cannot deal with certain Correlated Features because they are considered to be an overhead in terms of processing power on the Machine Learning system;
■ There are no Variance Minimization Techniques that are used, and thus it cannot make use of the "Bagging Technique";
■ It has a very limited set for Parameter Tuning;
■ It makes the further assumption that every unique feature in each and every dataset that is present and used for the Machine Learning system is unrelated to any other, and thus, it will not have any positive impact on other features which may be present in the datasets.

The KNN Algorithm

This is also known as the "K Nearest Neighbors" algorithm. This is also deemed to be a Supervised Machine Learning algorithm. It is typically used by those Machine Learning systems in order to specifically solve Classification and Regression scenarios. This is a very widely-used Machine Learning algorithm for the reason that it has two distinct properties, unlike the ones previously examined. They are as follows:

1) It is a "Lazy" Algorithm:
   It is lazy in the sense that this algorithm has no specialized training segments that are associated with it, and thus it makes use of all of the datasets that are available to it while it is training in its Classification Phase.
2) It is Non-Parametric by nature:
   This simply means that this specific algorithm never makes any assumptions about the underlying datasets.

In order to fully implement the KNN Algorithm for any kind of Machine Learning system, the following steps have to be taken:

1) Deploy the datasets, and initialize the "K" value to the preestablished set of the total number of nearest neighbors that are present. Also, any training and other forms of testing datasets must be deployed as well.

2) It is important to also calculate the values of "K" as well as the distance from the training datasets and the test datasets.
3) From within every point in the test dataset, you also need to compute the distance between the test datasets as well as each and every row for each of the training datasets as well.
4) Once the above step has been accomplished, then sort the "K" values in an ascending order format which is based upon the distance values that have been calculated previously. From this point, then choose the top "K" rows, and assign a specific class to it.
5) Finally, get the preestablished Labels for the "K" entries that you have just selected.

Another key advantage of the KNN Algorithm is that there is no learning that is typically required, and because of that, it is very easy to update as new datasets become available. This algorithm can store other forms of datasets as well by taking complex dataset structures and matching new learning patterns as it tries to predict the values of the various outputs. Thus, if any new types of predictions have to be made for the outputs, it can just use the pre-existing training datasets.

As we alluded earlier, various distances must be calculated for the KNN Algorithm. The most commonly used one is what is known as the "Euclidean Distance," which is represented by the following mathematical formula:

$$\text{Euclidean Distance}(X, Xi) = SQRT[(sum((X) - (xij^2)]$$

It should also be noted that other distancing formulas can be used as well, especially that of the Cosine Distance. Also, the computational complexity of the KNN Algorithm can also increase in tandem upon the size of the training dataset. This simply means that there is a positive, statistical relationship that exists: as the size increases, so will the complexity.

As mentioned, Python is very often used for Machine Learning, and the following code can be used to predict the outputs that the KNN Algorithm will provide:

```
Knn_predict <-function(test, train, k_value){
Pred <-c()
#LOOP – 1
For(I in c(1:row(test))){
    Dist = c()
    Char = c()
    Setosa = 0
    Versicolor = 0
    Virginica = 0
}
```

```
#LOOP – 2 – looping over trained data
For (j in c(1:row(train))){}
Dist <-c(dist, ED(test[I,], train [j,]))
Char <-c(char, as.character(train[j,][[5]]))
Df <-data.frame(char, dist$SepallLength)
Df <-df[order(df$dist.SepallLength),]
#sorting dataframe
     Df<-df[1:k_value,]

#Loop3: loops over df and counts classes of all neighbors
     For(k in c(1:nrow(df))){
If(as.character(df[k, "char"]) = = "setoasa"){
Setosa = setosa + 1
}else if(as.character(df[k,, "char]) = =
"versicolor"){
          Versicolor = versicolor + 1
          }else
          Virginica = virginica +1
          }
N<-table(df$char)
Pred = names(n)[which(n==max(n))]
Return(pred) #return prediction vector
}
#Predicting the value for K=1
K=1
Predictions <-knn_predict(test, train, K)
Output:
For K=1


[1]"Iris-virginica
```

(SOURCE: 2).

Unsupervised Learning

When it comes to Machine Learning, the Unsupervised Algorithms can be used to create inferences from datasets that are composed of the input data if they do not have Labeled Responses that are associated with them. In this category, the various models that are used (and which will be examined in much more detail) make use of the input data type of [X], and further, do not have any association with the output values that are calculated.

This forms the basis for Unsupervised Learning, primarily because the goal of the models is to find and represent the hidden trends without any previous learning cycles. In this, there are two major categories: Clustering and Association.

1) Clustering:

This typically occurs when inherent groups must be discovered in the datasets. But in this category, the Machine Learning system has to deal with a tremendous amount of large datasets, which are often referred to as "Big Data." With Clustering, the goal is to find any and all associations (which are hidden and unhidden) in these large datasets. The following are the major types of Clustering Properties that are very often used today in Machine Learning:

■ Probabilistic Clustering:
This involves grouping the various datasets into their respective clusters that are based upon a predetermined probabilistic scale.

■ K-Means Clustering:
This involves the clustering of all of the datasets into a "K" number of statistically mutually exclusive clusters.

■ Hierarchical Clustering:
This classifies and categorizes the specific data points in all of the datasets into what are known as "Parent-Child Clusters."

■ Gaussian Mixture Models:
This consists of both Multivariate and Normal Density Components.

■ Hidden Markov Models:
This technique is used to analyze all of the datasets that are used by the Machine Learning systems, as well as to discover any sequential states that could exist amongst them.

■ Self-Organizing Maps:
This maps the various Neural Network structures which can learn the Statistical Distribution as well as the Topology of the datasets.

Generative Models

These types of models make up the bulk of Unsupervised Learning Models. The primary reason for this is that they can generate brand new data samples from the same distribution of any established training dataset. These kinds of models are created and implemented to learn the data about the datasets. This is very often referred to as the "Metadata."

Data Compression

This refers to the process for keeping the datasets as small as possible. This is purely an effort to keep them as smooth and efficient as possible so as not to drain the processing power of the Machine Learning system. This is very often done through what is known as the "Dimensionality Reduction Process." Other techniques that can be used in this regard include those of "Singular Value Decomposition" and "Principal Component Analysis."

Singular Value Decomposition mathematically factors the datasets into a product of three other datasets, using the concepts of Matrix Algebra. With Principal Component Analysis, various Linear Combinations are used find the specific statistical variances amongst all of the datasets.

Association

As its name implies, this is actually a Rule-based Machine Learning methodology which can be used to find both hidden and unhidden relationships in all of the datasets. In order to accomplish this, the "Association Rule" is typically applied. It consists of both a consequent and an antecedent. An example of this is given in the matrix below:

Frequency Count	Items That Are Present
1	Bread, Milk
2	Bread, Biscuits, Drink, Eggs
3	Milk, Biscuits, Drink, Diet Coke
4	Bread, Milk, Biscuits, Diet Coke
5	Bread, Milk, Diet Coke, and Coke

(SOURCE: 2).

There are two very important properties to be aware of here:

■ The Support Count:
   This is the actual count for the frequency of occurrence in any set that is present in the above matrix. For example, [(Milk, Bread, Biscuit)] = 2. Here, the mathematical representation can be given as follows:
   X->Y, where the values of X and Y can be any two of the sets in the above matrix. For example, (Milk, Biscuits)->(Drinks).
■ The Frequent Item:
   This is the statistical set that is present when it is equal to or even greater than the minimum threshold of the datasets. In this regard, there are three key metrics that one needs to be aware of:
   1) The Support:
      This specific metric describes just how frequently an Item Set actually occurs in all of the data processing transactions. The mathematical formula to calculate this level of occurrence is as follows:
      Support[(X) →(Y)] = transactions containing both X and Y/The total number of transactions.

2) <u>Confidence</u>:

This metric is used to gauge the statistical likeliness of an occurrence having any subsequent, consequential effects. The mathematical formula to calculate this is as follows:

Confidence[(X) →(Y)] = the total transactions containing both X and Y/ The transactions containing X.

3) <u>Lift</u>:

This metric is used to statistically support the actual frequency of a consequent from which the conditional property of the occurrence of (Y) given the state of (X) can be computed. More specifically, this can be defined as the statistical rise in the probability level of the influence that (Y) has over (X). The mathematical formula to calculate this is as follows:

Lift [(X) →(Y)] = (The total transactions containing both X and Y) *)The transactions containing X)/The total fraction of transactions containing Y.

It should be noted that the Association Rule relies heavily upon using data patterns as well as statistical co-occurrences. Very often in these situations, "If/Then" statements are utilized. There are also three other Machine Learning algorithms that fit into this category, and they are as follows:

1) <u>The AIS Algorithm</u>:

With this, a Machine Learning system can scan in and provide the total count of the number of datasets that are being fed into the Machine Learning system.

2) <u>The SETM Algorithm</u>:

This is used to further optimize the transactions that take place within the datasets as they are being processed by the Machine Learning system.

3) <u>The Apriori Algorithm</u>:

This allows for the Candidate Item to be set as a specific variable known as "S" to generate only those support amounts that are needed for a Large Item that resides within the datasets.

The Density Estimation

This is deemed to be the statistical relationship between the total number of observations and their associated levels of probability. It should be noted here that when it comes to the outputs that have been derived from the Machine Learning system, the density probabilities can vary from high to low, and anything in between.

But in order to fully ascertain this, one needs to also determine whether or not a given statistical observation will actually happen or not.

The Kernel Density Function

This mathematical function is used to further estimate the statistical probability of a Continuous Variable actually occurring in the datasets. In these instances, all of the Kernel Functions that are present are mathematically divided by the sheer total of the Kernel Functions, whether they are actually present or not. This is meant to provide assurances that the Probability Density Function remains a non-negative value, and to confirm that it will remain a mathematical integral over the datasets that are used by the Machine Learning system.

The Python source code for this is as follows:

```
For I = 1 to n:
For all X;
Dens(X)
+ = (1/n) * (1/w) *K[(x-Xi)/w]
```

Where:

- The Input = the Kernel Function K(x), with the Kernel Width of W, consisting of Data Instances of x1 and xN.
- The Output = the estimated Probability Density Function that underlays the training datasets.
- The Process: This initializes the Dens(X) = 0 at all points of "X" which occur in the datasets.

Latent Variables

These variables are deemed to be those that are statistically inferred from other variables in the datasets that have no direct correlation amongst one another. These kinds of variables are not used in training sets, and are not quantitative by nature. Rather, they are qualitative.

Gaussian Mixture Models

These are deemed to be Latent Variable models as well. They are highly used in Machine Learning applications because they can calculate the total amount of data in the datasets, including those that contain Clusters. Each of the latter can be further represented as N1, ... NK, but the statistical distributions that reside in them are deemed to be Gaussian Mixture by nature.

The Perceptron

As you might have inferred, probably one of the biggest objectives of Artificial Intelligence, Machine Learning, and Neural Networks is to model the processes of the human brain. Obviously, we know that the human brain is extremely complicated, and we probably only have hit upon only 1 percent of it. Truth be told, we will never fully understand the human brain, and if we ever come to that point, it is safe to say that it will be literally centuries away.

As we know, the Central Processing Unit (CPU) is the main processing component of a computer. But if one were to equate this to the level of the brain, then the equivalence would be what is called the "Neuron." This will be covered in more detail on the chapter which deals with Neural Networks, but we will provide somewhat of an overview here, in this part of the chapter.

The human brain consists of literally billions and billions of neurons—according to some scientific studies there are as many as almost 90 billion of them. Research has also shown that the Neuron is typically much slower than that of a CPU in the computer, but it compensates for that by having such a high quantity of them, as well as so much connectivity.

These connections are known as "Synapses," and interestingly enough, they work in a parallel tandem from one another, much like the parallel processing in a computer. It should be noted that in a computer, the CPU is always active and the memory (such as the RAM) is a separate entity. But in the human brain, all of the Synapses are distributed evenly over its own network. To once again equate the brain to the computer, the actual processing takes place in the Neurons, the memory lies in the Synapses of the human brain.

Within the infrastructure of the Neuron lies what is known as the "Perceptron." Just like a Machine Learning system, it can also process inputs and deliver outputs in its own way. This can be mathematically represented as follows:

$$X_j = E, R, j = 1, \ldots d$$

Where:

D = the connection weight (also known as the "Synaptic Weight");

W_j = R is the specific output;

Y = the weighted sum of the inputs.

The sum of the weighted inputs can be mathematically represented as follows:

$$Y = d \sum j = 1 \; W_j X_j + W_o$$

Where:

W_o = the intercept value to further optimize the Perceptron Model.

The actual output of the Perceptron is mathematically represented as follows:

$$Y = W^{\wedge}t * X.$$

In this situation:

$$W = [W0, W1, \ldots Wd]^\wedge T$$

$$X = [1, x1, \ldots Xd^\wedge T.$$

The above-mentioned values are also known as the "Augmented Vectors," which include a "Bias Weight," which is statistically oriented, as well as the specific values for the inputs. When the Perceptron Model is going through its testing phase, the statistical weights (denoted as "W1") and the inputs (denoted as "X") will compute to the desired output, which is denoted as "y."

However, the Machine Learning system needs to learn about these particular statistical weights that have been assigned to it, as well as its parameters, so that it can generate the needed outputs. This specific process can be mathematically represented as follows:

$$Y = Wx + w0.$$

The above simply represents just one input and one output. This also becomes a solid linear line when it is embedded onto a Cartesian Geometric Plane. But, if there is more than just one input, then this linear line becomes what is known as a "Hyperplane." In this particular instance, these inputs can be used to implement what is known as a "Multivariate Linear Fit." From here, the inputs in the Perceptron Model can be broken in half, where one of the input spaces contains positive values, and the other input space contains negative values.

This division can be done using a technique which is known as the "Linear Discriminant Function," and the operation upon which it is carried out is known as the "Threshold Function." This can be mathematically represented as follows:

$$S(a) = \{1 \text{ if } a>0; 0 \text{ otherwise}\}$$

$$\text{Choose } \{C1 \text{ if } s(w^\wedge tx)>0, C2 \text{ otherwise}].$$

It should be noted that each Perceptron is actually a locally-based function of its various inputs and synaptic weights. However, actually deploying a Perceptron Model into the Machine Learning system is a two-step process. This can be mathematically represented as follows:

$$Oi = W^\wedge TI * X$$

$$Yi = \exp 0i / \Sigma k \exp 0k.$$

Training a Perceptron

Since the Perceptron actually defines the Hyperplane, a technique known as "Online Learning" is used. In this specific scenario, the entire datasets are not fed into the

Perceptron Model, but instead are given representative samples of them. There are two advantages to this approach, which are as follows:

- It makes efficient use of the processing power and resources of the Perceptron Model;
- The Perceptron Model can decipher rather quickly what the old datasets and the new datasets are in the training data.

With the "Online Learning" technique, the Error Functionalities that are associated with the datasets are not overwritten at all. Instead, the first statistical weights that were assigned are used to fine tune the parameters in order to further minimize any future errors that are found in the datasets. This technique can be mathematically represented as follows:

$$E^\wedge T(w|x^\wedge 1, r^\wedge 1 = \frac{1}{2} (r^\wedge t - y^\wedge t)^\wedge 2 = \frac{1}{2} \{r^\wedge 2 - (w^\wedge T X^\wedge 1)\}^\wedge 2.$$

The Online Updates can be represented as follows:

$$\text{Delta } W^\wedge tj = n(r^\wedge 1 - y^\wedge t) x^\wedge t * j$$

Where:
   N = the learning factor.

The learning factor is slowly decreased over a predefined period of time for a Convergence Factor to take place. But if the training set is fixed and not dynamic enough in nature, the statistical weights are then assigned on a random basis. In technical terms, this is known as a "Stochastic Gradient Descent." Under normal conditions, it is usually a very good idea to optimize and/or normalize the various inputs so that they can all be centered around the value of 0, and yet maintain the same type of scalar properties.

In a similar fashion, the Update Rules can also be mathematically derived for any kind Classification scenario, which makes use of a particular technique called "Logistic Discrimination." In this this instance, the Updates are actually done after each Pattern Variance, instead of waiting for the very end and then getting their mathematical summation.

For example, when there are two types of Classes that are involved in the Machine Learning system, the Single Instance can be represented as follows:

$$(x^\wedge 2, r^\wedge 2)$$

Where:

$$R^\wedge I = X^\wedge t \ E \ C1 \text{ and } R^\wedge 1 = 0 \text{ if } X^\wedge 1 \ E \ C2.$$

From here, the single output can be calculated as follows:

$$Y^1 = \text{sigmoid} (w^T, x^t).$$

From here, the Cross Entropy is then calculated from this mathematical formula:

$$E^t (w|x^t, r^t) = -r^t \log y^t - (1-r^t) \log (1-y^t).$$

All of the above can be represented by the following Python source code:

```
For i = 1, ... K
For j = 0, ... d
Wij ← rand (-0.01, 0.01)
Repeat
For all (x^t, r^t) E X in random order
For I = 1, ... K
Oi = 0
For j = 0, ... d
Oi ← Oi + Wijx^1
For I = 1, ... K
Y1 ←exp(oi)/∑k exp(0k)
For I = 1, ... K
For j = 0, ... d
Wij ← Wij + n(n^ti -y) * x^1j.
```

(SOURCE: 3).

The Boolean Functions

From within the Boolean Functions, the inputs are considered to be binary in nature, and the output value is normally 1 if the associated Function Value is deemed to be "True," and it possesses the value of 0 in other states of matter. Thus, this can also be characterized as a two-level classification problem, and the mathematical discriminant can be computed from the following formula:

$$Y = s(X1 + X2 - 1.5)$$

Where:
$$X = [1, x1, x2]^T$$
$$W = [-1.5, 1, 1]^T.$$

It is important to note at this point that the Boolean Functions typically consist of both statistical AND and OR Operators. They can separated in a linear fashion if the concept of the Perceptron is used. But the XOR operator is not available in Boolean Functions. Thus, they can be solved by the Perceptron as well. For this instance, the required inputs and outputs are given by the below matrix:

X1	X2	R
0	0	0
0	1	1
1	0	1
1	1	0

The Multiple Layer Perceptrons

Normally, the Perceptron typically consists of just one layer of statistical weights, and thus they can only operate in a linear fashion. They cannot handle the XOR statistical operator, where the mathematical discriminant is assumed to be nonlinear by nature. But, if the concept "Feedforward Networks" are made use of, then a "Hidden Layer" actually exists from within the Perceptron, which can be located between the input and the output layers.

Thus, these Multilayer Perceptrons can be used to deploy non-discriminant models into the Machine Learning system, and because of that, one can easily calculate the Nonlinear Functionalities of the various inputs. In this example, the input of "x" is thus fed into the input layer, and this activation process will propagate forward, and the Hidden Values (denoted by "Zh") are then calculated by this mathematical formula:

$$Z_h = \text{sigmoid}(w^{\wedge}\text{Th} *X) = 1/1 + \exp[- (\Sigma d\ j = 1\ W_{hj}X_j + W_{ho})],\ ^{\wedge}h = 1, \dots H$$

The output from the Machine Learning system (which is denoted as "Yi") is calculated by the following mathematical formula:

$$Y_i = V^{\wedge}T_i * Z = \Sigma H\ h = 1 * V_{ih}Z_h + V_{i0}$$

The following matrix demonstrates the various inputs that are used with the statistical XOR Operator. It is important to note that in this instance, there are two hidden units that actually deploy the two "AND'S," and the output takes any statistical "OR" condition of them:

X1	X2	Z1	Z2	Y
0	0	0	0	0
0	1	0	1	1
1	0	1	0	1
1	1	0	0	0

(SOURCE: 3).

The Multi-Layer Perceptron (MLP): A Statistical Approximator

From this point, the Boolean Functions can also operate a disunion of a unionized dataset. This statistical expression can be easily implemented into the MLP by making use of a Hidden Layer. Thus, each union can be incremented by a value of one Hidden Unit, and likewise, each disunion can be decremented by one value of the Output Unit.

This is statistically represented as follows:

$$X1 \text{ XOR } X2 = (X1 \text{ AND } - X2) \text{ OR } (-X1 \text{ AND } X2).$$

When it comes to Parallel Processing in the Machine Learning system, two MLPs can operate in tandem with two "ANDs," and yet another Perceptron can then statistically "OR" them together, thus forming a unionized set. This is represented statistically as follows:

$$Z1 = S(x1 - x2 - 0.5)$$

$$Z2 = S(-X1 + X2 - 0.5)$$

$$Y = s(Z1 + Z2 - 0.5).$$

Thus, the proof of Statistical Approximation is easily demonstrated with two Hidden Layers. For example, for every input, its statistical region can be delimited by a series of "Hyperplanes," by making use of the Hidden Units upon the Hidden Layer. Thus, the Hidden Unit which exists in the second layer then statistically "ANDs" them together, from which they are then bound to that specific region in the Machine Learning system.

From there, the weight of the connection from the Hidden Unit to the Output Unit will be equal in value to the predicted value. This process is also known sometimes as the "Piecewise Constant Approximation."

The Backpropagation Algorithm

It should also be noted that training the MLP system is virtually the same thing as training a single Perceptron. But in this situation, the resulting output is a nonlinear function by nature that is strongly correlated with its inputs. This process is also known technically as a "Gradient," and it is mathematically represented as follows:

$$VE/VWhj = (VE/VYi) * (VYi/VZh) * (VZh/VWhj).$$

It is interesting to note that the statistical errors actually "backpropagate" from the outer bands of the value of "Y" back to the various of, thus its name of the "Backpropagation Algorithm."

The Nonlinear Regression

In terms of the Machine Learning system, the Nonlinear Regression can be represented statistically as follows:

$$Y^Z = H\Sigma h = 1 \, Vh * Z^th + V0.$$

The second layer of the Perceptrons are associated with the Hidden Units and the correlated inputs; the "Least Squares Rule" can thus be used to literally update the Second Layer statistical weights with the following formula:

$$\Delta Vh = n\Sigma r * (r^1 - Z^t) * Z^th$$

But in order to update the First Layer statistical weights, the "Chain Rule" is now applied, which is as follows:

$$\Delta Whj = -n *(VE)/VWhj$$

$$N\Sigma t \, (VE^1/Vy^t) * (Vy^t/VzTh) * (VZ^th/VWhj)$$

$$N\Sigma t - [(r^2 - y^t)/VE^t] * [Vh/Vy^T|VZ^tn] * [Z^tH \, (1-1Z^th)x^tJ/ Vz^th|VWhj]$$

$$N\Sigma \, [(r^t - y^t)] * [VhZ^th] * [(1 - Zth) * x^tj].$$

With Chain Rule now firmly established by the above sequencing of equations, the statistical pattern of each direction can thus be computed in order to determine which of the parameters need to be changed in the Machine Learning system, as well as the specific magnitude of that particular change.

But, in the "Batch Learning Process," any changes in the magnitude are accumulated over a specific time series, and that change can only be made once a complete pass has been made through the entire Chain Rule. In the Chain Rule, it is also possible to have Multiple Output Units as well, in which case the Machine Learning system will have to learn them with the following mathematical formula:

$$Y^{\wedge}Ti = H\Sigma h+1 * VihZ^{\wedge}th + Vi0$$

However, the above formula only represents a one-time update. In order to keep the Machine Learning system update in real time on a 24/7/365 basis, the following set of statistical equations are thus needed, which are technically called the "Batch Update Rules":

$$\Delta Vih = n\Sigma t * (r^{\wedge}zi - y^{\wedge}ti) * Z^{\wedge}rh$$

$$\Delta Whj = n\Sigma [\Sigma t * (r^{\wedge}ti - y^{\wedge}ti)Vjh] * [Z^{\wedge}th (1-Z^{\wedge}th) * X^{\wedge}tj]$$

The Statistical Class Descriptions in Machine Learning

In the realm of Machine Learning, there are a number of these kinds of Discriminations, and they are reviewed further in this subsection.

Two Class Statistical Discrimination

If there are two classes of inputs that are used for the Machine Learning system, then only one output will be generated. This is mathematically represented as follows:

$$Y^{\wedge}t = sigmoid (H\Sigma h = 1 *VhZ^{\wedge}th + v0.$$

This further approximates the potential values of the outputs represented as follows:

$$P(C1|X^{\wedge}t)$$

$$P(C2|X^{\wedge}T) = 1 - y^{\wedge}t.$$

Multiclass Distribution

If there are an indefinite number of outputs to be computed by the Machine Learning system, the value of "K" (which represents the uncertain number of outputs) can be mathematically represented as follows:

$$O^\wedge ti = H\Sigma\ h = 1 * VihZ^\wedge th + Vi0.$$

It is also important to note that in this type of Class Discrimination, the outputs that are derived from the Machine Learning system can either be mutually exclusive or inclusive of one another. This can be statistically represented as:

$$X^\wedge ti = (Exp0^\wedge t1)\ /\ (\Sigma k\ ep\ 0^\wedge tk)$$

Multilabel Discrimination

It could also be the case that if there are multiple Labels that are used in the Machine Learning system for an input, and if there are an indeterminate amount of them (also represented as "K"), and if they are statistically mutually exclusive of one another, then this is represented as follows:

$$R^\wedge ti = \{1\ if\ x^\wedge r\ has\ a\ label\ of\ "I"\},\ \{0\ otherwise\}.$$

It should be noted that in these types of Discrimination situations, the traditional approach is to evaluate "K" as two separate and distinct Classification problems. This kind of scenario is typically found in linear models, especially when Perceptrons are used. Here, there will potentially be an indeterminate amount of "K" value-based models that are present, with a certain Sigmoid value-based output.

Thus, a Hidden Layer is now required in the Machine Learning system, so that the values for "K" can be trained separately from one another, especially if Multi-Layered Perceptrons are used. The case could also exist if there is a Hidden Layer that is common to all of the Perceptrons that even use the same datasets. If this does indeed happen, then the size of the datasets could also increase, thus greatly reducing the processing power of the Machine Learning system.

This phenomenon can be mathematically represented as follows:

$$Y^\wedge ti = sigmoid\ (H\Sigma h = 1 * VihZ^\wedge th + Vi0)$$

Where:
$Y^\wedge ti$, $I = 1, \ldots K$ are connected to the same $Z^\wedge Th$, $h = 1, \ldots H$.

Overtraining

If there is a Multilevel Perceptron that is being used, then there will most likely be an indeterminate number of Hidden Units (denoted by "H") and an indeterminate number of outputs (denoted by "K"), and they will also have a statistical weightage value of H(d+1). All of this will reside from within the first layer of the Multilevel

Perceptron (MLP), and also, there will be additional statistical weights that will be assigned to the second layer (denoted as "K(H+1)").

But, in those situations where the values of "d" and "K" happen to be predefined, then further optimization of the Multilevel Perceptron needs to be done before it can be implemented into the Machine Learning system. It is also important to keep in mind that if the MLP model is made too complex, then the Machine Learning system will take into account all of this extra "noise" that has been generated, and thus, will not be able to create an optimized output set per the requirements of the application in question.

This is especially true when a statistical model known as "Polynomial Regression" is used. It is a common practice, as it relates to Machine Learning, to increase the statistical order of magnitude that it already possesses. Also, if the total number of Hidden Units is large enough, the output will significantly deteriorate as well, thus further exacerbating the Bias/Variance in the Machine Learning system. This kind of phenomenon can also typically occur when the Machine Learning system is made to spend way too much time learning from the datasets, at least initially. Specifically, the Validation Error will pick up rather drastically, and this needs to be avoided at all costs.

For example, when the datasets are first fed into the Machine Learning system, they all have an initial statistical weight factor of almost 0. But, if the training goes for an exacerbated period of time, these weights then drift away from being 0, and become larger in size quickly. The end result is that this can greatly degrade the performance quality of the Machine Learning system.

The primary reason for this is that it will actually increase the total number of parameters in the Machine Learning system, thus even overriding the ones that have already been deployed into them. In the end, the Machine Learning system becomes way too complex by design, and the bottom line is that it will not deliver the desired set of outputs that are needed to get the project accomplished on time.

As a result, this process must be stopped early enough that the phenomenon known as "Overtraining" does not happen. Thus, the "perfect point" at which the initial levels of training should stop for the Machine Learning system is at the juncture where the optimal number of Hidden Layers in the Multilevel Perceptron is finally reached. But, this can only be ascertained by using the statistical technique known as "Cross-Validation."

How a Machine Learning System can Train from Hidden, Statistical Representation

As it has been reviewed earlier in this chapter, the Basic Regressor or Data Classifier in a Machine Learning system can be statistically represented as follows:

$$Y = h\Sigma j = 1 *(VjXj +V0).$$

If Linear Classification is used in the Machine Learning system, then one can merely look at the mathematical sign of "y" in order to choose from one of two classes. This approach is deemed to be Linear in nature, but you can go one step further to make use of another technique known as the "Nonlinear Basis Function." This can be statistically represented as follows:

$$Y = H\Sigma h = 1 *[VjO/h(x)]$$

Where:
    $O/(x)$ = the Nonlinear Basis Function.

Also, in a very comparable manner, this type of statistical technique can also be used for Multilevel Perceptrons, and this is mathematically depicted as follows:

$$Y = H\Sigma h = 1 *Vh0/(X|Wh)$$

Where:
    $0/(X|Wh)$ = sigmoid $(W^\wedge ThX)$.

There are also a number of key concepts that are important when a Machine Learning system makes use of hidden statistical representation. They are as follows:

1) <u>Embedding</u>:
   This is the statistical representation of a statistical instance that is found in a hidden space in the Multi-Layer Perceptron. This typically happens when the first layer (denoted as H < d) implements a Dimension Reduction property into the Machine Learning system. Further, the hidden units that reside here can be further analyzed by critically examining the statistical weight factors that are incoming to the Machine Learning system. Also, if the inputs are deemed to be statistically normalized, then this gives a pretty good indication of their relative importance and levels of priority in the Machine Learning system.

2) <u>Transfer Learning</u>:
   This occurs when the Machine Learning system consists of two different but interrelated tasks on hand that it is trying to accomplish. For instance, if the system is trying to solve the outputs that are needed for Problem X, and if there are not enough datasets for it, then you can theoretically train the Machine Learning system to learn off of the datasets that are being used to solve the outputs for Problem Y. In other words, you are literally transferring the Hidden Layer from Problem Y and implanting it into Problem X.

3) <u>Semi-supervised Learning</u>:
This scenario arises when the Machine Learning system has one small labeled dataset as well as a much larger unlabeled dataset. From here, the latter can be used to learn more about hidden spaces from the former. The end result is that this can then be used for initial training purposes.

Autoencoders

Another unique component of Multi-Layer Perceptrons what is known as the "Autoencoder." In this kind of architecture, the total number of inputs that are going into the Machine Learning system will equal the total number of outputs that will be generated. In this regard, the quantitative values of the outputs will also equal the quantitative values of the inputs. But, if the total number of Hidden Units is actually less than the total values of the inputs, then a phenomenon known as "Dimensionality Reduction" will occur.

It should be noted that the first layer in the Multi-Layer Perceptron is the "Encoder," and it is actually the values of these Hidden Units that make up underlying "Code." Because of this, the Multi-Layer Perceptron is thus required to ascertain the best approximation of the inputs in the Hidden Layers, so that it can be duplicated at a future point in time.

The mathematical representation of the Encoder is as follows:

$$Z^{\wedge}t = Enc(X^{\wedge}t|W)$$

Where:
W = the parameters of the Encoder.

From the above formula, the second layer from the Hidden Units in the Multi-Layer Perceptron now act as what is known as the "Decoder." This is mathematically represented as follows:

$$X^{\wedge}t = Dec(Z^{\wedge}t|V)$$

Where:
V = the parameters of the Decoder.

From here, the Backpropagation attempts to ascertain the best Encoder and the Decoder Parameters in a concerted effort to find the "Reconstruction Error." This can be computed as follows:

$$E(W, V|X) = \sum t \, ||x^{\wedge}t - x^{\wedge}t||^{\wedge}2 = \sum t||X^{\wedge}2 - Dec[Enc(X^{\wedge}2|W) * (V)]|| \, ^{\wedge}2.$$

When the Encoder is in the design phase, a piece of source code that is deemed to be of "small dimensionality" in nature, as well as an Encoder that has a value of Low Capacity is included in order to preserve the integrity of the datasets that are used by the Machine Learning system. But, there can be a part of the dataset that can be discarded due to noise or variance that is present. This was discussed at length in an earlier section of this chapter.

But, if both the Encoder and the Decoder are not in just one layer, but are found in multiple layers, the Encoder will then implement what is known as the "Nonlinear Dimensionality Reduction." It is also important to note that an extension of the Autoencoder is what is known as the "Denoising Autoencoder." This is the situation where extra noise or extra levels of variance are added in order to create so-called "Virtual Examples" in order for the Machine Learning system to learn off of as well, also including those of the datasets.

The inclusion of this extra noise or variance is done intentionally in order to forecast any errors that may take place when the final outputs are produced by the Machine Learning system. There is yet another extension as well, and this is known as the "Sparse Encoder." The purpose of this extra extension is to embed these extra noises, or variances, so that they are not long dimensionally, but rather they are "sparse" in nature.

Finally, another way that a Multi-Layer Perceptron can deploy Dimensionality Reduction into the Machine Learning system is through a process known as "Multidimensional Scaling." This can be mathematically represented as follows:

$$E(O|X) = \sum rt \; [||[g(x^\wedge r|O) - g(x^\wedge t|0)]|| - ||x^\wedge t - x^\wedge s| \; / \; ||x^\wedge r - x^\wedge s||.$$

The Word2vec Architecture

If the Autoencoder is deemed to be "noisy" enough, it will then be forced to create and further generate similar pieces of code because all of the outputs that are produced by the Machine Learning system should more or less be the same in value. This is, of course, largely dependent upon the specific type of application that it is being used for. For example, on a simplistic level, if there are different inputs that are used, then the same output must be created by the Machine Learning system.

The premise behind the above-mentioned example is known specifically as "word2vec architecture." Here the output is a qualitative one, such as that of a word; the input into the Machine Learning system is the context of that specific word. Also, if two separate words appear quite often from within the same context, then they should be similar as well. Thus, the overall purpose of this technique is to ascertain and locate a continuous, statistical representation for words that can be used in what is known as "Natural Language Processing," or "NLP" for short.

From this point onwards, there are actually two types of models that are used for the word2vec architecture, and they are known as the "CBOW" and the "Skip-Gram." The common features between these two are the following:

■ The d-dimensional input;
■ The d-dimensional output;
■ If H < d has an "X" number of Hidden Units and an "X" number of Hidden Layers, then this will closely resemble an Autoencoder (as reviewed in the last subsection).

But these two models also differ from each other in the way we define the terms of the context for the word. In the CBOW model, all of the specific words that are used are averaged together to form a binary representation of them. Thus, this can also become an input for the Machine Learning system. But, in the Skip-Gram model, all of the words that are used are averaged together one at a time, and as a result, they form different training dataset pairs that can also be used by the Machine Learning system.

In the end, it has been determined that the Skip-Gram model works far better than the CBOW model for Machine Learning systems. However, there are also a number of ways in which the word2vec technique can be improved upon, and they are as follows:

■ Words such as "the" or "with," which are quite frequently used, can be used fewer times in order to make the Machine Learning system more efficient;
■ Both the computational and processing times of the Machine Learning system can be further optimized and made much more efficient by first taking a statistical sample of the output. This is also known technically as "Negative Sampling."

Application of Machine Learning to Endpoint Protection

The world has become increasingly dependent on an ever-growing cyber infrastructure. Not only do our computers and smart devices connect us to our family, friends, employers, governments, and the companies from which we buy goods and services, but also our infrastructure is becoming more automated and computerized, including all modes of transportation, power generation and distribution, manufacturing, supply chain logistics, etc. Securing all of this cyber infrastructure has become essential to having an efficient and safe existence. Many attack vectors exist, so any cybersecurity strategy needs to be broad and deep. This is commonly referred to as "defense in depth." Because endpoint devices such as personal computers and smart phones are so numerous and under the control of multitudes of individual users, they are one of the weakest links in the infrastructure security chain. Protecting endpoints from being infected by malware is a critical arrow in the cybersecurity quiver. In this section, we will explore how machine learning can be used to help detect and prevent malware infections on endpoint devices.

Note that anti-malware software is often referred to as "anti-virus" software, even though malware comes in many different forms beyond just viruses—for example: worms, Trojan horses, adware, spyware, ransomware, etc. Malware also has many different purposes. While some are merely malicious and annoying pranks, most have some form of economic or national security motivation. The malware may be attempting to generate advertising revenue or redirect purchases to specific websites, to steal valuable information about individuals for resell, to steal money from financial institutions or credit cards, to steal intellectual property or competitive information, to encrypt valuable data for ransom, or even to steal computation cycles to mine cryptocurrency. Nation states and terrorist groups use malware to gain access to important intelligence information or to inflict damage to the infrastructure of an adversary, like the Stuxnet worm, which caused Iranian centrifuges to destroy themselves while enriching uranium.

Since the "Morris worm" infected 10 percent of the internet back in 1988, the battle between malware creators and anti-malware software has been one of constant escalation of detection and prevention followed by updated attacks circumventing those protections. Beginning in the early 1990s, the primary mechanisms for detecting malware have relied on some form of signature detection. For example, the earliest detection approach simply examined the binary code to detect modifications that caused code execution to jump to the end of the file to run the malicious software, a pattern not used by benign software. The battle has escalated from there.

Today, anti-malware software companies deploy a multitude of "honeypot" systems which have known security vulnerabilities and appear to be systems of interest to attackers to attract and obtain samples of new malware. Once new malware is captured in a honeypot, they are analyzed by threat analysts to develop "signatures" of these new examples of malware. These new signatures are then deployed to the endpoints containing their product to detect and block these new variants. The simplest and most common form of signature is to compute a cryptographic hash (e.g. MD5, SHA-1, SHA-2, SHA256 …) of the binary file and distribute that to the endpoints to block any files with the same hash. The cryptographic hash is designed so that it is highly unlikely that benign software will have the same hash and, therefore, will not be accidentally blocked. However, changing only a single bit within the malware binary will generate a completely different hash making it very easy for malware creators to generate multiple copies of the same malware with different hash signatures (known as "polymorphic" malware). Malware that creates its own copies with slight differences is known as "metamorphic."

"Fuzzy" hashing techniques can be used to thwart some of these simple modifications to the malware binary and still detect these metamorphic versions. Context Triggered Piecewise Hash (CTPH) [Source a] is an example of this approach. Rather than compute a single hash across the entire file, a hash is generated for many segments of the file. In this case, a single bit change would only affect one of the hashes, leaving the remaining hashes to identify the malware sample. Even in this case, multiple small changes throughout the file can result in different hashes for each segment of the file.

To get around these sorts of simple signature alteration strategies, anti-malware software derives more sophisticated signatures based on structure and features within the file that are more difficult for the malware creator to change while still not flagging benign software as malware. An example of this the "import hash" (or imphash – source b). An import table is generated for each executable for every function that the executable calls from another file. The way that this import table is generated allows for the computation of a hash that can identify families of related malware, even though their file hash or CTPH are different.

Even more complex forms of creating signatures are possible, but this process is dependent on human threat analysts, making it time-consuming and error prone. During the time it takes to derive and distribute signatures for new malware (also known as "zero-day malware"), all signature endpoints are vulnerable to attack. Depending on the novelty of the new malware sample, the exposure window can run from days to weeks (much like developing a new vaccine for COVID-19 takes longer than developing one for next fall's seasonal flu). A Machine Learning model that can detect zero-day malware without human intervention can eliminate this window of vulnerability to zero-day malware.

This window of vulnerability is not the only problem with human-identified, signature-based approaches to malware detection. Another vulnerability is the dependence on the ability to constantly update each endpoint with the latest list of signatures. For endpoints that are almost always connected to the Internet, this is not an additional risk. However, if the endpoint has sporadic connection to the Internet or is in a highly secure network that is never connected to the Internet, this dramatically increases the window of vulnerability to zero-day malware. Again, a Machine Learning model that can detect zero-day malware without human intervention can address this issue since it does not require periodic signature updates to be effective at detecting and blocking malware.

Before a piece of malware has detonated, detection is a binary classification problem (e.g. is this file clean or malicious?) with a very large number of labeled samples making it an ideal problem for Machine Learning. Once a file has been classified as malware, the threat analyst needs to determine what actions should be taken. This will be partially determined by the type of malware the file represents (e.g. worm, virus, trojan, ransomware, adware, etc.). Multiclass classification of the malware samples also lends itself well to a Machine Learning approach. In theory, any of the well-known Machine Learning classification approaches can be used. The most common options are the following and are described in more detail earlier in this chapter:

■ Random Forest;
■ Gradient-Boosted Trees;
■ Support Vector Machines;
■ Bayesian Networks;
■ K-Nearest Neighbors;
■ Logistic Regression;
■ Artificial Neural Networks.

The selection of the appropriate Machine Learning approach is heavily influenced by the constraints of this particular problem. For example, while some of the file characteristics relevant in classifying malware are numeric values (e.g. file size, entropy, etc.), you will see in the feature selection discussion that many more of them are categorical in nature (e.g. API calls used, Registry keys modified, etc.) rather than numerical. Not only does the Machine Learning approach need to deal with categorical features, but it also needs to be robust to features that are not always present and have no meaningful way to be imputed.

Training a Machine Learning model is done offline, so the amount of computer resources that are being used is typically not a relevant constraint. However, once the model has been trained, making a prediction on a file is significantly constrained by the endpoint device which must run the prediction. The prediction algorithm must limit how much CPU, Memory, and Battery Power are consumed since the endpoint device has other applications that must be able to run at the same time. Furthermore, if the prediction must complete before a new file can begin execution, the prediction latency must be very low so as to not impact the productivity of the endpoint user. Selection of a Machine Learning model that uses compute resources very efficiently is a critical design decision.

Decision tree algorithms (e.g. Random Forest and Gradient-Boosted Trees) have some decided advantages in classification of malware because they naturally handle categories in the structure of each decision node and many malware features are categorical. Furthermore, once trained, Decision Trees are relatively lightweight on compute and memory usage compared to Bayesian Networks and Artificial Neural Networks, and they generally produce better predictions than the other options.

Feature Selection and Feature Engineering for Detecting Malware

Since Machine Learning models learn from their training data, selecting the proper data is critical to building an effective model. The model is trying to learn the "malware signal" buried in the noise of the rest of the file's content, thus the training data needs to include whatever signals malware usually present. The process of selecting this data is called feature selection and feature engineering. Picking and engineering features that are different between malware and clean files is essential. Fortunately, this process can be guided by the very things that human threat analysts use to identify malware. This section will describe examples of the kinds of features that are often used to build Machine Learning malware classification models.

Common Vulnerabilities and Exposures (CVE)

Whenever a new exploit of an operating system, browser, or application is discovered, the details are submitted to the MITRE Corporation, which is funded by the National Cyber Security Division of the United States Department of Homeland Security to maintain a list of known security exposures available to the public. MITRE assigns each a unique "CVE number." The Common Vulnerability Scoring System (CVSS) is a free and open industry standard for assessing the severity of these CVEs. These CVEs are leveraged by malware to gain access to computer systems to accomplish their ultimate tasks. Because of this, CVEs are often not disclosed to the general public until the vendor responsible for the CVE has had the chance to release a patch or fix that eliminates the vulnerability or exposure.

In the early days of anti-malware detection, identifying code that exploited CVEs was one of the more effective ways to detect malware. Fast forward to today where tens of thousands of CVEs are reported every year. Even if threat analysts could keep up with this onslaught, by the time they release signatures for these CVEs, the vendors responsible for these exposures will have already released fixes for them so that a well-patched system is no longer vulnerable. This also makes CVEs very poor features for training a Machine Learning model. The model could learn all known CVEs but would have very little chance of predicting CVEs in the future. Fortunately, CVEs are really only the "keys" that malware uses to unlock the computer system. Even though these "keys" are all different, once inside the system, malware goes about its appointed task which is more easily detectable than the CVE used to gain access in the first place. The clues for these activities can be detected with the following types of features (Source c).

Text Strings

While malware primarily consists of executable code, they also contain predefined data fields and other text data that can help reveal malware. These text strings can include the name of the author, file names, names of system resource used, etc. For more sophisticated malware that attempts to obfuscate these clues, histograms of non-alphanumeric characters and string lengths (either unusually short or long) can help detect these techniques. While strings can yield important features for training a malware model, extracting them from executable code can be computationally expensive, especially for larger files.

Byte Sequences

Another effective set of features for detecting malware is to analyze the executable file at the byte level. A popular approach is to compute a histogram of n-grams. An n-gram is a sequence of n bytes in length. For example, a trigram (3-gram) could be the byte sequence "04 A7 3C." Since computational complexity for counting n-grams is exponential with n, this feature calculation is typically limited to bigrams and trigrams. This simple approach is surprisingly effective in distinguishing some forms of malware from benign executables.

Opcodes

The binary instructions that the CPU executes are called opcodes (operation codes). Parsing the code section of an executable file in the same way that the CPU does enables the calculation of the frequency at which each opcode is used. Likewise, histograms of n-grams of opcodes can be computed on sequences of opcodes. Malware will often make more frequent use of certain opcodes than the typical benign application. A recent example would be malware that is exploiting cache side-channel attacks enabled by design flaws in speculative code execution in modern CPUs such as Meltdown and Spectre (source e and f). These attacks make use of special cache manipulation opcodes that most applications do not use. However, extracting opcodes from an executable requires a decompiler which is computationally expensive, so is more appropriate for offline malware detection.

API, System Calls, and DLLs

Malware can also raise suspicions through examining the other software and system resources they use. Use of certain APIs/System Calls or the way the API/System Call is being used are important clues. Likewise, the list of Dynamic-Linked Libraries (DLL) used by the executable and the imphash discussed earlier can be used to summarize some of this information and provide telltale signs. For example, the Spectre/Meltdown examples mentioned previously rely heavily on accurate execution timing information and will make more frequent calls to the timer system calls than benign software.

Entropy

Sophisticated malware often makes use of encryption or compression in an attempt to hide the very features that would give it away. Encryption and compression increase the randomness of the binary data. Information entropy is a measure of the uncertainty in a variable's possible outcomes or its randomness. By computing the entropy of sections of the code, sections that have been encrypted or compressed can be detected. An executable file with a significant amount of entropy is a strong indication that the file is malware. However, compression is also used by benign applications like executable packers such as UPX, so high entropy has to be combined with other features to yield accurate predictions.

Feature Selection Process for Malware Detection

As with most Machine Learning applications, the feature selection process is the most important to developing a good model. This requires a careful set of experiments where a set of features are generated and used to train a model using a set of files selected for training. That model is then tested against files not included in the training set to determine its efficacy for out-of-sample files. A variety of techniques can be used to determine the importance of each feature to the prediction being made by the model. This is known as "feature importance." Features with near-zero importance can be removed and a new model trained to confirm that efficacy will not be impacted. Features that are highly correlated with each other can also be pared down in a similar fashion to achieve an optimal set of features that still achieve the desired efficacy. This is particularly important for features that are computationally expensive to calculate. For example, 4-grams are generally better at distinguishing malware from benign files but are more complex to compute than trigrams. Experimentation will determine whether the additional efficacy is worth the computational complexity. The generation of new types of features and experimentation are the keys to constant improvement of malware detection models.

Feature Selection Process for Malware Classification

Once a file has been predicted to be malware, a security/threat analyst will then want to know what type of malware has been detected since the response required for adware is very different than for ransomware, for example. This is a multi-class classification problem that can use most of the same Machine Learning techniques as malware detection, but with a different set of constraints. Malware detection requires a very quick prediction so that user experience is not impacted while the model is determining whether it is safe to launch an application. This means that malware prediction needs to be made in hundreds of milliseconds. Once a malware detection has been determined, execution of that file will be blocked and the security/threat analyst will not need to know the malware type for many seconds or minutes. In fact, the classification algorithm doesn't even need to be executed on the endpoint but could be sent to a separate server for classification.

Not only are the constraints on computation and memory very different for malware classification but the optimal feature selection is very likely different, as well. First, some features that distinguish malware from benign applications are common between different types of malware and will not be helpful. Other features may be common with benign software but are useful to distinguish different types of malware. Finally, given the more relaxed constraints for a malware classification model, features that were too expensive to compute on the endpoint can now be used in the malware classification model. Again, the generation of new types of features and experimentation are the keys to constant improvement of malware classification models.

Training Data

As with any Machine Learning model development, the resulting models are only as good as the data used for training. Fortunately, samples of malware are readily available in the millions, but that is not enough. Training a good binary classifier requires a representative sample of benign software. Benign samples from major software providers like Apple, Google, and Microsoft are relatively easy to obtain. Some smaller software providers only provide copies to paying subscribers. Applications developed for internal use at corporations are very difficult to obtain. This is even worse for document files. The vast majority of benign document files are generated by businesses or consumers and are not publicly available.

Furthermore, malware detection is a very unbalanced binary classification problem. The ratio of benign files to malignant files is >> 1M:1. If the training set is similarly imbalanced, the model will be biased to predicting benign since that is the right answer >99.9 percent of the time. So, the training set needs to be more evenly balanced between malignant and benign files than is found in real life. Note that the balance cannot go too far in the other direction or the model will be biased to predicting malignant over benign. Within this relatively balanced training set, the sample of benign and malignant samples need to be as diverse as possible to produce a model that will predict well in deployment. Constant grooming and improvement of the training set by incorporation of classes of files that are mis-predicted is essential for improving the efficacy of malware detection models.

Tuning of Malware Classification Models Using a Receiver Operating Characteristic Curve

An ideal malware classification model would always block malware and never block benign software. However, even the best models will have False Negatives (failure to detect malware) and False Positives (detecting benign software as malignant). If the False Positive rate is too high, the user will get frustrated by having their legitimate work interrupted by the model "crying wolf" too often. On the other hand, a model with a high False Negative rate is little better than having no model at all. Most modeling techniques have a confidence level associated with their prediction. This confidence level can be used to set a threshold for when a malware prediction results in the file actually being blocked (e.g. only block software when the model is >90 percent confident in its malware prediction).

A common technique used to set this threshold is to use a Receive Operating Characteristic (ROC) curve. This is a curve made by plotting the True Positive rate (malware correctly predicted) versus the False Positive rate (benign software predicted as malignant) for each confidence level threshold. Figure 1 is an example of two different ROC curves for two different models. The top right corner reflects setting the threshold such that all software is predicted as malware (i.e. malware confidence threshold = 0). At this setting, 100 percent of all malware will be detected, but 100 percent of benign software will be misidentified as malware. The bottom left corner is the opposite extreme where nothing is detected as malware (i.e. confidence threshold = 100 percent). The rest of the curve reflects the impact of adjusting the confidence threshold between these two extremes.

ROC curves provide a strong visual indication of the predictive power of a model. A perfect model would have a ROC "curve" that is a vertical line on the y-axis connected to a horizontal line along the top of the plot. Random guessing would yield a diagonal line from the origin to the top right corner. The closer the ROC curve is to the top left corner, the more predictive the model is. In fact, the Area Under the Curve (AUC) is often used as a metric to compare the effectiveness of a model. In Figure 1, the model with the ROC 1 curve is much more predictive than the one represented by the ROC 2 curve.

An effective malware detection algorithm needs to achieve very high levels of efficacy. A model that flags benign software as malware 10 percent of the time (False Positive rate of 0.1) would be very annoying for most users. The ROC 2 model only achieves a True Positive rate of 50 percent if the threshold is set to yield a 10 percent False Positive rate. In contrast, the threshold for the model represented by ROC 1 can be set to a 1 percent False Positive rate and still achieve a True Positive rate in the high 90 percent range.

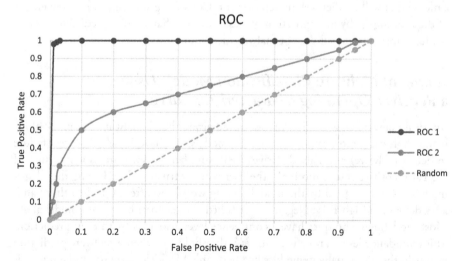

Different customers may have different sensitivities to False Positive vs True Positive rates. For example, a sophisticated, high-security customer might prefer a higher False Positive rate in exchange for a higher True Positive rate, so the threshold adjustment may be exposed to the customer to select. An endpoint protection product may also offer different actions based on the confidence threshold. If the model is highly confident that a sample is malware, the file may be immediately quarantined. If the model is slightly less confident, it may leave the file alone and alert the Security Analyst to determine what to do.

Detecting Malware after Detonation

The safest time to detect malware is before it is allowed to execute. However, even the best models will miss detecting some malware before execution. The next layer of protection is to detect malware that is already active on the endpoint. Many of the same features and techniques used for static file analysis could be used to analyze the in-memory footprint of each active process. When malware is active in memory, it will likely have decrypted any encrypted parts of its code that it was trying to hide. This makes entropy as a feature less useful, but many of the other features may become more effective since more of the malware's actual code and data are now exposed in the clear. Still, any malware that escaped detection in the static file analysis model has a pretty good shot at not being detected by only these same features.

Once malware is active, models that detect anomalous behavior can be more effective at detecting the presence of malware. By observing things like CPU, memory, network, file, and registry update activity for unusual activity, malware can reveal itself. Some unusual malware activity can be anticipated like uploading significant amounts of data, modifying sensitive registry keys, or updating critical areas of storage (e.g. the boot record), which a model can look for explicitly.

For other activity that is more subtle, an anomaly detection model is required. Unlike the supervised models described for malware detection and classification, anomaly detection requires an unsupervised modeling approach since labeled samples of the malicious behavior are unlikely to be available. Some unsupervised algorithms include:

- Clustering algorithms (k-means, DBSCAN, HDBSCAN, etc.);
- Anomaly detection (Local outlier factor, Isolation Forest);
- Normal behavior modeling (Various neural network autoencoder algorithms, …).

In all of these approaches, the key thing is for the model to have been trained on enough "normal" data to be able to detect something that is "not normal." These models all learn some representation of what the normal relationship between all of the features has been in the past. Once a new relationship is detected, then the model makes an "abnormal" prediction. Whether this abnormal condition is caused by malware or merely a "new normal" behavior that has not been seen before will be up to the Security Analyst to figure out.

For endpoints that are relatively locked down and are typically doing the same kinds of things over and over (e.g. an embedded process controller), anomaly detection of this sort can be very effective. For more general-purpose endpoints (e.g. an individual's PC), where new applications are being installed and new websites are being accessed, the risk of False Positives goes up quite a bit and can result in the dreaded "cry wolf" syndrome.

Summary

With the availability of a very large, well-labeled set of training data and relevant extracted features, developing a malware detection model using machine learning is very achievable. As these types of models become more prevalent on deployed endpoints, we can be sure that malware creators will find ways to circumvent detection and create the next round of escalation in this never-ending war.

Applications of Machine Learning Using Python

As you have seen throughout this book thus far, the heart of Artificial Intelligence and all of the subsets that reside within it (Machine Learning, Neural Networks, and Computer Vision), is the data and the sets in which they "live in." An Artificial Intelligence is only as good as the datasets that it uses in order to come up with the desired outputs.

In Chapter 1, we examined in great detail the importance of data, and the great care that must be used to select the right data pieces that are needed for your Artificial Intelligence application(s). In the first half of Chapter 2, we also examined in great detail the types of the various datasets that can be used, from the standpoint of computational statistics. We also reviewed the types of statistical as well as mathematical concepts that are needed to further optimize these kinds of datasets.

Optimization in this regard is a very critical step before the datasets are fed into the Machine Learning system. For example, as we have learned, if you have too much data, then the system will overtrain due to the excessive data that is present, and will most likely present a series of outputs that are highly skewed, well beyond what you were either anticipating or expecting.

Datasets with too much data in them can also tax the processing as well as the computational powers of the Machine Learning system. It is important to keep in mind that the ideal conditions for having your Machine Learning system deliver your desired outputs is for it to be constantly fed datasets on a 24/7/365 basis. This is enough to put a burden on the system in and of itself. Therefore, the process of cleansing and optimizing the datasets in order to get rid of excess or unneeded is an absolute must.

In the chapters in this book thus far, whenever an Artificial Intelligence system or Machine Learning system was used as a reference point, it was assumed that a technology was already in place, not developed from scratch per se. In this regard, it can be further assumed that such systems were made readily available by having them ready to deploy from a Cloud-based platform.

In other words, these applications of both Artificial Intelligence and Machine Learning are made available as a "Software as a Service," or "SaaS" offering. But also keep in mind that many Machine Learning applications can also be built from scratch as well, in order to fully meet your exacting requirements. In order to do this, the Python programming language is made use of quite often.

As we continue looking at various types of applications, we will provide two separate examples of just how you can build a very simple Machine Learning application using Python on two different market sectors:

- The Healthcare Sector;
- The Financial Services Sector.

The Use of Python Programming in the Healthcare Sector

Given the world that we live in right now with COVID-19 and both the human and economic toll that it has taken worldwide, many people have lost their jobs, and many others have been furloughed, without any guarantees that their particular job will be in place once things have gradually started to open up. In this regard, the use of chatbots has now become important, not just for E-Commerce and online store applications, but even for the healthcare industry as well.

In fact, these technological tools are now being used to help doctors and nurses in the ER to, at a certain level, help diagnose patients and even provide some treatment recommendations. In this section, we will examine further how to build a very simple chatbot using the Python language. But first, it is important to give a high level overview of just how Machine Learning and chatbots are being used in conjunction with one another today.

How Machine Learning is Used with a Chatbot

It is important to keep in mind that with a chatbot, you can interact with it one of two ways, and possibly even both:

- Text chats;
- Voice commands.

In order to accommodate both of these scenarios, chatbots make use of the concepts of both Machine Learning (ML) and Natural Language Processing (NLP). Machine Learning is what is used to create intelligent answers and responses to your queries as you engage in a conversation with it.

One of the key advantages of using Machine Learning in this aspect is that it can literally learn about you as you keep engaging with it over a period of time.

For example, it builds a profile of you and keeps track of all of your conversations so that it can pull it up in a matter of seconds for subsequent chat sessions, and later on, down the road, it can even anticipate the questions that you may ask of it so that it can provide the best answer possible to suit your needs.

By doing it this way, you never have to keep typing in the same information over and over again.

NLP is yet another subbranch of AI, and this is the tool that is primarily used if you engage in an actual, vocal conversation with a chatbot. It can easily replicate various human speech patterns in order to produce a realistic tone of voice when it responds back to you. Whether you are engaging in either or both of these kinds of communication methods, it is important to note that chatbots are getting more sophisticated on an almost daily basis.

The primary reason for this is that they use a combination of very sophisticated, statistical algorithms and high-level modeling techniques, as well as the concepts of data mining. Because of this, the chatbot can now interact on a very proactive basis with you, rather than you having to take the lead in the conversations, thus making it flow almost seamlessly.

As a result of using both Machine Learning and NLP, chatbots are now finding their way to being used in a myriad of different types of applications, some of which include the following:

- Merchant websites that make use of an online store;
- Mobile apps that can be used on your Android or iOS device;
- Messaging platforms;
- Market research when it comes to new product and service launches;
- Lead generation;
- Brand awareness;
- Other types of E-Commerce scenarios;
- Customer service (this is probably the biggest use of it yet);
- Healthcare (especially when it comes to booking appointments with your doctor);
- Content delivery.

The Strategic Advantages of Machine Learning In Chatbots

As one can infer, there are a plethora of advantages of using this kind of approach for your business. Some of these include the following:

1) You have a 24/7/365 sales rep:

As mentioned earlier, there is no need for human involvement if you have an AI-driven chatbot. Therefore, you have an agent that can work at all times of the day and night that can help sell your products and services on a real-time basis. In other words, it will never get tired and will always be eager to serve!

2) It cuts down on expenses:

By using a chatbot, you may not even have to hire a complete, full-time customer service staff. Thus, you will be able to save on your bottom line by not having to pay salary and benefits. But keep in mind, you should never use a chatbot as a total replacement for your customer service team. At some point in time, you will need some of them around in order to help resolve complex issues or questions if the chatbot cannot do it.

3) Higher levels of customer satisfaction:

Let's face it, in our society, we want to have everything right now and right here. We have no patience when we have to wait for even a few minutes to talk to a customer support rep on the other line. But by using a chatbot, this wait is cut down to just a matter of seconds, thus, this results in a much happier customer and in more repeat business.

4) Better customer retention:

When you are able to deliver much needed answers or solutions to desperate customers and prospects, there is a much higher chance that you will be able to keep them for the long-term. This is where the chatbot comes into play. Remember, you may have a strong brand, but that will soon dissipate quickly if you are unable to fill needs in just a matter of minutes.

5) You can reach international borders:

In today's E-Commerce world, there are no international boundaries. A customer or a prospect is one that can purchase your products and services from any geographic location where they may be at. If you tried to do this with the traditional customer service rep model, not only would this be an expensive proposition, but representatives would have to be trained in other languages as well. Also, the annoyance factor can set in quite rapidly if the customer rep cannot speak the desired language in a consistent tone and format. But the AI-driven chatbot alleviates all of these problems because they come with foreign language processing functionalities already built into them.

6) It can help triage cases:

If your business is large enough where you need to have a dedicated call center to fully support it, the chances are that your customer service reps are being bombarded with phone calls and are having a hard time keeping up with them. If you deploy a chatbot here, you can use that to help resolve many of the simpler to more advanced issues and queries. But if something is much more advanced and a chatbot cannot resolve it, it also has the functionality to route that conversation to the appropriate rep that can handle it. In other words, the chatbot can also triage conversations with customers and prospects if the need ever arises.

An Overall Summary of Machine Learning and Chatbots

The following matrix depicts the advantages of using an AI driven chatbot versus using the traditional virtual assistant:

Functionality	AI driven Chatbot	Virtual Assistant
FAQs easily answered	Yes	Yes
Can understand sophisticated questions	Yes	No
Can create a customized and personable response	Yes	
It can learn more about you from previous conversations	Yes	No
It can greatly improve future conversations with you	Yes	No

The Building of the Chatbot—A Diabetes Testing Portal

In this particular example, the primary role of the chatbot is to help greet a particular patient and guide them through a series of questions in order for them to submit a blood test in order to determine if this individual has diabetes or not. It is important to keep in mind that it is not the chatbot that will actually be conducting this kind of test, rather the patient will have to sit separately at an automated testing machine in order for the blood test to be carried out.

As it has been described in great length in these first two chapters, it's very important to make a Decision Tree first, as this will guide the software development team in creating the software modules, as well as the source code that resides within it. Since the example we are giving in this subsection is rather very simple, the resulting Decision Tree is relatively straight forward as well.

The following depicts this Decision Tree:

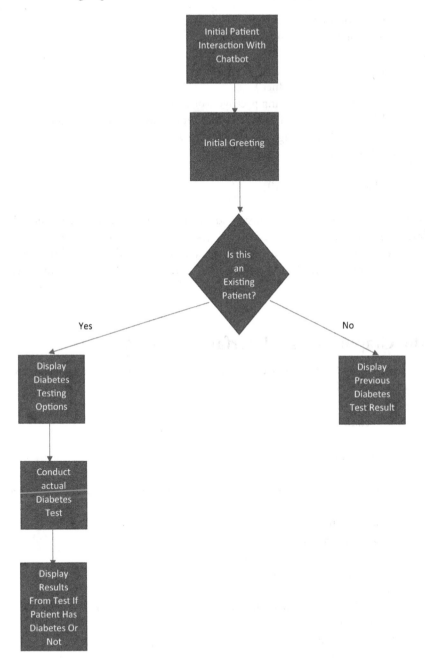

The Initialization Module

The initialization Python code is:
Install using the following commands:

```
Import nltk
Nltk.download ('wordnet')
[nltk_data] Downloading package wordnet to
[nltk_data] C:\Users\PMAUTHOR\Appdata\Roaming\nltk_data ...
[nltk_data] Unzipping corpora\wordnet.zip
Out[4]: True
Import nltk
Nltk.download ('punkt')
```

NOTE: The above Python source code will actually pull up a Graphical User Interface (GUI) library and various images so that the patient can interact seamlessly with the chatbot. Also included is a specialized "dormant" function that will put the chatbot to sleep if it has not been in active use for an extended period of time.

The Graphical User Interface (GUI) Module

The next package is the source code that will help create the above mentioned GUI in order to help the patient out:

```
# -*- coding: utf-8 -*-
"""
@author: RaviDas
"""
#Loading tkinter libraries which will be used to in the GUI of the medial
    chatbot
Import tkinter
From tkinter import *
From tkinter.scrolledtext import *
From tkinter import ttk
Import time
From PIL import Image Tk, Image
Import tkinter
#Loading random choices in our Chatbot program
Import random
```

The Splash Screen Module

After the initial GUI has been presented to the patient by the above described Python source code, the next step is to create a "Splash Screen" that will welcome the patient to this particular medical hospital. The Python source code to do this is as follows:

```
#Splash Screen
Splash = tkinter.Tk ()
Splash.title ("Welcome to this Diabetes Testing Portal, brought to you by
    Hospital XYZ")
Splash.geometry ("1000 X 1000")
Splash.configure (background = 'green')
W = Label(splash, text = "Hospital XYZ Diabetes Testing Portal\nloading ...,
    font = "Helvetica", 26), fg = "white", bg = "green"
w.pack ()
splash.update ()
time.sleep (6)
splash.deiconify ()
splash.destroy ().
```

The Patient Greeting Module

After the overall welcome GUI has been presented to the patient, the next step is to create a specialized window that specifically greets the patient, using their first and last name. The Python source code to do this is as follows:

```
#Initializing tkinter library for GUI Window show up window = tkinter.Tk ()
S = tkinter.Scrollbar (window)
Chatmsg.focus_set ()
s.pack (side = tkinter.RIGHT, fill = tkinter.Y)
chatmsg.pack (side = tkinter.TOP, fill = tkinter.Y)
s.config (command = chatmsg.yview)
chat.config (yscrollcommand = s.set)
input_user = String Var ()
input_field = Entry (window, text = input_user_
input_field.pack (side = tkinter.BOTTOM, fill = tkinter.X)
bot_text = "Welcome to the Hospital XYZ Diabetes Testing Portal\n"
chatmsg.insert (INSERT, 'Bot:%s\n' % bot_text)
bot_text = "Press enter to continue "
chatmsg.insert (INSERT, 'Bot:%s\n' % bot_text)
chat.msg.focus ().
```

The Diabetes Corpus Module

In real world scenarios and applications, especially when it comes to dealing with Natural Language Processing, there is a concept that is known as a "Corpus." In simpler terms, this is nothing but a collection of the related jargon and other forms of lexicons that are used by a specific industry. So, in our chatbot example using Python programming, there will be a good amount of medical terms that are used if this chatbot were to be actually deployed in a real world setting, such as in a doctor's office, outpatient center, or even in a hospital setting.

To go through each type of medical terminology that could be used with a medical chatbot is out of the scope of this book, but to give you an example of how it can be created in the Python programming language, the following demonstrates how to create what is known as a "Diagnostics Corpus," in order to examine a patient who could potentially have diabetes:

```
#Diagnostics Corpus for medical chatbot
Greet = ['Hello, welcome to the Hospital XYZ Diabetes Testing Portal', 'Hi,
    welcome to the Hospital XYZ Diabetes Testing Portal', 'Hey, welcome to
    the Hospital XYZ Diabetes Testing Portal', 'Good Day, welcome to the
    Hospital XYZ Diabetes Testing Portal']
Confirm = ['Yes', 'Yay', 'Yeah', 'Yo']
Membered = ['12345', 12346', 12347', 12348', '12349']
Customer = ['Hello', 'Hi', 'Hey']
Answer = ['Please select one of the options so that I can help you', 'I truly
    understand and sympathize with your anxieties, but please input an appro-
    priate response']
Greetings = ['Hola, welcome to the Hospital XYZ Diabetes Testing Portal
    again', 'Hello, welcome to the Hospital XYZ Diabetes Testing Portal again',
    'Hey, welcome to the Hospital XYZ Diabetes Testing Portal', 'Hi, welcome
    to the Hospital XYZ Diabetes Testing Portal']
Question = ['How are you?', 'How are you doing?']
Responses = ['I am OK', 'I could be doing better', 'I feel sick', 'I feel anxious',
    'I am fine']
Another = ["Do you want another Diabetes Test?"]
Diabetes tests = ['Type 1 for the hbAic Test', 'Type 2 for the Blood Viscosity
    Test', 'Type 3 for the Heart Rate Test', 'Type 4 for the Blood Oxygen Test',
    'Type 5 for the Blood Pressure Test']
Testresponse = ['1', '2', '3', '4', '5', '6']
```

NOTE: As you can see from the simple Python programming source code up above, there are many different kinds of responses that are presented to the patient, depending upon the depth of their language skills, and their vocabulary that they use in everyday conversations with other people. As mentioned, this is only a simple example, and if this were to be actually deployed in a real world medical setting, many other responses would have to be entered into the Python source code as well. Also, other foreign languages would have to be programmed in as well, primarily that of Spanish.

The Chatbot Module

In this specific module, we now further examine the underlying constructs of the source which now make up the actual Diabetes Chatbot application:

```
#Global variable to check first time greeting
Firstswitch = 1
Newid = '12310'
Memid = 0
Def chat (event):
      Import time
      Import random
      Global memid
      Condition= ""
      #Greet for first time
      Global firstswitch
If (firstswitch==1):
      Bot_text = random.choice (greet0
      Chatmsg.insert (INSERT, 'Bot:%s\n' %bot_text)
      Bot_text = "If you are an existing patient of Hospital XYZ, please enter
            in your Patient ID: or enter no if you are a new patient"
      Chatmsg.insert (INSERT, 'Bot:%s\n' %bot_text)
      Firstswitch = 2
If (firstswitch = 1):
      Input_get = input_field.get().lower()
      If any (srchstr in input_get for srchstr in membered):
            Memid = input_get
            Bot_text = "Thank you for being a loyal and dedicated patient of
                  Hospital XYZ\n Please choose the type of service that is most
                  suited for your visit this time from the following menu in order
                  to continue with the diagnostics procedure\ nType 1 for the
                  hbAic Test\ nType 2 for the Blood Viscosity Test\ nType 3 for the
                  Heart Rate Test'\ nType 4 for the Blood Oxygen Test\ nType 5
                  for the Blood Pressure Test'\ nType 6 to Exit the Diabetes Testing
                  Portal\n\n"
Elif (input_get=="no"):
      Memid = newid
```

```
        Bot_text = "Your new Member Identification Number is: " + newid
            + "Please remember this for future reference since you are a new
            patient. \n Please choose the type of service that is most suited for
            your visit this time from the following menu in order to continue
            with the diagnostics procedure\ nType 1 for the hbAic Test\ nType 2
            for the Blood Viscosity Test\ nType 3 for the Heart Rate Test'\ nType
            4 for the Blood Oxygen Test\ nType 5 for the Blood Pressure Test'\
            nType 6 to Exit the Diabetes Testing Portal\n\n"
Elif any (srchstr in input_get for srchstr in testresponse):
        Bot-text = "Please place any of your fingers up on the Fingerprint Panel
            as indicated above in order to proceed with your Diabetes Test"
        Chatmsg.insert (INSERT, 'Bot:%s\n' % bot_text)
        Delaycounter = 0
        For delaycounter in range (0,10):
            Bot_text = str (delaycounter)
            Time.sleep (1)
            Chatmsg.insert (INSERT, 'Bot:%s\n' % bot_text)
        Bot_text = "Please wait for a few minutes, we are analyzing your Diabetes
            Test, and will present you with the results shortly\n"
        Chatmsg.insert (INSERT, 'Bot:%s\n' % bot_text)
            Time.sleep(2)
            If (input_get=="1):
                Hba1c = random.randit (4, 10)
                Bot_text    =    "Member    Identification    Number:"    +
                    str(memidnum) + "Your hbaa1c
                Test resultis: "+ str(hba1c)
                If (hba1c>=4 and hbaic<=5.6):
                    Condition= "You do not have Diabetes"
                Elif (hba1c>5.7 and hba1c<=6.4):
                    Condition = "You are prediabetic, please consult your
                        Primary Care Physician as soon as possible"
                Elif (hba1c>6.5):
                    Condition = "You are diabetic, please consult your
                        Primary Care Physician as soon as possible"
                Bot_text = bot_text +" Your condition is: "+condition
                Chatmsg.insert (INSERT, 'Bot:%s\n % bot_text)
                Elif (input_get==2):
                    Viscosity=random.randit (20,60)
                    Bot_text = "Member Identification Number: " +
                        str(memidnum) + "Your Blood Viscosity Level test
                        result is " +str(viscosity)
                Elif (input_get==3):
                    Viscosity=random.randit (20,60)
```

```
            Bot_text = "Member Identification Number: " +
            str(memidnum) + "Your Heart Rate Level test result
            is " +str(heatrate)
Elif (input_get==4):
        Viscosity=random.randit (20,60)
        Bot_text = "Member Identification Number: " +
        str(memidnum) + "Your Blood Oxygen test result is "
        +str(oxygen)
Elif (input_get==5):
        Systolic = random.randit (80,200)
        Diastolic = random.randit (80,110)
        Bot_text = "Member Identification Number: " +
        str(memidnum) + "Your Blood Pressure Level test
        result is: Systolic: " +str(systolic)"
        " Diastolic: " + str(diastolic)
Elif (input_get==6):
        Import sys
        Window.deiconfy ()
        Window.destroy ()
        Sys.exit (0)
        Else:
                From nltk.stem import WordNetLemmatizer
        Import nltk
        If ((not input_get) or (int(input_get)<=0)):
                Print ("Did you just press Enter?") #print some info
        Else:
                Lemmatizer = WordNetLemmatizer()
                Input_get = input_field.get().lower()
                Lemvalue = lemmatizer.lemmatize(input_get)
                Whatsentiment = getSentiment(lemvalue)
                If (whatsentiment=="pos"):
                        Bot_text = answer[0]
                        #print ("Positive Sentiment")
                Elif (whatsentiment=="neg"):
                        Bot_text = answer[1]
                #print ("Negative Sentiment")
                Chatmsg.insert (INSERT, '%s\n' % lemvalue)
                #bot_text = "I do not understand what you mean!"
        Chatmsg.insert (INSERT, '%s\n' % lemvalue)
        #label = Label(window, text = input_get)
        Input_user.set(")
        #label.pack()
        Return "break"
```

The Sentiment Analysis Module

It should be noted that a key component of chatbots that makes use of Machine Learning is what is known as "Sentiment Analysis." It can be technically defined as follows:

> Sentiment analysis is contextual mining of text which identifies and extracts subjective information in source material, and helping a business to understand the social sentiment of their brand, product, or service while monitoring online conversations. However, analysis of social media streams is usually restricted to just basic sentiment analysis and count based metrics.

(SOURCE: 4).

As one can see from the above definition, at its most simplistic level, the purpose of using Sentiment Analysis is to try to gauge, with scientific certainty, the mood of the prospect or the customer. In the case of our example, the basic premise is to gauge just exactly (to some degree of certainty) how either the existing patient and/ or the new patient is feeling. It is important to keep in mind that Sentiment Analysis can be quite complex, and translating all of that into a production mode chatbot will take many lines of Python source code.

But for purposes of the chatbot that we are building in this subsection, we will demonstrate on a very simplistic level what the Python source code will look like:

```
#Sentiment Analyzer using NLP
Def getSentiment(text):
    Import nltk
    From nltk.tokenize import word_tokenize
    #nltk,download ('punkit')
    #Step1 – Training data building from the Diabetes Corpus Module
    Train = [(thanks for an outstanding diabetes report", "pos"),
    ("Your service is very efficient and seamless", "pos"),
    ("As a patient, I am overall pleased with the services that have been
        provided", "pos")
    ("I did not know that I actually had Diabetes until after I took this series
        of tests", "neg",)
    ("The service could have been a little bit quicker—perhaps too much to
        be processed", "neg"),
    ("Hospital XYZ was not easy for me to find", "neg"),
    ("Hospital XYZ was very easy for me to find", "pos"),
    ("I do not quite believe the results of the tests that were conducted—I
        will seek a second medical opinion", "neg"),
```

("I wish there was more human contact at Hospital XYZ, everything seems to be too automated", "neg"),

("Can I actually talk to a human medical expert here?!", "neg"),

("The test results from the Diabetes tests are good", "pos"),

("Hospital XYZ has a good level of medical service", "pos"),

("Hospital XYZ has a great level of medical service", "pos"),

("Hospital XYZ has a superior level of medical service", "pos"),

("Hospital XYZ has an amazing array of medical technology", "pos"),

("This Diabetes Report cannot be true by any means", "neg"),

("This testing procedure will be very expensive for me—I am not sure if my medical insurance will even cover this", "neg"),

("I cannot believe that I have Diabetes based upon this report", "neg"),

("Does this mean I have to take special Diabetic medication and prescriptions?", "neg"),

("Will I have to take either injections or oral medication on a daily basis?", "neg"),

("My lipids are getting much worse than expected—should I see my Primary Care Physician?", "neg"),

("Hospital XYZ has very poor level of service", "neg"),

("Hospital XYZ has a poor level of service", "neg"),

("Hospital XYZ has a bad level of service", "neg"),

("Hospital XYZ is extremely slow with service and medical report processing", "neg"),

("Hospital XYZ is very slow with service and medical report processing", "neg"),

("Hospital XYZ is slow with service and medical report processing", "neg"),

("My Diabetes actually got worst with these tests than with previous ones", "neg"),

("I don't believe this Diabetes Report", "neg"),

("I don't like the sound of this Diabetes Report", "neg"),

("I am in Diabetes Limbo here", "neg"),

```
#Step 2 Tokenize the words to the dictionary
    Dictionary = set(word.lower() for passage in train for word in word_
    Tokenize (passage[0]))
#Step 3 Locate the word in training data
    T = [({word: (word in word_tokenize(x[0])) for word in dictionary),
    X[1]) for x in train]
#Step 4 – the classifier is trained with sample data
    Classifier = nltk.NaiveBayesClassifer.train(t)
    Test_data = "oh my gosh what is this???"
    Test_data_features = {word.lower(): (word in word_tokenize (test_data.
    Lower ()))) for word in dictionary}
```

```
        Print (classifer.classify(test_data_features))
        Return classifier.classify(test_data_features)
    #Start the program chat and put in loop
    Input_field.bind ("<Return>", chat)
    Tkinter.mainloop()
```

NOTE: The source for this Python code comes from (SOURCE: 5).

Overall, this section has examined the use of Python source code to build, in essence, a very primitive prototype of a chatbot that makes use of Machine Learning in a medical environment. It is important to keep in mind that the chatbots that are used in a real-world setting in production mode will actually require millions upon millions of lines of Python source, given the depth and the complexity of the application in question.

The Building of the Chatbot—Predicting Stock Price Movements

Probably one of the biggest uses of Artificial Intelligence is that of the Financial Industry. In this regard, it is most often used to try to predict stock price movements so that financial traders, hedge fund managers, mutual fund managers, etc. can make profitable trades not only so that they can make more money in the respective portfolios that they manage, but also to ensure that their clients do the same.

This is actually a field that is best left for Neural Networks, but Machine Learning can also be used just as well. In this section, we build a very simple Python-based model in order to help try to predict what future stock price movements could potentially look like. It is important to keep in mind that no system ever has or ever will predict these kinds of movements with a 100 percent level of accuracy.

The best an individual can do is to try to estimate the range in which a future stock price could fall in, and from their make the best educated extrapolations possible. Thus, in this regard, the concepts of statistics are very often called upon, such as that of the Moving Average and Multiple Regression Analysis.

The S&P 500 Price Acquisition Module

Before you can start writing the Python source code, you first need to gain access to a Stock Market Price Feed. In this instance, you will need an API that can connect directly and integrate with the Python source code. For the purposes of building this series of modules, you will need to get the Pandas Data Reader, which is available at this link:

pandas-datareader.readthedocs.io/en/latest/remote_data.html

The below Python source code demonstrates how you can get the S&P 500 data to load up, and it gives you the relevant stock prices that you need:

```
#-" -coding: utf-8 -*-
AUTHOR: RaviDas
====
Input numpy as np
Import pandas as pd
#import pandas.io.data as web
From pandas_datareader import data, wb
Sp500 = data.DataReader ('^GSPC, data_source= 'yahoo', start='5/18/2020'
End = '7/1/2020')
#sp500 = data.DataReader ('^GSPC, data_source= 'yahoo')
Sp500.ix ['5/18/2020']
Sp500.info()
Print(sp500)
Print(sp500.columns)
Print(sp500.shape)
Import matplotlib.pyplot as plt
Plt.plot(sp500['Close'])
#now calculating the 42nd day as well as the 252 day trend for the index
Sp500['42d' = np.round(pd.rolling_mean(sp500['Close'], window=42),2)
Sp500['252d' = np.round(pd.rolling_mean(sp500['Close'], window=252),2)
#Look at the Data
Sp500[['Close', '42d', '252d']].tail()
Plt.plot(sp500[['Close', '42d', 252d']])
```

Loading Up the Data from the API

The following module depicts the Python source code in order to load up more financial data from the specified API, as described in the last subsection:
Pip install Quandi

```
#-*-coding: utf-8 -*-
@author: RaviDas
Import quandl
Quandl.ApiConfig.api_key = 'INSERT YOUR API KEY HERE'
# get the table for daily stock prices and,
# filter the table for the selected tickers, columns within a time range
# set paginate to True because Quandl limits the tables from the API to 10,000
    per call
```

```
Data = quandl.get_table ('WICKI/PRICES', ticker = ['AAPL', 'MFST',
   'WMT']
      Qopts = {'colums': ['ticker', 'date', 'adj_close']},
      Date = {'gte': '5-18-2020', 'lte': '5-18-2020"],
         Paginate=True)
Data.head()
# create a new dataframe with 'date' column as index
Now = data.set_index('date')
#use pandas pivot function to sort aj_close by tickers
Clean_data = new.pivot (columns='ticker')
#check the head of the output
Clean_data.head()
Import Quandl
Quandl.ApiConfig.api_key = 'z1bx8q275VanEKSOLJwa'
Quandl.AiConfig.api_version = '5-18-2020'
Import Quandl
Data = qunadl.get ('NYSE/MSFT')
Data.head()
Data.columns
Data.shape
#This stores the stock price data in a flat file
Data.to_csv("NYSE_MSFT.csv")
#A basic statistical plot of the MSFT price data over the certain timespan
Data['Close'].plot()
```

The Prediction of the Next Day Stock Price Based upon Today's Closing Price Module

As the title of this subsection implies, you are using the financial stock information that you have loaded up in the last module in order to try to gauge what the price of a certain stock will be when the NYSE opens up the next morning based upon the previous day's closing price:

```
Import numpy as np
Import pandas as pd
Import os
#Change your directory to wherever the actual financial dataset is stored at
Os.chdir ("E:\\") # Change this to your directory path or wherever you
   downloaded the financial stock price information from the API based
   dataset.
#Loading the dataset of the particular company for which the prediction is
   replaced
```

```
Df=pd.read_csv ("StockPriceSP500DDataset.csv", parse_dates=['Date'])
Print(df.head(1))
Print(df.columns)
Out[*]
Unamed: 0 Date Opening Price High Low Closing Price Total Number of
    Shares Traded
Index ([u'Unamed: 0', u'Date', u'Opening Price' u'High', u 'Low', u'Closing
    Price', u'Total Number of Shares Traded'
Dtype = 'object'
Df.shape
```

The Financial Data Optimization (Clean-Up) Module

In this particular module, the financial data that has been collected from the SP500 API (as reviewed previously) is now "cleaned up" in order to provide a more accurate reading of future financial stock prices:

```
#Checking to see if any financial data optimization, or clean-up is further
    required
Df.isnull().any()
#df=df.dropna()
#df=df.replace("NA", 0)
Df.types
Out[96]:
Date datetime64[ns]
Open float64
Close float 64
Dtype: object
```

The Plotting of SP500 Financial Data for the Previous Year + One Month

As the title implies, this module plots the specified SP500 financial data from the previous year, with a lag time of one month included:

```
#Now plot the SP500 financial data for just the entire previous year and
    one month
Df['Date'].dt.year==2019
Mask=(df['Date'] > 1-1-2019 & (df['Date']] <= '12/31/2018')
Print(df.loc[mask])
Df2018=df.loc[mask]
Print(df2018.head(5))
Plt.plot(df2018['Date'], df2018['Close'])
```

The Plotting of SP500 Financial Data for One Month

This module plots the specified SP500 financial data for just a one month time span:

```
#Plotting the last 1 month data from the SP500
Mask = (df['Date'] > '12-13-2017') & (df['Date'] <= '12-24-2018')
Print(df.loc[mask])
Dfdec2017=df.loc[mask]
Print(dfdec2018.head(S))
Pt.plot(dfdec2018['Date'], dfdec2018['Close'])
```

Calculating the Moving Average of an SP500 Stock

As mentioned earlier in this section, one of the statistical tools that is used to help predict a future stock price is that of the Moving Average. The following Python source code demonstrates how this can be done:

```
#Now calculating the Moving Average of A Stock In The SP500
#Simple Moving Average Of Just One Year
Df2019['SMA'] = df2018['Close'].rolling(window=20).mean()
Df2019.head(2S)
Df2018[['SMA', 'Close']].plot().
```

Calculating the Moving Average of an SP500 Stock for just a One Month Time Span

This Python source code below is almost the same as the previous module, but for just one month:

```
# Now calculating the Moving Average of A Stock In The SP500 for just a one
    month time span
Dfdec2019['SMA'] = dfdec2019['Close'].rolling(window=2).mean()
Dfdec2019.head(25)
Dfdec2019[['SMA', 'Close']].plot()
```

The Creation of the NextDayOpen Column for SP500 Financial Price Prediction

While all of the other previous modules are important, this one is more crucial because this is the next step before the actual SP500 financial price prediction can take place:

```
#Now creating the NextDayOpen Column for the SP500 stock price
    prediction
Ln=len(df)
Lnop=len(df['Open'])
Print(lnop)
Ii=o
Df['NextDayOpen']=df['Open']
Df['NextDayOpen]=0
For I in range(o,ln-1):
    Print("Open Price: ", df['Open'][i]
    If i!=0
        Ii=i-1
Df['NextDayOpen'] [ii]=df['Open] [i]
Print(df['NextDayOpen'][ii])
```

Checking for any Statistical Correlations that Exist in the NextDayOpen Column for SP500 Financial Price Prediction

It is important to note at this point that before any SP500 financial price information can be predicted, it is very crucial to check to see if there are any statistical
correlations with the prices that have been collected by the previous module. The
primary reason for this is that if any correlation does exist, it can greatly skew the
price prediction for any given stock. Thus, this must be carefully checked for, as
demonstrated by the following Python source code:

```
#Checking to determine if there is any statistical correlation from the financial
    information collected by the last module
Dfnew=df[['Close', 'NextDayOpen']]
Print(dfnew.head(5))
Dfnew.corr()
Out[110];
In [111];
```

The Creation of the Linear Regression Model to Predict Future SP500 Price Data

In this last Python source code module, we now approach the very last step: that
of creating the statistical Linear Regression model that could potentially be used to
predict financial price movements in the SP500:

```
#The creation of the Linear Regression Model for predicting price movements
    in the SP500
#Importing the variables
```

```
From sklearn import_cross validation
From sklearn.utils import shuffle
From sklearn import linear_model
From sklearn.netrics import mean_squared_error_Y2_score
#Creating the features and target dataframes
Pricedfnew['Close']
Print(price)
Print(dfnew.columns)
Features = dfnew[['NextDatOpen']]
#Shuffling the data
Price = shuffle (price, random_state=0)
Features = shuffle (features, random_stated=0)
#Dividing the SP financial data into Training Mode and Test Mode
X_train,, X_test, y_train, y_test= cross_validation.train_test_
Split(features, price, test_size=0.2, random_state=0)
#Linear Regression Model on SP500 financial price information
Reg= linear_model.LinearRegression()
X_train.shape
Reg.fit(X_train, y_train)
redDT.fit(X_train, y_train)
y_pred= reg.predict(X_test)
y_pred= regDT.predict(X_test)
print ("Coefficients: ", reg.coef_)
#Calculating the Mean Squared Error
Print("mean squared error: ",mean_squared_error(y_test, y_pred))
#Calculating the Variance Score
Print ("mean squared error: ",r2_score(y_test, y_prod))
#Calculating the Standard Deviation
Standarddev=price.std()
#Predict the Opening Price of the SP500 and the Opening Volume
#In the predict function, please enter the first parameter for the Opening Price
    of the SP500 and the 2nd Volume in US Dollars
SP500ClosePredict=reg.predict ([[269.05]])
#180 is the Standard Deviation of the difference between the Opening Price
    and the Closing Price of the SP500
So this range
Print("Stock Likely To Open at: ",SP500ClosePredict, "(+-11)")
Print("Stock Open between: ", SP500ClosePredict+standarddev," & "
SP500ClosePredict-standarddev)
Name: Close, Length: 5911, dtype: float64
Index([u'Close', u'NextDayOpen'], dtype='object')
('Coefficients: ", array([0.98986882]))
```

('mean squared error: ', 313.02619408516466
('Variance Score: ', 0.994126802384695)
('SP500 Stock likely to open at: ', array([269.34940985]), '(+-11)')
('SP500 Stock Open between: ', array([500.67339591]), ' & '
Array([38.02542379]))

Overall, these separate Python source code modules, when all integrated together, will form the basis of a mode in which to help predict the price movements of the SP500, and from there, make both the relevant and profitable trading decisions. Once again, just like with the Diabetes Portal Chatbot Model, the Python source code here is only a baseline example.

Millions more Python programming lines will be needed in order to put this into a production mode in the real world. Plus, the model that will have to refined and optimized on a real time basis in order to keep it fine-tuned.

Source for the Python source code: (SOURCE: 5).

Sources

1) Taulli T: Artificial Intelligence Basics: A Non-Technical Introduction, New York: Apress; 2019.
2) Graph, M: Machine Learning, 2019.
3) Alpaydin E: Introduction to Machine Learning, 4th Edition, Massachusetts: The MIT Press; 2020.
4) Towardsdatascience: https://towardsdatascience.com/sentiment-analysis-concept-analysis-and-applications-6c94d6f58c17
5) Mathur P: Machine Learning Applications Using Python: Case Studies from Healthcare, Retail, and Finance. New York: Apress; 2019.

Application Sources

FireEye: "Threat Research: Tracking Malware with Import Hashing." www.fireeye.com/blog/threat-research/2014/01/tracking-malware-import-hashing.html
Kocher P, Horn J, Fogh A, Genkin D, Gruss D, Haas W, Hamburg M, Lipp M, Mangard S, Prescher T, Schwarz M, Yarom, Y: "Spectre Attacks: Exploiting Speculative Execution." <spectreattack.com/spectre.pdf>
Kornblum, J: "Identifying Almost Identical Files Using Context Triggered Piecewise Hashing", *Digital Investigation*, Volume 3, Supplement, September 2006, pages 91–97.

Lipp M, Schwarz M, Gruss D, Prescher T, Haas W, Fogh A, Horn J, Mangard S, Kocher P, Genkin D, Yarom Y, Hamburg M: "Meltdown: Reading Kernel Memory from User Space." <meltdownattack.com/meltdown.pdf>

Shalaginov A, Banin S, Dehghantanha A, Franke K: "Machine Learning Aided Static Malware Analysis: A Survey and Tutorial." <arxiv.org/pdf/1808.01201.pdf>

Ucci D, Aniello L, Baldoni R: "Survey of Machine Learning Techniques for Malware Analysis." <arxiv.org/abs/1710.08189>

Chapter 3

The High Level Overview into Neural Networks

So far in this book, the first two chapters have provided a very deep insight into what Artificial Intelligence (Chapter 1) is actually all about, and how Machine Learning (Chapter 2) is starting to make a huge impact in Cybersecurity today. In the last chapter, we took a very extensive look at both the theoretical and applicable aspects of Machine Learning. In the second half of chapter two, two specific examples were further explored as to how Machine Learning can be used, making use of the Python programming language.

The examples that were examined included creating a Diabetes Testing Portal for an outpatient clinic (or for that matter, even a full-fledged hospital), and creating a tool to help predict the next day's price for a certain stock in the S&P 500, one of the largest financial trading institutions here in the United States. But there is yet another subcomponent of Artificial Intelligence that is also gaining attention very quickly, which is that of Neural Networks.

In Chapter 1, we provided an overview and a technical definition into what it is all about, but we devote the entirety of this chapter to Neural Networks. It will examine this topic from both the theoretical and application standpoints, just like the last chapter. Long story short, Neural Networks is the part of Artificial Intelligence that tries to "mimic" the thought and reasoning process of the human brain.

But before we do a deep dive into this, it is first very important to provide the high level overview.

The High Level Overview into Neural Networks

The Neuron

As just described, probably the biggest objective of Neural Networks is to mimic the thought and reasoning processes of the human brain. It is very important to keep in mind that this does not just involve examining the structure of the brain at a macro level, but the intent is to go as deep as the layer of the neuron, which is deemed to be the most basic building block of the human brain.

In many ways, the human brain can be considered to be like a Network Infrastructure, which consists of many types of network connections. And in any given lines of network communication, it is always the data packet which is at the heart of this process. In a manner very similar to that of the human brain, it is the data packet which acts as the neuron. Just like the data packet, the neuron also consists of a central body, which is known as the "nucleus." In fact, this is very much analogous to the header, information/data packet, and trailer that make up the entire of the data packet.

It is at the level of the nucleus where all of the computational processes take place. But it is important to keep in mind that it is not just one single neuron that generates all of this power. Rather, the human brain consists of literally billions of these neurons, in order to come up with all of the reasoning and logical thinking that it can do for one human being. In other words, it is the collective of these billions of neurons that constitute the makeup of the human brain.

Take, for example, once again, the data packet. It is not just one data packet that allows us to communicate over the Internet, rather it is the collective powers of hundreds or even thousands of them which lets us interact not only with just other websites, but other individuals as well, especially when we send emails, text messages, and chat messages (for example, when you make use of a chatbot at an E-Commerce site).

So, the question that remains now is, how are all of these billions of neurons connected amongst one another, so that it seems like that our thought, logical, and reasoning processes seem to be so seamless? Well, the answer comes from the various electrical triggers, which are sent from one neuron to the next in a sequential fashion. In more physiological terms, these electrical triggers are essentially an electrochemical process, which typically consists of ion exchange and transmission that takes place in between these billions of neurons.

This is achieved by passing these electrical triggers along an axonomic geometric plane as well as through the diffusion of neurotransmitter molecules over what is known as the "Synaptic Gap." But, it is important to keep in mind that the communications that take place between neurons is not a direct electrical conduction, but rather through these ionic charges, as just described. So in other words, on a very simplistic level, when one neuron communicates with another neuron, the lines of communications first originate at the nucleus of the neuron.

From there the charge moves out onto the axon, and then from there to the synaptic junctions that are located at the endpoints of the axon. The lines of communications (from one neuron to another neuron) go out to a much deeper level, which are known as the "Dendrites," also referred to as the "Soma." The communications that take place from one neuron to another have been clocked at an astounding three meters per second.

Now, take this example of how one just one neuron communicates with another, but multiply it by a factor of 1,000,000,000 times. This is now what forms the entire thought, logical, and reasoning processes of the human brain, and thus, it is referred to as the "Biological Neural Network."

In this regard, in the previous two chapters, we have discussed how different inputs for an Artificial Intelligence system all have different statistical weight values that are assigned to them. But when it comes to the physiology and anatomy of the human brain, all of these weights have the same statistical value that are assigned to each and every one of the billions of neurons that exist from within it. But these are the inputs that are going into the human brain, as these are technically the stimuli that we see in the external world, as it is captured by the human eye. It is very important to note that the interconnections between the neurons (as just previously described) do not have equal, statistical weights that are assigned to them. Rather, they have different values, which are technically deemed to be either "Excitory" or "Inhibitory" in nature. For example, the former will speed the communications that take place from one neuron to the next, whereas the latter can actually block these communications, as its name implies. But obviously, these varying statistical weights cannot be manually assigned to them, rather they are determined by the variances, or the differences, in the chemical transmitters as well as the modulating substances that exist from within the neuron itself, and also in the axons that exist in the synaptic junctions.

It is this specific weighting of varying levels as just described which forms the basis for what are known as the "Artificial Neural Networks," also known as the "ANNs" for short. Although the average speed of communications between one neuron to the next is deemed to be at three meters per second, this can now vary given the effects of both the "Excitory" and "Inhibitory" states of the neuron. Now, these differences can range as low as 1.5 meters per second to as high as five meters per second.

The Fundamentals of the Artificial Neural Network (ANN)

Although Neural Networks may sound like a new piece of techno jargon in the world of Cybersecurity, the truth of the matter is that it actually has its origins going all the back to the 1940s, more specifically, 1943. During this time frame, numerous scientists came up with some working foundations for Neural Networks, and in the end, six of them have still been around even up to this day. They are as follows:

1) The specific activity of a Neuron in an ANN takes what is known as an "all or nothing" approach. This simply means that it is either used all the way to help predict the results of the output, or it is not used at all.

2) In the ANN, if there is fixed number of neural synapses that have a statistical weighting of greater than one, it must be "excited" within a pre-established time period (this concept was further reviewed in the last sub section).
3) The only acceptable delays in an ANN system are those of Synaptic delays.
4) If a Synapse is deemed to be "inhibitory" in nature (this was also reviewed in detail in the last subsection), then the only preventative action that can take place from within the ANN is to stop the action of one Neuron at a time in the system.
5) The interconnections that are found within an ANN do not, and should not change over a period of time.
6) The Neuron is actually composed of a binary format in the ANN system.

Another key theorem as it relates to ANNs which is still widely used today is known as the "Hebbian Learning Law." It too was founded in 1949, and it is specifically stated as follows:

> When an Axon of Cell A is near enough to excite the levels of Cell B, and when Cell A takes an active participation in the transmitting of Cell B, then some growth process or metabolic change as the level of Cell A is increased which increases its particular efficiency level.
>
> **(Graupe, 2019)**

In other words, there is a one to one (1:1) direct, mathematical relationship between Cell A and Cell B. The more active Cell B becomes in the ANN system, then that will have a direct and positive impact upon both the workload and the productivity of Cell A, which will enhance the overall processes of the ANN system in order to derive the desired outputs.

Later on, in the 1960s and in the 1980s, two more theoretical constructs were also formulated, which are even applied to ANN systems that are being used today. They are as follows:

1) The Associative Memory Principle, also known as the "AM" (1968):
   This states that if an Information Vector (which will consist primarily of the source code and other various patterns [such as that of qualitative datasets]) is used in the ANN system, then that can also be considered to be an input in order to further modify the statistical weights that have been assigned to them so that they can more closely be correlated with the datasets that they have been associated with.
2) The Winner Take All Principle, also known as the "WTA" (1984):
   The constructs of this principle state that if there is a certain grouping of Neurons (denoted as "N"), and if they are all receiving the same type of Input Vector, then only one Neuron needs to be fired in order to further optimize the computational and processing capabilities of the ANN system. This Neuron will then be further designated as the one whose statistical input weights will best fit into the ANN system so that the desired outputs can thus be achieved.

In other words, if it only takes one particular Neuron to complete a specific function, then there is no practical need to have multiple Neurons to carry out the same type of functionalities from within the ANN system.

It is important to note that these above two theorems as just described have actually been proven scientifically to exist within the processes of the human brain, or "Biological Neural Network."

After the six principles and the above two theorems were developed, the basic structures for the ANN systems were then formulated. These are also used in ANN systems today. They are as follows:

1) <u>The Perceptron</u>:
   This was reviewed in great detail in the theoretical component of Chapter 2.
2) <u>The Artron</u>:
   This is also referred to as a "Statistical Switch-based Neuron Model," and it was developed in the late 1950s. The Artron is deemed to be a subset of the Neuron, in that it is only used to help further automate the processes from within the ANN system. It does not have its own Neuron-based architecture.
3) <u>The Adaline</u>:
   This is also referred to as the "Adaptive Linear Neuron," and was developed in the early 1960s. This is actually an artificial-based Neuron. It should be noted that this only refers to one Neuron, and not a series of them that form a more cohesive network.
4) <u>The Madaline</u>:
   This was developed in 1988, and it is actually based upon the Adaline, as just reviewed. However, the Madaline consists of many Neurons, not just one. This is also called the "Many Adaline."

Eventually, the above four components led to the creation of the foundation for the ANN systems that are being used today. They are as follows:

1) <u>The Backpropagation Network</u>:
   This is a multiple layered ANN, in which the Perceptron is the main vehicle that is being used to calculate the desired outputs from the ANN system. It uses various "Hidden Layers," and the mathematical crux for this kind of ANN system is the "Richard Bellman Dynamic Programming Theory."
2) <u>The Hopfield Network</u>:
   This was developed by a scientist known as John Hopfield in 1982. This kind of ANN system has many layers to it as well, but what separates it from the Backpropagation Network is that the "feedback" from the Neurons that are used in the ANN system are also used to compute the values of the desired outputs. The statistical weights that are assigned to the inputs are based upon the Associative Memory Principle, as just described.

3) The Counter Propagation Network:

This ANN system was created in 1987, and the mathematical foundations for it lie in what is known as the "Kohonen Self-Organizing Mapping," also known as the "SOM." This system makes further usage of the Winner Take All Principle, also previously described. It also makes use of what is known as "Unsupervised Learning," and it is very often used when fast results are needed from the calculated outputs.

4) The LAMSTAR:

This is an acronym that stands for the "Large Memory Storage and Retrieval Network." This is also known as a "Hebbian" type of ANN system, in that various SOM layers and WTM components are also used. In order to assign the statistical weights to the inputs in the ANN system, a concept known as the "Kantian-based Link Weights" is used. It is primarily used to interlink the multiple layers of the Neuron, which then allows the ANN system to integrate the inputs of other various types and dimensions. A unique feature of the LAMSTAR is that it also makes use of what is known as a "Feature Map" which actually displays the activity of the Neurons firing from within the ANN system. It also makes use of "Graduated Forgetting." This simply means that this kind of ANN system can still continue seamlessly even if there are large chunks of data that are missing in the respective datasets.

The Theoretical Aspects of Neural Networks

The Adaline

As it was reviewed in the last subsection, the Adaline (which is actually an acronym for **AD**aptive **LI**near **NE**uron) is not only one of the most critical aspects of an ANN system, but it is one of the key building blocks for what is known as the "Bipolar Perceptron." Mathematically, it can be represented as follows:

$$Z = Wo + n \sum t=1 \ WiXi$$

Where:

Wo = A statistically biased term to the training functionality of the ANN system.

When the Adaline is actually applied to an ANN system, the desired output can be computed as follows:

$$Z = \sum I \ WiXi.$$

The Training of the Adaline

It should be noted that the specific training for any ANN system, at a very simplistic level, simply involves the process of assigning various statistical weights to all of the inputs that are being used to derive the needed outputs. Technically, this is actually known as the "Adaptive Linear Combiner," or the "ALC" for short. In other words, this is simply the linear-based summation that is common amongst all of the elements in the "Bipolar Perceptrons." This kind of training can be mathematically represented as follows:

Given an "X" number of training sets where X1 ... Xl; d1 ... dL

Where:

$$Xi = (X1 ... Xn)T * I; I = 1, 2, ... L$$

Where:
I = the Ith numerical set;
N = the total number of inputs;
Di = the desired output of the specific Neuron in question.

This then results in the final ANN training algorithm, which is mathematically represented as follows:

$$J(w) = E(e^2 *k) = 1/L *L \sum k=1 * c^2 *k$$

Where:
E = the statistical expectation;
Ek = the statistical training error;
K = the iterative, numerical sets that are used by the ANN system.

It is important to note that in order to optimize the statistical weights that are assigned to the ANN system, a concept known as "Least Mean Squares" is utilized. From a statistical standpoint, it can be represented as follows:

$$VJ = 0J/0W = 0$$

Further, the statistical weights that are assigned to the inputs of the ANN system in this specific scenario can be also statistically represented as follows:

$$W^LMS = R^{-1} * p.$$

The Steepest Descent Training

Another statistical technique that is used by the ANN systems of today is called the "Steepest Descent Training." This technique makes an attempt to use the statistical weights that have been assigned to the inputs in one particular dataset and approximate, or estimate, that for the next dataset in question. The procedure for doing this is as follows:

$$L > n+1$$

Where:
    N = the total number of inputs that are used by the ANN system.

From the above, a "Gradient Search Procedure" is then established, which is mathematically represented as follows:

$$w(m+1) = w(m) + Vw*(m)$$

Where:
    Vw = the change, or statistical variation.

This variation can be mathematically computed as follows:

$$Vw(m) = uVJw(m)$$

Where:
    U = the statistical rate parameter.

Finally, the training used by the ANN system is mathematically represented as follows:

$$VJ = [0J/0W1 / 0J/0Wn]^\wedge T.$$

The Madaline

As it was stated earlier in this chapter, the "Madaline" is actually a further extension of the "Adaline," in that there multiple layers that exist within its infrastructure. The actual structure of the Madaline is different form the Adaline in the sense that the outputs that are produced from the former are not incomplete by any means. In other words, only complete outputs can be yielded by the ANN system. In order to train the Madaline, a specific procedure known as the "Madaline Rule II" is very often made use of today.

This technique is based upon the statistical theorem known as the "Minimum Disturbance Principal." It consists of various distinct phases, which are as follows:

1) All of the statistical weights that are assigned to the inputs of the ANN system initially have at first very low, random values that are associated with them. In other words, a specific training dataset—such as where Xi(i=1,2 ...)—is only applied mathematically at one vector at a time to the inputs of the ANN system in question.

2) Any number of incorrect statistical bipolar values at the output layer of the Madaline is counted one at a time, and is also noted by the Error "E" in any given vector that also acts as an input.

3) For any Neurons that may exist at the output layer of the Madaline, the following sub-procedures are also made use of:

   a. The threshold of the activation function is denoted as "Th." In other words, for every input that exists in the ANN system, the first unset Neuron is actually selected, and is also denoted as "ABS[z-th]." This means that the values of these Neurons must consist of an absolute from a mathematical standpoint. So for example, if there is an "L" number of inputs that are vector-based, then this selection process can be mathematically represented as follows: n * L values of Z. This is the specific node that can actually reverse its polarity by even the slightest of variances, thus its technical name is the "Minimum Distance Neuron." It is picked from the corresponding value of "ABS[z-th]."

   b. Next, the statistical weights of each Neuron in the ANN system are changed so that the bipolar output (denoted as "Y") also changes in the same linear format.

   c. The inputs that are mathematically vector-based are once again propagated to the output of the ANN system.

   d. If there are any changes or variances in the statistical weights that are assigned, then the earlier statistical weights are then restored back to the Neuron, and in turn will go to the next mathematical vector that is associated with the next small disturbance or variance, to the next Neuron.

   e. Steps with a – d until all of the total number of output errors are totally reduced to the lowest level that is possible.

4) Step 3 is repeated for all of the layers of the Neuron that exist within the ANN system.

5) If there are any Neurons that exist at the Output Layer, then steps 3 and 4 are correspondingly applied for those Neuron pairs in which their analog-based node outputs are close to the value of "0."

6) Also for any other Neurons that exist at the Output Layer, steps 3 and 4 are also applied for "Triplet Neurons" in which their analog based node outputs are close to the value of "0."

7) After the last step has been accomplished, the next mathematical vector is assigned to the "Lth level" in the ANN system.

8) Step 7 is repeated for any combinations of those "L"-based mathematical vectors until the training of the ANN system is deemed to be at an optimal and satisfactory level.

It should be noted at this point that these procedures (Steps 1–8) can be repeated for sequencing of Neurons, for example even "Quadruple Neurons." Once again, in these instances, all of the statistical weights that are assigned to the Neurons are set to a very low threshold value. For example, these specific values can either be positive or negative, well within the range of -1 to +1. For optimal testing and training purposes, the total number of Hidden Layers in the Neurons should be at least three, and preferably even higher.

Based upon this detailed description of the Madaline, it is actually what is known as a "Heuristic Intuitive Method." In other words, the values of the outputs that are produced by the ANN system should not be expected to live up to what is actually desired. It also very prone to degradation if any datasets are not optimized and cleansed—this process was also reviewed in Chapter 1. But in the end, it is both the Adaline and the Madaline that has created the foundation for many of the ANN systems that are currently in use today.

An Example of the Madaline: Character Recognition

In this subsection, we examine an actual case study using the Madaline in a Character Recognition scenario. In this example, there are three distinct characters of 0, C, and F. These have been translated into a mathematical binary format, in a six-by-six Cartesian Geometric Plane. In this particular instance, the Madaline is trained and further optimized with various kinds of techniques, and the Total Error Rate as well as the statistical Convergence is also noted and recorded.

The training of the Madaline uses the following procedures:

1) A training dataset of is created with five sets each of 0s, Cs, and Fs.

2) This is then fed into the Madaline.

3) The statistical weights for the inputs of the Madaline are then assigned randomly to numerical range of -1 to +1.

4) A mathematical based hard-limit transfer function is then applied to the Madaline for each Neuron within it, which is represented as follows:

$$Y(n) = \{1, \text{ if } X > 0; -1, \text{ if } X < 0\}.$$

5) After the above step, each output that has been computed is then passed onto a subsequent input to the next successive layer.

6) The final output is then compared with the desired output, and the Cumulative Error for the 15 distinct characters (as described in Step 1) is then calculated.

7) If the Cumulative Error is above 15 percent, then the statistical weights for those specific Neurons whose output values are closest to zero is then corrected using the following mathematical formula:

$$WEIGHTnew = WEIGHTold + 2 * constant*output\ of\ the$$
$$previous\ layer * error.$$

8) The statistical weights for the inputs are then updated and a new Cumulative Error is then calculated.

9) Steps 1–8 are repeated until there is no more Cumulative Error, or until it is deemed to be a reasonable or desirable threshold.

10) The test dataset that is fed into the Madaline is constantly being updated with brand new statistical weights (for the inputs) and from there, the output is then calculated by determining the overall optimization of the Madaline.

The Backpropagation

The Backpropagation (aka "BP") Algorithm was actually developed way back in 1986. The goal of this algorithm was to also deploy statistical weight of varying degrees to the datasets and use them to train the Multi-Layer Perceptrons. This then led to the development of Multi-Layered ANNs. But unlike the Adaline or the Madaline just extensively reviewed in the last two subsections, the hidden layers do not have outputs that are easily accessible.

So, the basic premise of the BP Algorithm is to establish a certain, comprehensive methodology that can be used to set up and implement intermediate statistical weights to the inputs that are used by the ANN system, in order to train the Hidden Layers that reside within it. The BP Algorithm is mathematically derived by the following process:

1) The initial Output Layer is first computed, in which the intermediate layers of the ANN system cannot be accessed. This is represented mathematically as follows;

$$E = V\ \tfrac{1}{2}\ \Sigma k\ *(Dk - Yk)\char94 2 = \tfrac{1}{2}\ \Sigma k * e\char94 2k$$

Where:
K = 1 ... N;

N = The total number of Neurons that reside in the Output Layer.

2) The Steepest Gradient is then calculated as follows:

$$Wkj \ (m+1) = Wkj(m) + VWkj(m).$$

3) Next, a statistical based "Down Hill Direction Minimum" is then mathematically computed as follows:

$$Zk = \Sigma j \ Wkj^\wedge xj.$$

4) The output of the Perceptron is calculated as follows:

$$Yk = Fx(Zk).$$

5) Using the principles of substitution, a Nonlinear Function for the ANN system is mathematically defined as follows:

$$Oe/OWkj = (0e/0zk) * (0zk/0Wkj).$$

6) Finally, the final Output Layer of the ANN system is represented mathematically as follows:

$$0z/0Wkj = 0e/0Zk*X2(p) = 0z/0ZrYj(p-1).$$

Modified Backpropagation (BP) Algorithms

As the title of this subsection implies, the goal is to introduce some of level of risk or bias into the BP Algorithms. The idea is to help make the training datasets more varied, so that the ANN system can calculate robust outputs that are deemed to be acceptable. In other words, the goal is to keep the ANN system optimized on a macro level by introducing some variance into it, so it can learn better with future datasets that are fed into it.

In order to accomplish this specific task, the level of biasness is introduced into the inputs, with some sort of mathematical constant that is associated with it, such as either +1 or +B. This level is calculated as follows:

$$Bi = Woi*B$$

Where:

Woi = the statistical weight that is assigned to the input of the associated Neuron.

As noted previously, this level of variance can hold either a positive or a negative mathematical value.

But in order to make sure that there is not too much variance introduced that can drastically skew the outputs from the ANN system, two techniques can be used: Momentum and Smoothing.

The Momentum Technique

With this, a Momentum Term is simply added to the ANN system, which is as follows:

$$VWij \, ^\wedge(m) = N0 \, (r)Yj * (r\text{-}1) + aVwij \, ^\wedge (m\text{-}1)$$

$$Wij^\wedge(m+1) = Wij^\wedge(m) + Vwj^\wedge(m).$$

The Smoothing Method

This is mathematically represented as follows:

$$Vwij^\wedge(m) = aVWij^\wedge(m\text{-}1) + (1\text{-}a)0i \, (r)Yj *(r\text{-}1)$$

$$Wij^\wedge(m+1) = Wij^\wedge(m) + NAWij^\wedge(m).$$

There are also other techniques like the above two just described, and they are as follows:

1) Enhancing the mathematical range of the Sigmoid Function from 0 to +1 to a range of -0.5 to +0.5.
2) Further enhancing the step size of the ANN system so that it does not get "stuck" in a processing loop, which can lead to "Learning Paralysis."
3) Using the tools of convergence and applying it to the "Local Minima" of the ANN system. This should only be used when there is a statistical probability that moving the ANN system will cause the application to degrade over a certain period of time.
4) Making use of a modified or "enhanced" BP Algorithm. This can be used to catalyze the speed of the Convergence and further reduce any form of variance. This technique only takes into account the mathematical signs of the Partial Derivates to compute the statistical weights, rather than assigning Absolute Values.

A Backpropagation Case Study: Character Recognition

We review once again with Character Recognition, but this time with Neural Networks. In this particular instance, the model is primarily made up of three distinct layers, with two Neurons apiece for each layer. There are also two hidden layers with 36 distinct inputs assigned to the ANN system. The Sigmoid Function for this can be represented as follows:

$$Y = 1/1 + \exp(-z).$$

The above mathematical representation can also be considered a "Neuron Activation Function." Statistical input weights have also assigned, with some variance allowed (as reviewed previously), to the ANN system. It has been further trained to recognize the distinct characters of the following: "A," "B," and "C." But, in order to fully optimize the ANN system, additional characters have also been introduced, which include the following: "D," "E," "F," "G," "H," and "I." Finally, in order to confirm if any statistical errors can be captured, three additional characters have also been assigned which include the following: "X," "Y," and "Z."

The BP Algorithm was used to further explore this study. The ultimate goal of the BP Algorithm is to fundamentally reduce the sheer amount of noise, or errors, that have been associated with the Output Layer. From here, a series of mathematical-based vector inputs has been applied to the ANN system via the BP Algorithm, and they have been assigned to all of the input values. These have then been subsequently forward-propagated to the Output Layer.

The statistical weights that have been assigned have also been adjusted by the BP Algorithm. Throughout the entire ANN system-processing lifecycle, these steps have been used over and over again, with the following, mathematical iteration:

$$(m+2).$$

The entire process comes to an end when the particular Convergence has been reached.

A Backpropagation Case Study: Calculating the Monthly High and Low Temperatures

Although Neural Networks and the BP Algorithm can be used virtually in about any kind of industry, it has found a particular usefulness in the field of meteorology. For example, these kinds of models can help to determine future weather patterns, especially when it comes to tornadoes, severe thunderstorms, torrential rainfall, cyclones, typhoons, hurricanes, and even the global warming hotspots on the planet. It can also be used for agricultural meteorology as well, especially when it comes to predicting the effects of temperatures on crops, particularly for grains like wheat, corn, and soybeans.

This algorithm can also be used to predict how saturated or dry certain agricultural producing regions will be on a worldwide basis. As the title of this subsection implies, this next case study will further examine how an ANN system with the BP

Algorithm can be used to predict both low and high temperatures on a daily basis. In this particular instance, certain other variables are also taken into consideration, which include the following:

- The rate of water evaporation;
- The relative humidity;
- The wind speed;
- The wind direction;
- The precipitation patterns;
- The type of precipitation.

For this case study, a multi-layered ANN system has been created which has been implemented with the BP Algorithm. With the latter, it consists of all three items: 1) An Input Layer; 2) A Hidden Layer; and 3) An Output Layer. It should be noted that there are Neurons which are located in both the Hidden Layers as well as the Output Layers. Collectively, they mathematically represent the summation of the products of both the incoming inputs that are going into the ANN system, as well as their associated statistical weights.

The BP Algorithm has been mathematically formulated based upon the principle of the Least Square Method, also known as the "LSM." It should be noted that the overall performance and optimization of the ANN system coupled with the BP Algorithm is computed by the Mean Square Error methodology. This is statistically represented as follows:

$$F(x) = E(e^2) = E[(t-a)^2]$$

Where:

F(x) = the overall system performance;

E = the statistical error that lies amongst the target, or desired, outputs, which are denoted by "t" and "a."

In this particular case study, the BP Algorithm is actually heavily reliant upon the first statistical input weight matrices that have been to assigned to all of the layers of the ANN system, as just previously described. These matrices have been preestablished with small numerical values with a range denoted as "[a,b]." It is important to note that these weight matrices are further optimized by the following mathematical formula:

$$W * (k+1) = W(k) + W(k)$$

Where:

VW(k) = the product of the statistical error that is present at a certain, specified iteration in the ANN system.

At this point, the BP Algorithm is then mathematically transposed into the Hidden Layer region of the ANN system. This is used to calculate the level of sensitivity, or variation, of the optimized weight matrices for every single Hidden Layer that is present in the ANN system. In this case, the level of variance, or sensitivity, is denoted as "m+1," and it is mathematically calculated as follows:

$$S * (m+1) = -2 * F'(n) * e$$

Where:

    E = the statistical error;

    F'(n) = the diagonal lines in the Cartesian Geometric Plane.

A more optimized mathematical model to calculate the level of variance, or sensitivity, is given as follows:

$$Sm = Fm(nm) = W * (m+1)' * S * (m+1)$$

Where:

    Fm(nm) = the mathematical derivative long the "m" layer in the Cartesian Geometric Plane.

But, in order to update the weight matrices in an iterative fashion, the following mathematical formula is used:

$$Wm + (k+1) = Wm(k) - a * Sm * (am-1)'$$

Where:

    A = the current learning rate of the ANN system.

In return, the data from the various datasets that have been fed into the ANN system will be placed at the Output Layer, associated either with a Log Sigmoid Function or a Pure Linear Function.

Overall, in this particular model, the BP Algorithm consists of 252 overall inputs, arranged as follows, according to this schematic:

■ One Input Layer with 200 Neurons;
■ Three Hidden Layers consisting of 150, 100, and 50 Neurons each;
■ An Output Layer which has 12 Neurons to mathematically produce 12 different target outputs.

Initially, the datasets that were used by the ANN system had to be optimized. In order to reach this goal, they were either categorized as an Average Monthly Temperature High, or a Low Monthly Temperature. They were also categorized by their respective annual years, which was how the outputs that were computed by the ANN system displayed the results.

After the above step was accomplished, it was then fed into the ANN system. Two different types of BP Algorithms were used, which represented the High Temperatures and Low Temperatures, respectively. From here, the datasets were then transmitted to the Input Layer and the three Hidden Layers that were present in the ANN system, all associated with a Log Sigmoid Function. It should be noted that the Pure Linear Function was chosen over the Log Sigmoid Function because this model did not have specific characters that were contained in the datasets. Only the Log Sigmoid Functions can handle this kind of qualitative data.

The Hopfield Networks

In all of the ANN system configurations that we have examined so far in this book, only the concept of "Forward Flow" has been introduced. This simply means that only a unimodal flow was looked at, in particular going only from input to output. In more technical terms, this is known as a "Nonrecurrent Interconnection." One of the primary advantages of this is that, to a certain degree, it can offer network stability. But in an effort to more closely replicate the thought, logical, and reasoning processes of the human brain, a so-called "Feedback" mechanism needs to be incorporated as well.

Thus, this feature also needs to be included into an ANN system as well. This is where the role of the Hopfield Neural Network comes into play as it consists of a "Forward Flow" as well as a "Feedback" mechanism. But the primary disadvantage here is that the network stability in the ANN system cannot be assured or guaranteed at all. Therefore, some sort of mechanism needs to be implemented in order to counter these effects.

Thus, it is important to point out that while Hopfield Neural Networks traditionally consist of only one Layer, the "Feedback" mechanism in the end actually makes it a Multi-Layered one. Also, the Hopfield Neural Network has been recognized amongst the first to solve what are known as "Non-Convex-based Decisions."

In the Hopfield Neural Network, the mechanism that has been designed and implemented to counter the effects of stability is a delayed feature. In a sense, this kind of delay is also present in the human brain as well. This is actually exhibited in time delays in both the Synaptic Gap and the subsequent firing of the Neuronic activity that stems from it.

Because of the Multi-Layer approach that is taken in the output of the Hopfield Neural Network, it can also be considered to be binary in nature as well. The mathematical representation of this is as follows:

$$Zj = \sum i = -WijYz(n) + Ij; n = 0, 1, 2 \ldots$$

$$Vj(n+1) = \{1 \lor Zj > Thj; 0 \lor Zj < Thj$$

OR

$$1 \lor Zj(n) > Thj$$

$$Yj(n) \lor Zj = Thj$$

$$0 \lor Zj < Thj$$

Thus, in this regard, a Binary Hopfield Neural Network can be considered to be a "T" state system, in which the outputs technically belong to a four-state set, represented as follows:

$$\{00, 01, 10, 11\}$$

As a result, when a Hopfield Neural Network has a vector that is inputted into it, network stabilization will occur at any of the above four states, with the exact one being ultimately decided by the statistical weights that are assigned to each input. This is further described in the next subsection.

The Establishment, or the Setting of the Weights in the Hopfield Neural Network

The Hopfield Neural Networks make use of the principles that are known as the "Associative Memory" (aka "AM"), and the "Bidirectional Associative Memory" (aka "BAM"). Mathematically, these both can be represented as follows:

$$XiER^{\wedge}m; YiEr^{\wedge}n; i = 1, 2, \ldots L$$

$$W = \sum I \, YiXi^{\wedge}t$$

Where:
> W = the weight connections between the "x" and the "y" elements of the input vectors.

Also, the above equations can be considered an "Associative Network," which is mathematically represented as follows:

$$W = L\sum i=1 \ XiXi^Ti \ \text{over "X" number of input vectors.}$$

The above is also known as the "BAM," as just previously discussed, because all of the Xi values are closely correlated with the input vectors denoted as "W."

Earlier in the last subsection, it was noted that Hopfield Neural Networks are initially a Single Layer at the input stage, and this can be mathematically represented as follows:

$$W = L \sum i=1 \ XiXi^T$$

Where:

$$Wij = WJi \ V \ I, j.$$

However, in order to completely meet the network stability demands with a one Layer input in the Hopfield Neural Network, the following equation needs to be utilized:

$$Wii = 0 \ V \ i.$$

But, if the Hopfield Neural Network needs to be converted over so that binary inputs—denoted as "x(o,1)"—can produce mathematical values in the -1 to +1 numerical range, then the following mathematical formula must be used:

$$W = \sum I *(2Xi-1) \ (2Xi -1)^T.$$

Calculating the Level of Specific Network Stability in the Hopfield Neural Network

The concept of introducing Network Stability was introduced in some detail in the last subsections. In this subsection, we go into more detail about it, especially in the way it can be computed for an ANN system making use of a Hopfield Neural Network. Previous research has told us that Network Stability can be guaranteed to even higher levels if the "W" matrix of the statistical input weights is geometrically symmetrical in nature, and if the diagonal lines that cross it are close to "0" as possible. This is mathematically represented as follows:

$$Wij = Wji \ Vi, j$$

Where:

$$Wu = V i.$$

The fundamental theory for the above two equations comes from what is known as the "Lyapunov Stability Theorem," which states that if Network Stability is used in a mathematical energy function in the ANN system, and if it can be further refined so that it will decrease over time, Network Stability can then be considered to be a prime model for the ANN system in question.

But, in order for this to occur, the following conditions must be met first:

- Condition 1:
  Any finite changes that occur in the Network System denoted as "Y" will output a finite increase in "E," at a rate of positive correlation.
- Condition 2:
  "E" is constrained by the mathematical equation below:

$$E = \sum I \, THjYj - \sum j \, I2yj - \tfrac{1}{2} \sum I \sum j=/1 \, WijYjYi$$

Where:
   I = the "ith" Neuron;
   J = the "jth" Neuron;
   Ij = an external input to Neuron "J";
   THj = the statistical threshold for Neuron "J."

Now, how the "Lyapunov Stability Theorem" can prove the particular Network Stability of an ANN system is as follows:

In the first step, the value of "W" is proven to be geometrically symmetric with all of the diagonal elements in the Cartesian Geometric Plane being at the value of "0," as described before. These are both accomplished with the following two mathematical equations:

$$W = W''t$$

$$Wii = o \, Vi$$

Where:
   The Absolute Value of [Wij] is bounded for the numerical sets that exist in the set of "I, J."

In the second step, the value of "E" mathematically satisfies the condition of "A" by considering a change, or variance, to be done in just one region of the Output Layer, which is mathematically represented as follows:

$$Yk(n+1).$$

The Variance is further computed as follows:

$$Ven = E(n+1) - E(n)$$

$$= [Yk(n) - Yk(n+1)] * [\Sigma i=/k \, WikYi(n) + Ik - Thx]$$

But, assuming that a binary-based Hopfield Neural Network is used, the following three statistical conditions must also be met:

$$Yk(n+1) = \{1 \ldots VZk(n) > Thk; \, Yk(n) \ldots VZk(n) = Thk; \, 0 \ldots VZk(n) < Thk$$

Where:

$$Zk = \Sigma WikYi + Ik.$$

Finally, in the end, only two types of variances can occur in the ANN system, which are statistically represented as follows:

$$\text{If } Yk(n) = 1, \text{ then } Yk(n+1) = 0;$$

$$\text{If } Yk(n) = 0, \text{ then } Yk(n+1) = 1.$$

How the Hopfield Neural Network Can Be Implemented

In this subsection, we now provide a summary as to how the Hopfield Neural Network can be deployed into the ANN system.

Overall, the statistical weights of the inputs that are assigned must satisfy the following mathematical formula:

$$W = W\Sigma i=1 * (2Xi - 1) * (2Xi - I)^{\wedge}T.$$

Now the computation of the Hopfield Neural Network can be accomplished, assuming a "BAM" component resides within it, by using the following methodology:

1) The statistical weights of Wij are assigned to the mathematical matrix denoted as "W," where Wii = o Vi and Xi are the actual training vectors that are being used.
2) An unknown weighted input pattern, denoted as "X" is set to:

$$Yi(0) = Xi$$

Where:
Xi = the "ith" element of mathematical vector "X."

3) Step #2 can be statistically represented as follows:

$$Yi(n+1) = Fn[Zi(n)]$$

Where:
Fn = the Activation Function which is represented as follows:

$$Fn(z) = \{1 \ldots Vz > Th; \text{Unchanged} \ldots Vz = Th; -1 \ldots Vz < Th\}$$

$$Zi(n) = \sum i=1 \ WijYi(n)$$

Where:
N = the possible range of numeric integers which can be found in the iteration denoted as (n = 0, 1, 2 ...).

NOTE: the above iterations keep repeating until a specific Convergence has been reached, in which the changes in $Yi(n+1)$ can be closely correlated with $Yi(n)$ below some pre-established threshold value.

4) Steps 1–3 are repeated for all of the elements of any unknown mathematical vectors. This is done until the next element of the unknown mathematical vectors is at 100 percent in the ANN system.

5) But after all of this, if any other unknown mathematical vectors are subsequently discovered, then this entire process, which encompasses Steps 1–4, is repeated yet again.

The Continuous Hopfield Models

It should be noted at this point that all of the concepts associated with the Hopfield Neural Network have been discrete in nature. However, they can also be transformed into a continuous state by making use of the following mathematical model:

$$Yi = f1(AZi) = 1/2 * [1 + \tanh(AZi)].$$

In the above model, a differential equation can be used to delay the timing that transpires between the Input Layer and the Output Layers of the ANN system. This can be done with the following mathematical equations:

$$\sum j=/I \ Tij - Zi/Ri + Ii = 0$$

$$C * Dzi/Dt) = \sum j=/1 * (TijYj) - (Zi/Ri) + (Li)$$

Where:

$$Yi = Fn(Zi).$$

A Case Study Using the Hopfield Neural Network: Molecular Cell Detection

In the world of biological sciences, a concept known as "Intracellular Microinjection" is a very typical procedure that is made use of in order to manipulate various types of cell cultures. In this regard, any sort of "Micromanipulation" processes for a single cellulite structure is very important in the field of In-Vitro Toxicology, Cancer, as well as HIV-based research. But, in order to actually stimulate the cell, one of the most important obstacles to overcome is determining the accurate, geometrical shape of the actual cell.

In terms of Contour Extraction, a number of other fields have been closely examined, such as that of Image Processing. Determining the edge structure of the cell has made use of such techniques as Gradient-based detectors, one of which is known specifically as the "Prewitt, Sobel, and Laplace" concept. Other edge structure techniques have been proposed as well, such as the mathematical-based 2nd Derivative Zero Crossing Detector or even some other sorts of computational methods, such as the "Canny Criteria."

But given the other obstacles, such as cell texture, cell noise, the blurring of images, scene illumination, etc., these techniques just described cannot output results with a strong level of statistical confidence. Also, the source image of the cell in question could be represented as broken edge fragments which possibly cannot be detected at all. Even the data that is discovered by the cellular edge can be skewed by the pixels that are extracted from the image of the cell that has been captured.

Also, all of these techniques just described typically require some sort of "post-processing" optimization as well. In other words, active contours of the cell need to be captured, and as a result, a new technique known as "Snakes: Active Contour Models" was proposed back in 1988, and in fact, it has been used quite widely . Some of the things it can do include the following:

■ Edge detection of the cell;
■ Shape modeling of the cell;
■ Segmentation of the cell;
■ Pattern recognition/Object tracking of the cell.

The "Snake" technique is thus able to produce closed and active images of the cellular membrane, and can even be further segmented and divided for a much closer examination. At this point, the "Snake" technique can also be incorporated into the Hopfield Neural Network, and the mathematical representation of this union can be represented as follows:

$$Esnake = |S2\ [AEcount(v) + BEcurv(v) + TEimage] * ds$$

Where:

A, B, T = the relative influence of the energy term in the ANN system;

Ecurve = the statistical smoothness term;

Econt = the statistical continuity term;

Eimage = the energy level that is associated with the external force in order to attract the properties of the "Snake" concept to the needed image contour of the cellular membrane.

As one can see, the Energy Component is a very important one in this specific example of the Hopfield Neural Network, and this can be mathematically represented as follows:

$$Esnake = N\Sigma i{=}1\ \{A[(Xi - Xi{-}1)^\wedge 2 + (Yi{-}Yi{-}1)^\wedge 2 + B[(Xi{-}1{-}2Xi + Xi{+}1)^\wedge 2$$
$$+ (Yi{-}1{-}2Yi + Yi{+}1)^\wedge 2 - Tgi\}$$

Where:

N = the total number of nodes that are in the "Snake";

Gi = the value of the image gradient at the point of Xi, Yi.

In this case study, a two-dimensional (2D) Binary Hopfield Neural Network is used, and from that, the Neurons are updated at predetermined time intervals using the following mathematical formula:

$$Wik = N\Sigma i{=}1\ M\Sigma j{=}1\ Tikjt^\wedge Vjt + Iik\ Vi = g(Uih)$$

$$G(Utk) = \{1, \text{ if } Utk = max(Uth;\ h = 1,2\ ...,\ M\ 0, \text{ otherwise})$$

Where:

N = the total number of "Snakes" nodes;

M = the total number of neighboring points that have to be considered for each of the nodes that reside within each and every Neuron that is used by the ANN system.

The "Snakes" method can be used to diminish the level of Energy, and this can be computed as follows:

$$E = {-}1/2\ N\Sigma i{=}1\ M\Sigma k{=}1\ N\Sigma j{=}1\ M\Sigma l{=}1\ *Tikjt^\wedge Vjk^\wedge Vjt - N\Sigma\ i{=}1$$
$$M\Sigma\ k{=}1\ IikVih.$$

The above can then be mapped to the Hopfield Neural Network as follows:

$$Tikjt -[(4A + 12B)^\wedge 0ij -(2A+8B) * Oi+1j - (2A + 8B) * 2Bbi+2j + 2Bb-1) * [XikKjt + YikYjt]]$$

$$Iik = TGik.$$

It should be noted that in this model, feedback connection can become quite unstable (as discussed in the previous subsections), and in order to minimize this risk, any Neuron Outputs that can contribute to the minimization of the total energy of the ANN system are accepted. Finally, the ANN system consists of the following:

- 16 Nodes (denoted as "N=16");
- A 50 point radial line in the Cartesian Geometric Plane (denoted as "M=50");
- The total number of Neurons in the ANN system is 800 (denoted as "N X M").

Counter Propagation

The Counter Propagation (CP) Neural Network was first researched and discovered back in 1987. When compared to that of the Backpropagation network as reviewed in the last section, it is extremely fast, in fact by a factor of well over 100 times as fast. But, the downside to this is that it cannot be used for a wide range of applications; it can only be used for a certain number. The primary reason for this is that faster speeds require, of course, much more processing power on part of the ANN system.

The CP is actually a combination of both the "Self-Organizing" and the "Outstar" networks. One of the key advantages of using the CP Neural Network is that it is quite useful for generalization purposes, in the sense that it is very good at trying to predict what the outputs will look like from the ANN system. In this regard, it is very good for mathematical input vectors that are deemed to be either partially completed or even partially incorrect by nature.

The two primary concepts that underpin the CP Neural Network are the Kohonen Self-Organizing Map Layer (also known as the "SOM"), and the Grossberg Layer, which are examined in closer detail in the next two subsections.

The Kohonen Self-Organizing Map Layer

This is also known as the "Winner Take All" layer of an ANN system. In other words, for just one mathematical input vector, the output is only "1," while all of the others are deemed to have a value of "0." Further, it is important to note that no other training vectors are required for the Kohonen SOM. The output for this is represented by the following mathematical formula:

$$Kj = m\Sigma i=1 \ WijXi = W^TiX; \ WjV \ [W1j \ ... \ Wmj)^T$$

$$XV \ [X1 \ ... \ Xm]^T$$

Where:
    J = q, 2, ... p,p;
    M = the statistical dimensions of the input vectors.

In order to fully determine what the next Neuron will look like after the first one (denoted as "j=h"), this can be mathematically represented as follows:

$$Kh > Kj=/h.$$

But, if the Neurons are to be defined as a specific iteration, then the following equation is used to compute this specific series:

$$Kh = m\Sigma i=1 WihXi = 1 = W^ThX.$$

The Grossberg Layer

This is actually deemed to be a statistically weighted output layer of the SOM Layer. But, in this specific Layer, the total number of Neurons must be at least half of the value of the different classes that are used by the ANN system, and further, this representation must be binary in nature. This can be accomplished by the following mathematical formula:

$$Gq = \Sigma IKiViq = K^TVq; \ k \ V \ [k1 \ ... \ kp]^T$$

$$Vq \ V \ [V1q \ ... \ Vpq]^T$$

Where:
    Q =1 1, 2, ..., r, r. This is the actual binary representation, as just previously stated.

Now, as eluded to before, the SOM Layer makes use of the "Winner Take All" approach. This is mathematically represented as follows:
    {Kh = 1; ki = /0] if any of these two conditions are met, then the "Winner Take All" can be mathematically computed as follows:

$$Gq = p\Sigma I = 1KijVjq = khUhq = Vhq.$$

How the Kohonen Input Layers are Preprocessed

The following steps are required to accomplish this process:

The statistical normalization of the Kohonen Layer Inputs are calculated as follows:

$$X^{\wedge}ri = Xi/SQUAREROOT \ \Sigma jX^{\wedge}2j.$$

Now, the training of the Kohonen Layer happens in the following process:

1) The Normalization of the input vector "X" is done to obtain input vector X';
2) The Neuron value at the level of the Kohonen Layer is calculated as follows:

$$(X')^{\wedge}T * Wh = K'h.$$

3) Finally, all of the statistical weights of the input vectors at the Kohonen Layer are calculated as follows:

$$K'h = \Sigma I \ X^{\wedge}iWih = X'iWih = X^{\wedge}ji + X^{\wedge}i2 + \dots X'm$$
$$* Whm = (X')^{\wedge}T * Wh.$$

How the Statistical Weights are Initialized in the Kohonen Layer

Once the Preprocessing phase has been completed as detailed in the last subsection, the initialization process, as the title of this subsection implies, is mathematically computed below.

All of the statistical weights are assigned to the same value, calculated as follows:

$$N * (1/SQUAREROOT \ N)^{\wedge}2 = 1.$$

In order to add a specific variance to this (also as discussed previously in this chapter), the following mathematical formula is used:

$$X^{\wedge}*I = TXi + (1-T) * (1/SQUAREROOT \ N).$$

But, there are also methods with which to add extra noise, and these are as follows:

1) Adding more noise to the Input Vectors;
2) Making use of statistical Randomized Normalized Weights;
3) The selection of the best representation of the Input Vectors, and using them as the initial weights. The end result is that each Neuron will be initialized one mathematical vector at a time.

The Interpolative Mode Layer

It should be noted that a typical Kohonen layer will only hold onto what is termed the "Wining Neuron." But, the Interpolative Mode Layer will hold back a certain group of Kohonen-based Neurons in a given class of input vectors. In this regard, the outputs of the ANN system will be statistically normalized to a preestablished weight; all of the other outputs will set back to zero.

The Training of the Grossberg Layers

The outputs of the Grossberg Layer are mathematically computed as follows:

$$Gi = \sum j \, VijKj = VshKh = Vih$$

$$Gi = \sum j \, VijKj = VshKh = Vih.$$

Any further statistical weight adjustments are done as follows:

$$Vij(n+1) = Vij(n) + B[Ti-Vij(n)kj]$$

Where:
  Ti = the desired outputs of the ANN system;
  N+1 = the Neurons that are set to be at the value of "1";
  Vij = the random input vectors are set to a value of "1" for each Neuron in the ANN system.

The Combined Counter Propagation Network

It has been reviewed that the Grossberg Layer can be used to train the various outputs of the ANN system to "converge" amongst one another, whereas the Kohonen Layer is basically what is known as a "Pre-Classifier" in the sense that it also accounts for what are known as "Imperfect Inputs." In other words, the latter remains unsupervised, while the former remains in a supervised state from within the ANN system.

Also, Neurons that lie within the Grossberg Layer will literally converge onto the appropriate target input, and this will be simultaneously applied to the Kohonen Layer as well. In fact, this is how the term "Counter Propagation" has evolved. This is primarily the result of the deployment of the target input being applied to the Kohonen Layer at the same time.

But, one key drawback of Counter Propagation is that it requires that all of the various input patterns be of the same kind of dimensionality in the Cartesian Geometric Plane. Because of this, the Counter Propagation cannot be used for more applications on a macro or general level.

A Counter Propagation Case Study: Character Recognition

In this case study, the primary goal is to recognize three numerical values as follows: "0," "1," "2," and "4." As the title of this subsection implies, it also makes use of the Counter Propagation technique. In terms of training, a dataset consisting of an eight-by-eight dimensionality is utilized, with Bit Errors in the range of 1, 5, 10, 20, 30, and 40 values being used.

In terms of setting the statistical weights, the following procedure is established:

1) Obtain all of the relevant training dataset vectors that lie in this mathematical permutation: X_i, $I = 1, 2, \ldots L$
2) For each of the relevant vectors belonging to the permutation established in the last step, the following sub-procedures are also utilized:
   ■ Normalize each and every X_i, $I = 1, 2, \ldots L$ with the following mathematical permutation: $X_i^\wedge t / SQUAREROOT (\sum X^\wedge 2j)$;
   ■ Calculate the average vector as $X = (\sum X_j^\wedge 1)/N$;
   ■ Normalize the average vector so that $X, X' = X/SQUAREROOT (\sum X^\wedge 2j)$;
   ■ Establish the Kohonen Neuron weights to $W_k = X$;
   ■ Set the Grossberg Neuron weights to $(W1kW1k \ldots W1k)$ so that it is completely adjusted to the output vector denoted as "Y."
3) Steps 1–2 keep repeating in an iterative process until all of the training datasets are propagated in their entirety across the entire ANN system.

Finally, the test datasets are generated by a random procedure, with the following formula:

$$testingData = getCPTTesting (trainingData, numberOfBitError, numberPerTrainingSet)$$

Where:
   numberOfBitError = the expected number of Bit Errors;
   numberPerTrainingSet: used to specify the expected size of the testing dataset;
   testingData: used to obtain other output parameters, as well the test dataset.

The Adaptive Resonance Theory

The Adaptive Resonance Theory was developed in 1987, and it is known as "ART" for short. The primary purpose of this theory is to create, develop, and deploy an ANN system with regards to Pattern Recognition or Classification Behavior that matches very closely to the Biological Neural Network (BNN). In other words, a main goal with ART is to develop an ANN system with what is known as "Plasticity." Whenever the ANN system learns a new pattern, it will not use that to replace other previously learned patterns. In essence, the ANN system becomes a central repository of everything that it has learned and will continue to learn in the future.

The ART network consists of the following components:

- A Comparison Layer;
- A Recognition Layer;
- A Gain Element that feeds its output to "g1";
- A Gain Element that feeds its output to "g2";
- A Reset Element (this is where the Comparison Layer is evaluated and compared against the "Vigilance Value," which is nothing but a level of tolerance specifically designed for the ANN system.

Each of the above components are reviewed in more detail in the next few subsections.

The Comparison Layer

In this specific layer, a Binary Element is entered into the Neuron of the Comparison Layer, with the following mathematical permutation:

$$(j = 1 \ldots m; m = \dim(X)).$$

A statistical weight is also assigned to this Neuron by the following statistical formula:

$$Pj = m\Sigma I = 1 \ TijTi$$

Where:

R_i = the "ith" iteration of the "m" dimensional output vector of "r";

n = the total number of Categories that need to be recognized in the ANN system.

Also, it should be noted that that all of the Comparison Layer Neurons will receive the same mathematical Scalar Output denoted as "Gi," based upon the following permutation:

$$Cj(0) = Xj(0).$$

The Recognition Layer

This actually serves as another variant of the "Classification Layer." The various inputs that it receives are mathematically derived from the "n" dimensional weight vector "d." This is mathematically computed as follows:

$$Dj = m\Sigma I = 1 \ BjiCi = bj^\wedge T \ C; \ Bj \ V \ [Bj1 \ ... \ Bjm]$$

Where:

I = 1, 2, ... m;
J = 1, 2, ... n;
M = dim(x);
N = the number of Categories.

In the Recognition Layer, there is a property known as the "Lateral Inhibition Connection." This is where the output of each Neuron (denoted as "I") is connected via an "inhibitory" connection-weighted matrix, denoted as follows:

$$L = \{Lij\}, \ I = /j$$

Where:

Lij < 0 to any other Neuron in the ANN system (denoted as "j"). The end result is that Neuron with a large mathematical output will supersede all of the other Neurons with a lower mathematical threshold value.

Another key concept that should be noted is that of the "Positive Reinforcement." This is where a positive feedback loop in the ANN system (denoted as "Ijj > 0) is used in such a way that each mathematical output of the Neuron (denoted as "Rj") is literally fed back with a positive value statistical weight in order to further reinforce the output (as just described) if it is to fire another Neuron in a sequential, iterative fashion.

The Gain and Reset Elements

These kinds of elements use the same type of Scalar Outputs as all of the Neurons in the ANN system. This is statistically represented as follows:

$$G2 = OR(x) = OR(x1 \ ... \ Xn)$$

$$G2 = OR(or) \ U \ OR(x)$$

$$= OR(r1 \ ... \ rN) \ U \ OR(x1 \ ... \ Xn)$$

$$= g2 \ U \ OR(r).$$

In other words, if there is at least one input element of "X" where it is equal to 1, then g2 = 1. Or, if there are any other elements of g2 = 1, but there are no elements of "r" then g1 = 1, or else g1 = 0. The bars on the top are statistical-based negation factors, the "U" also represents a logical, statistical intersection. Equally, if OR(x) then OR(r) will always be equal to zero as well.

Also, the "Reset Element" will carefully evaluate the degree of correlation that exists between the input of vector "X" and the output of vector "C," with the following permutation:

$$N < N0$$

Where:

> N0 = the preestablished initial tolerance value, also technically known as the "Vigilance Value."

The Establishment of the ART Neural Network

The first step in the process of creating an ART-based Neural Network is the initialization of the statistical weights. In this matrix, the Comparison Layer (CL) is first initialized, and this is denoted by "B." To start this part, the following mathematical formula is used:

$$Bij = < E/E + 1 -1 \ Vij.$$

This must meet the following permutations:

$$M = dim(x);$$

$$E > 1 \ (typically \ E=2).$$

The RL weighted matrix, denoted as "T" is then initialized so that:

$$Tij = 1 - Vi,j.$$

From here, the tolerance level (denoted as "Rjo") is decided with the following formula:

$$0 < N0 < 1.$$

It is important to note that a high N0 will yield a specific statistical discrimination, but in contrast, a lower N0 threshold permits for a more collective grouping of patterns in the ANN system that are not similar in nature. Thus, the ANN system may actually first start with a much lower N0 value, and from there raise it up as needed and/or required.

The Training of the ART Neural Network

The training first starts with the establishment of the weighted matrix of "B," which represents the side of the RL, and "T," which represents the side of the Comparison Layer (CL). Furthermore, the ART Neural Network could be impacted by several iterations of input vectors, in which there is no time to match up a specific input vector with another corresponding value that has an average, denoted as "X."

The parameters to set up the training of the ART Neural Network are set up as follows:

$$Bij = Eci/E + 1 + k\sum Ck$$

Where:

  $E > 1$;

  Ci = the ith component of an input vector "C," where the value of "j" will then be associated with the Winning Neuron, which is denoted as "Rj."

Also, the parameter denoted as "Tij" of "T" is established by the following mathematical formula:

$$Tij = Ci\ Vi = 1 \dots m, m = dim(X), j = 1, \dots n.$$

In this specific instance, "j" represents will represent Winning Neuron.

The Network Operations of the ART Neural Network

After the training of the ART Neural Network has been accomplished, the next phase is then to launch the network compatibility, or operations of the system. To start this specific process (which is the first step), the iteration of "0" (where $X = 0$), is represented by the following mathematical equation:

$$G2(0) = 0 \text{ and}$$
$$G1(0) = 0.$$

Next (in the second step), if an input vector where $X = /0$ then the output vector denoted as "r" to the Comparison Layer is the one that will govern all of the layers in the ANN system. This is denoted as "r(0) = 0." Later on, if an input vector where $X = /0$, then there will be no specific Neuron that will have no more of an advantage of other Neurons in the ANN system.

In the third step, only RL-related Neurons will fire. Thus, in this regard, if $Rj = 1$, and $Ri = /j = 0$ will determine which input vector (denoted as "r") will become the output of the RL side of the ANN system. But, if several Neurons have the same value of "d," then the first Neuron will be chosen that has the lowest possible value, which is denoted as "j."

If multi-dimensional statistical input weights are used, the inputs that are specific to the Comparison Layer will be determined by the following mathematical formula:

$$Pj = Tj; Tj, \text{ of input vector "T."}$$

The winning Neuron will be denoted as "Pj = 0."

In the fourth step, a statistical classification is viewed as the "Reset Element" of the ANN system. As a result, all Classification processes will then halt. Because of this, there will be a huge variance between the input vectors of "p" and "x," respectively. This will lead to a very low "N" value, which is subsequently what is known as the "Reset Element" of the ANN system. This is done in such a way that N < N0. Because of this, if all of the Neurons are weighted with the same kinds of statistical inputs, a different Neuron in the RL component will then technically win. But, if there is no Neuron that actually corresponds to the input vectors in the ANN system within the stated level of variance, then the next step is immediately followed.

In the fifth step, a previously unknown Neuron will be assigned the statistical weight vectors denoted as "Tj" and "Bj" in order to associate it with the input vector of "X." A key advantage here is that the overall ANN system and the learning networks that it possesses will not "lose," or "forget," of any previously learned patterns. Not only will these be retained, but other new patterns that are learned will be added on top of this in the ANN system. This process is very similar to that of the Biological Neural Network (BNN).

Finally, in the last and sixth step, the procedure just detailed previously will then further statistically categorize all of the classes and the patterns that have been trained so far in the ANN system.

The Properties of the ART Neural Network

The following list summarizes some of the best features of the ART Neural Network, as well as what separates it from other Neural Networks as described so far in this chapter:

1) Once this specific network stabilizes, the property known as "Direct Access" will become very similar to the "Rapid Retrieval" functionalities that are found in the Biological Neural Network (BNN).
2) The Search Process will help to statistically normalize the Winning Neuron.
3) The training datasets of the ART Neural Network are deemed to be stable so that they will not cross over once the Winning Neuron has been ascertained.
4) The training will then stabilize into a finite number of statistical iterations.

However, there are certain disadvantages to the ART Neural Network, which are as follows:

1) It makes use of both Gain and Reset Elements, which literally have no relevance to the Biological Neural Network.
2) It is quite possible that if missing Neuron, it could then totally eradicate the entire learning processes that have been gained by the ANN system.

Further Comments on Both ART 1 & ART 2 Neural Networks

It should be further noted that the ART Neural Network is actually subdivided further into the ART 1 and ART 2 types of Neural Networks. Here is a summary of the distinct features of them:

1) The ART 1 Neural Network:
   - It makes use of a multilayer structure;
   - It makes use of a feedback mechanism, but a different one than is utilized in the Hopfield Neural Networks;
   - It makes use of BAM training datasets;
   - It makes of use of the "Winner Take All" concept;
   - It makes use of Inhibition;
   - It makes use of the Reset Function;
   - It possesses a Plasticity Feature;
   - It does not perform up to its optimal levels when at least one or more Neurons are missing or even malfunctioning in the ANN system;
   - It is non-transparent, in other words, it still suffers of being viewed as a "Black Box."

2) The ART 2 Neural Network:
   - It is designed specifically to make use of Analog, or Continuous Training inputs;
   - It does not require a previous setup or deployment;
   - Patterns (such as those of qualitative datasets) can be added as the ANN system is still in operation;
   - Also, the above-mentioned patterns can be categorized and classified before they are piped into the ANN system;
   - The mathematical matrices of "B" and "T" are also scalable enough so that they can further expanded into the ANN system if the need ever arises.

An ART 1 Case Study: Making Use of Speech Recognition

In this particular case study, the concepts of Speech Recognition are used to distinguish between the following words:

- Five;
- Six;
- Seven.

Using the current Neural Network design, these words are passed onto a mathematical array of what are known as "Five Band Pass Filters." The energy that is further derived from the outputs of the ANN system is then statistically averaged into intervals of 20 milliseconds over five iterations, which culminates a total of 100 milliseconds. Also, a five-by-five matrix is implemented into a Cartesian Geometric Plane, which consists of binary values of 0s and 1s, which are associated with the spoken words detailed up above.

Also a reference input matrix is compiled by the end user's repetition of each of these spoken words, spoken 20 times each. This is then averaged over 20 millisecond iterations.

This application makes use of the C programming language, which is as follows: Display

> "5", "6", or "7" (zero random noise) – choose input pattern (patterns are in three groups:
>> 5 patterns which represent the word "5" when it is used in different types of pronunciations:
>> "6" similar to "5"
>> "7" similar to "6"
> Pattern # (0-random) -There are ten different input patterns that strongly correlate from the spoken words of "5", "6" and "7", thus choose one
> Create new pattern for: - specify how many patterns need to be assigned

END OF PROGRAM
Also, the following variables are used in the C source code:

> PATT = the stored patterns;
> PPATT = the previous inputs that are correlated with the speech patterns in the Comparison Layer of the ANN system;
> T = the statistical weights that are assigned to the Neurons that are in the Comparison Layer;
> TO = the statistical weights of a Neuron that is in the Comparison Layer and also correlated with the Winning Neuron that is found at the Recognition Layer;
> TS = the status of the Recognition Layer Neurons;
> BO = the statistical input to the Neurons in the Recognition Layer;
> C = the outputs that are generated from the Recognition Layer in the ANN system;
> INP = the input vector;
> NR = the total number of patterns that are stored in the weights of both the Comparison Layer and the Recognition Layer;
> GAIN = a stored pattern that correlates with 1 input and 2 inputs when there are no stored patterns in the ANN system
> SINP = the total number of "1" values that are present in the input vector;
> SC = the total number of "1" values that are present in the Output Layer of the ANN system;

STO = the total number of "1" values that are chosen for the speech patterns of the chosen words;

MAXB = the mathematical pointer which is used to best associate all of the input vectors that are present in the ANN system.

A modified version of the ART 1 Neural Network is given as follows:

$$D \text{ (modified)} = \min(D, D1)$$

Where:

D = the regular D of ART 1'

D1 = c/p; where also p = the number of 1 values in the chosen, speech of the three numbers, as described previously.

An example of this includes the following:

Input Vector 1111000000; x = 4

Chosen pattern 1111001111; p = 8

Comparison Layer 11110000000 = 4

This will give the following product, calculated as follows:

$$D = c/x = 4/4 = 1.0 \text{ in regular ART-1}$$

$$D1 = c/p = 4/8 = 0.5$$

$$D \text{ (modified)} = \min(D, D1) = 0.5$$

The Cognitron and the Neocognitron

The Cognitron is a specialized type of Neural Network that has been created and designed for the deployment of Recognition Patterns. In order to accomplish this specific task, the Cognitron-based Neural Network makes total use of both the Inhibitory and Excitory Neurons. This was first conceived of back in 1975, making use of an Unsupervised Neural Network. In this instance, this model was meant to mimic the process of initiating the retina (which is located in the back of the eye). This was considered to be a "Deep Learning" type of experiment, and this concept will be further explored in more detail later in this chapter.

The Neocognitron was developed in the early 1980s as well. This was done in order to further broaden the scope of the Cognitron, both in terms of functionality as well as optimization. This laid the groundwork for the creation of what is known as the "Convolutional Deep Learning" kind of Neural Network, which occurred in 1989.

In terms of the composition of the Cognitron, it primarily consists of many layers and even sub-layers of both the Inhibitory and Excitory Neurons. The connections between both of these types of Neurons is only established to those that have been already created in the layer below them in the ANN system. The technical term for this is known as the "Connection Competition" of the Neuron. In other words, the connections are established from a bottom-up approach, versus the traditional top-down approach.

In order to optimize the training of the ANN system, not all Neurons are used or fired; rather, the training is reserved specifically for a class of Neurons known as the "Elite Group." These are Neurons that are devoted to a specific task and to creating a specific kind of output from the ANN system. It should also be noted that the Neurons in the "Elite Group" are those that have been previously trained as well. In the bottom-up approach in terms of Neuron connectivity, there is very often overlap that is experienced. This is where a Neuron may also be associated with other interconnections.

This kind of overlap can cause performance degradation from within the ANN system; therefore, the concept of "Competition" is used to overcome this overlap. At this point, those connections between the Neurons that are deemed to be "weak" in nature will be automatically disconnected. With "Competition," there is also a sense of redundancy introduced, so that these disconnections will not impede any other processes that are currently occurring from within the ANN system.

The structure of the Cognitron has been designed so that it is based upon the principle of Multilevel architecture, and the Neurons that are in between two specific layers are further designated as L-I and L-II, in an iterative fashion, denoted as "2n." These iterations can be represented as follows:

- L-I1;
- L-II1;
- L-I2;
- L-II2.

The Network Operations of the Excitory and Inhibitory Neurons

The specific Output of the Excitory Neuron is mathematically computed as follows: For the Excitation Neuron Inputs:

$$Xi = \sum k\ AikYk;$$

For the Inhibitory Neuron inputs:

$$Zi = \sum k\ BikVk$$

Where:

Yk = the output from the previous layer in the ANN system;

Vj = the output from the Inhibitory Neuron from the previous layer in the ANN system;

Aik and Bik = the appropriate statistical weights that have been assigned, and are also further adjusted when a specific Neuron is deemed to be more "active" than the others.

When the above two mathematical formulas are combined amongst one another, the total, or overall, aggregate output from the ANN system is calculated as follows:

$$Yi = f(Ni)$$

Where:

$$Ni = (1+Xi)/(1+Zj) - 1 = (Xi-Zi)/(1+Zi)$$
$$f(Ni) = \{Ni \ldots \text{ for } Ni> 0; 0 \ldots \text{ for } Ni<0\}.$$

For the Inhibitory Neuron Inputs

The outputs of these Neurons are mathematically computed as follows:

$$V = \Sigma I \ CiYi;$$

$$\Sigma iCi = 1.$$

The Initial Training of the Excitory Neurons

The initial datasets that are used are first assigned to the Excitory Neurons in a series of statistical iterations based upon the following formula:

$$Obi = (q\Sigma j \ AjiY^2j)/(2v^*); \quad Obi = \text{the change in Bi}$$

Where:

Bi = the statistical weights of the connections that are established between the Inhibitory Neuron that is located in layer "L1" and the "ith" Excitory Neuron located in layer "L2." It should be noted here that "Σj" actually represents the mathematical summation of the weights from each and every Excitory "L1" Neuron all the way to the "ith" Neurons at layer L2.

The above equation has been developed on the assumption that there will always be active Neurons in the ANN system. However, in the off chance that there is no activity whatsoever, then the following two equations automatically supersede:

$$Oaji = q^rCjYj$$

$$Obi = q'Vi$$

Where:

$$Q^r < q.$$

In summary, there is a positive correlation that exists between the Inhibition output and its statistical weight; as one increases, the other will also increase by an equal level or amount.

Lateral Inhibition

Another key concept here is that of "Lateral Inhibition." This is where a specific Neuron is located in each of the Competition Layers of the ANN system. In this regard, the Inhibitory Neuron actually obtains its statistical inputs from the Excitory Neurons in one specific layer given the weights that it has just been assigned, and is denoted as "Gi." This is represented as follows:

$$V = \sum iGiYi$$

, Where:
    Yi = the output of the Excitory Neuron.

From, here the output of V from the L2 Inhibitory Neurons is calculated as follows:

$$O/I = f[1+Yi/1+V] - 1.$$

The Neocognitron

Now that we have extensively reviewed the Cognitron, it is important to go into more detail as to what the Neocognitron is all about. As stated previously, this is considered to be a much more advanced version of the Cognitron. It has a hierarchal structure and is specifically geared toward understanding how human vision is actually processed.

In the hierarchal structure, there are two groups of layers, which are composed of both Simple Cells and Multilayered Cells. There is also a thick layer that resides between these two Cellular-based structures. In this three-tiered approach, the number of total Neurons actually decreases in a top-down fashion. This has been specifically designed so that the Neocognitron can overpower the various recognition issues that were experienced by the Cognitron, and even succeed where it failed. This includes images that are in the wrong kind of position or that have any sort of angular distortions associated with them.

Recurrent Backpropagation Networks

Backpropagation Neural Networks were introduced and reviewed in extensive detail earlier in this chapter. Now, a recurrent functionality can be added into it, and with it, the specific output from the ANN system can be automatically fed back into the inputs of the ANN system. It should be noted that this can be achieved only in small iterations. This concept was actually introduced back in 1986 and 1988, and finally fully implemented into the Backpropagation Neural Networks in 1991.

With this kind of deployment, there are also a very minimal number of Hidden Layers from within the ANN system. In this configuration, delay mechanisms are introduced so that the various Feedback Loops will be totally independent of each other between each iteration, also known technically as "epochs." So, once the first time interval has been completed, the outputs are then fed back into the inputs that are associated with them. Interestingly enough, any errors that are correlated with the outputs from the ANN system can also cycle back as direct inputs for the next iteration in the ANN system. For example, if an ANN system receives the inputs denoted as "X1" and "X2" respectively, this will count as the first-time iteration.

After this, the statistical weights for the inputs are also computed in the Backpropagation Neural Network, and from here, they are all added together with no further adjustments made to them until the first iteration has actually completed its cycle.

Then the outputs, denoted as "Y1" and "Y2" respectively, are cycled back into the ANN system to be used as inputs once again in the second iteration. This process keeps repeating until the ANN system has learned from the new datasets that have been fed into it.

Fully Recurrent Networks

These are actually very similar to the Recurrent mechanisms just previously discussed. However, there is one primary difference. Rather than the outputs of the ANN system being fed back as inputs, they are fed back as Layers. So, at the end of the first iteration, the Output Layer will be fed back as the Input Layer into the ANN system. Thus, the Recurrent Neurons are also transposed in this same manner as well.

Continuously Recurrent Backpropagation Networks

In this particular situation, the Recurrent Mechanism that is present in the Backpropagation Network keeps going on literally forever, but each time the based iteration becomes shorter in nature. Mathematically, this can be represented as follows:

$$T(DYi)/(Dt) = -Yi + g (Xi + \Sigma j\ WijVj)$$

Where:
   T = the time constant coefficient;
   Xi = the external input;
   G = the Neuron activation function;
   Yi = the output from the ANN system;
   Vj = the outputs of the Hidden Layers of the Neurons from the ANN system.

Stability is also introduced here as well, and is mathematically represented as follows:

$$Yi = g(Xi + \Sigma j\ WijVj).$$

Deep Learning Neural Networks

As its name implies, Deep Learning Neural Networks, also known as "DLNNs" are specialized Neural Networks in which a certain level of deep learning is actually attained. Specifically, Deep Learning can be defined technically as follows:

> Deep learning is a subset of machine learning where artificial neural networks, algorithms inspired by the human brain, learn from large amounts of data. … Deep learning allows machines to solve complex problems even when using a dataset that is very diverse, unstructured, and inter-connected.
>
> **(Forbes, n.d.)**

For example, Deep Learning examines datasets that are far more complex than other types of Neural Network systems that have been reviewed so far in this book. Deep Learning can probe much deeper into very complex datasets that are both qualitative and quantitative in nature. It can also probe for and discover hidden trends in the datasets that will help to greatly optimize the outputs that are generated by the ANN system, in an effort to get the desired results.

Deep Learning can also parse, filter through, and analyze those particular datasets in a much more powerful manner that makes use of various kinds of mathematical algorithms that typically include the following:

- Other forms of Logical computing methods;
- Linear methods;
- Nonlinear methods;
- Other forms of analytical methods;
- Heuristic methods;
- Deterministic techniques;
- Stochastic techniques.

Based upon this, another technical definition of Deep Learning can be offered as follows:

> DLNNs are a specific class of Machine Learning techniques that exploit the many layers of nonlinear-based information for the processing of both supervised and unsupervised feature extraction, and for pattern analysis and classification.
>
> **(Graupe, 2019)**

Most of the Neural Networks examined so far in this book, although complex by design, are still used for applications that are considered to be rather "simple" in nature. It is important to note that the word "simple" being used is very subjective in nature, and what may seem to be straightforward to one entity may actually appear to be complex to another entity. With this in mind, Deep Learning is typically used in those "heavy" kinds of Neural Network applications in which literally Terabytes or even Petabytes of datasets are needed in order to feed meaningful input into the ANN system in question.

Given the gargantuan nature of the datasets, one of the key components that is absolutely critical for the ANN system is that of maintaining a high level of what is known as "Integration." This simply means that given the huge breadth, diversity, and scope of these enormous datasets, they all must work together in a seamless fashion so that the ANN system can literally "digest" them all in an efficient and unified fashion, so that the outputs that are generated will not be skewed or biased in any way, shape, or form.

Also with Deep Learning, these kinds of ANN systems must be able to learn quickly, despite the enormous size of the datasets that are being fed into them. They must be able to intake these kinds and types of datasets on a constant basis, depending upon the requirements that have been set forth. Also, Deep Learning tries to mimic, or replicate, the actual human brain to the greatest extent that is possible.

Actually, the concepts of Deep Learning are really nothing new. The interest in this grew as scientists started to explore the concepts of Machine Learning (which was the main focal point in Chapter 2) and how it can be used to process large amounts of data as well. Also, the concepts of Deep Learning were first implemented into those ANN systems that made use of the principles of Backpropagation. This was first introduced in 1986.

It was Convolutional Neural Networks (also known as "CNNs") that became the first to adopt and deploy the concepts of Deep Learning. The motivating catalyst for creating the CNN was an attempt to model the visual cortex of the human brain. Because of this, the CNNs that were deployed have primarily been limited to commercial applications that made heavy usage of imaging.

It should be noted that the first CNN to make use of Deep Learning took actually three entire days to process all of the datasets that were fed into it. Although this appears to be drastically slow by today's standards, back in 1989, that was a very quick turnaround for that particular ANN system. Once it was proven that Deep Learning could be applied to both visual and imaging applications, the next step for it was to be used for Speech Processing and Speech Recognition types of applications. These made use of yet another technique which is known technically as "Support Vector Machine"-based mathematical algorithms, or "SVMs" for short.

The next major breakthrough for the principles of Deep Learning came about in 1996, when the concept for what is known as the "Large Memory Storage and Retrieval Neural Network" (also known as "LAMSTAR" or "LNNs" for short) was created. In this situation, this type of configuration was established in order to make certain predictions, investigations, and detections, as well as operational-based decisions from a wide and varied range of large datasets. They included the following characteristics:

- Deterministic;
- Stochastic;
- Spatial;
- Temporal;
- Logical;
- Time series;
- Quantitative/Qualitative.

It should be noted that the theoretical constructs for the LAMSTAR originated all the way back in 1969 with a Machine Learning tool that was first introduced. It made various attempts to replicate the interconnections of the Neurons that exist between the different layers and cortexes of the human brain. In order to undertake this enormous objective, it made use of very sophisticated modeling techniques which included the following:

- The integration and ranking of parameters;
- Coprocessing;
- Stochastic;

- Analytics;
- Entropy;
- Wavelets.

The processing and computational power for this kind of ANN system came from the following theoretical constructs:

- The Hebbian-Pavlovian Principle;
- The Kohonen Winner Take All Approach;
- Parallel Computing.

Another version of the LAMSTAR came out in 2008, and it has been appropriately called the "LAMSTAR-2" or the "LNN-2" for short. This was developed to overcome some of the shortcomings of the LAMSTAR, and this version offers much greater computational and processing power.

The Two Types of Deep Learning Neural Networks

Apart from the other Neural Network configurations thus far covered in this chapter, there are two other specialized ones as well that are also considered to be Deep Learning Neural Networks, and they are as follows:

1) The Deep Boltzmann Machines (DBM):
   These are considered to be stochastic kinds of Neural Networks. They were first introduced and deployed in 2009, and are basically unsupervised by nature. In order for the ANN system to learn from the datasets that are inputted into it, a concept known as "Thermodynamic Equilibrium" is utilized, which is based upon the Gibbs-Boltzmann statistical distribution. The actual learning process is done through a special technique called "Log-Likelihood," based upon gradient maximization. In other words, the statistical errors between the datasets and the ANN system model is very carefully analyzed. A key drawback of the DBM is that it requires an exorbitant amount of both computational and processing power, and thus it has a very limited scope in terms of application deployment.
2) The Deep Recurrent Learning Neural Networks (DRN):
   This kind of Deep Learning Neural Network makes specific use of the Backpropagation technique (as reviewed in extensive detail earlier in this chapter). They are stacked in a linear pattern at varying time intervals, and are also fed into the inputs of the ANN system. These are also too slow for wide scale application deployment, as they require the coupling of other mathematical algorithms into the learning component of the ANN system. However, it should be noted that the DRN has been very successful in modeling various languages.

The LAMSTAR Neural Networks

The LAMSTAR Neural Network was actually reviewed in the last subsection. Essentially, there are two of them, known as the "LAMSTAR-1" and the "LAMSTAR-2," respectively. These kinds of Neural Networks are specifically designed for applications devoted to retrieval, analysis, classification, prediction, and decision-making. They are also meant to be used with datasets that are extremely large in nature, which cannot be processed as easily with the other Neural Network configurations examined thus far in this chapter. Thus, in this regard, the add-on tool that is most favored for these LAMSTAR Neural Networks is that of the of the Kohonen Self-Organizing Map (SOM).

Also, the LAMSTAR Neural Networks are designed to handle both quantitative and qualitative data, when they are multidimensional in nature, and even incomplete in many areas. Also, this kind of Neural Network is deemed to be what is known as an "expert intelligent system," in which the datasets are continually being refined and optimized in order to get the desired outputs. The LAMSTAR Neural Networks can be used to help estimate any type of missing data in the datasets through the techniques of both interpolation and extrapolation.

These kinds of Neural Networks are deemed to be very transparent in nature, thus helping to alleviate the notion of the "black box" phenomenon that is so often associated with any kind of Neural Network. The primary reason for this is that LAMSTAR Neural Networks have a unique method in which the statistical weights are assigned to their respective inputs. In other words, these kinds of Neural Networks have been proven to be very successful with those applications that typically deal with decision-making and recognition applications.

When it comes to LAMSTAR Neural Networks, the outputs of the Neurons are typically calculated based upon this mathematical formula:

$$Y = f[p\Sigma I = 1 \ WijXij]$$

Where:

   $F(x)$ = the nonlinear function;
   Wij = the Associative Memory weights that have been statistically assigned to the inputs.

It should also be noted that in this situation, the specific firing of the Neurons takes an all or nothing approach. By making use of the unique assignment of statistical weights to the inputs, LAMSTAR Neural Networks take into account not only the values that are stored in the memory of the ANN system, but also the various correlations that take place between them as well. Also, when the Neuron fires at a point in time when the next time series iteration is about to occur in the ANN system, the statistical weightage of these correlations also increases by a proportional nature.

It is these connections that also serve LAMSTAR Neural Networks' ability to both interpolate and extrapolate, as examined previously, without having to reprogram the ANN system in its complete entirety.

The Structural Elements of LAMSTAR Neural Networks

When it comes to the actual storage of datasets and their inputs, the LAMSTAR NNs make use of the Kohonen SOM modules, and these are further ingrained by making use of the Associative Memory principle. As noted, the reason why the LAMSTAR NNs can deal with such huge datasets is their usage of simple, mathematical computational algorithms that are further dispersed at these linkages. This simply translates into less processing and computational power that is needed. These links, or connections, are also considered to be the main driver in the entire ANN system, by further connecting the SOM modules together.

Because of all these various linkages and connections that are deployed in the ANN system, it now to a certain degree resembles the Central Nervous System (CNS) of the human brain. Further, in most of the systems that are SOM-based, each and every Neuron is closely examined for its particular closeness to any numerical range of the input vectors that are currently present in the entire ANN system. But in the LAMSTAR NNs, only a smaller grouping of Neurons (denoted as "q") can be checked, which of course is a big disadvantage in this regard. The determination of these particular sets is governed by the links, or connections, that are present in the ANN system.

It should also be noted at this point that the main engine of the LAMSTAR NNs is the actual, mathematical summation of all these links, or points, of connections just reviewed thus far. Also, the statistical weights that are assigned to them are actually updated in real time with the sheer amount of traffic that is present on these link and connection nodes in the ANN system.

The Mathematical Algorithms That Are Used for Establishing the Statistical Weights for the Inputs and the Links in the SOM Modules in the ANN System

Whenever a new input is added into the ANN system, especially those of the training datasets, the LAMSTAR NNs will carefully examine all of the storage weight vectors for each module (denoted as "i"), and compare those with the statistical weights that could be potentially assigned to the inputs of the datasets. From this close examination, the "Winning Neuron" (as discussed previously throughout this chapter) is then computed with the following mathematical formula:

$$D(j,j) = ||Xj\text{-}Wj|| < ||Xj\text{---}Wk = /j|| = d(j,k).$$

Also, these statistical weights as just described can be further adjusted if need be, in order to gain as much optimization and reliability as possible. This is done with another specialized mathematical technique, and this is technically known as the "Hamming Distance Function" (denoted as "Dmax"), and it can be represented as follows:

$$Dmax = max[d(xiWi)].$$

Also, as mentioned previously in the last subsection, the LAMSTAR NNs contain many interconnections, or links, between the input layers and the output layers of the ANN system. Although these links can be considered "dynamic" in nature, they too need to be updated for optimization as well as reliability. Once again, this is done by assigning these various interconnections different statistical weight values, and they can be thus computed and assigned according to the following formulas:

$$Li,j/k,m * (t+1) = Li,j/k,m^\wedge(t) + VL;$$

$$Li,j/k,m * (t+1) = Li,j/k,m^\wedge(t+1) \ VM, \ s=/1;$$

$$L(0) = 0$$

Where:
   Li,j/km = represents the links of the Winning Neuron (denoted as "I") in the output module (denoted as "j").

The statistical weights as described in the above equations can also help to regulate the flow input from the dataset in the ANN system so that only the needed processing and computational power is used, and not any more. In many applications that actually make use of the LAMSTAR NNs, the only interconnections or links that are considered for updating are those that reside in between the SOM layers and the outputs of the ANN system. But the interconnections, or links, between the various SOM modules do not get updated whatsoever.

Also as mentioned previously, of the key components of the LAMSTAR NNs are those of "Forgetting," and "Inhibition." In terms of the former, this, which is incorporated with what is known as the "Forgetting Factor," denoted as "F," can be reset at various, predetermined intervals. This can be denoted as k = sK, s = 0, 1, 2, 3, etc., where K represents a predetermined numerical, constant value. This is mathematically represented as:

$$L * (k+1) = FL(k)$$

Where:
   0 > F > 1 = the preset Forgetting factor.

It is important to note at this point that another mathematical algorithm can also be substituted for the above equation, and this is known as the "Forgetting Algorithm," where the value of L(k) is reset at every k = sK, s = 0, 1, 2, 3, etc. This algorithm can be represented as follows:

$$F(i) = (1-z)^{\wedge}1 \; L(k), \; 0 < z <<<< 1$$

$$I = (k-sK)$$

Where:

Z = the highest numerical value to achieve "Ks < k," so that "i" is started from scratch at the value of 0, and subsequently increasing in value at every iteration in the ANN system.

With regards to "Inhibition," this must be ingrained and programmed into the ANN system before it can be executed in the production environment. With respect to the LAMSTAR NNs, it is typically included by pre-assigning the selected Neurons in the input layers.

An Overview of the Processor in LAMSTAR Neural Networks

As it was reviewed earlier in the previous subsections, LAMSTAR NNs make use of what is known as "Deep Learning." With this extra functionality, it can compute the outputs by making use of a specialized processor in order for the ANN system to be used in much larger and complex types of applications. Also, in order to facilitate the processing power and computational speeds, the ANN system can avail itself to the concepts of parallel processing.

The processor of the LAMSTAR NNs is often found in the inputs of the SOM layer of the ANN system.

The Training Iterations versus the Operational Iterations

With the typical ANN system, one of its greatest advantages of it is that it can keep training nonstop on a 24/7/365 basis, as long as it is constantly being fed clean and robust datasets. But as it has been pointed out before in previous subsections, this not the case with LAMSTAR NNs. These can only operate in an iterative cycle mode. In other words, the LAMSTAR NNs can only run and operate in testing and operational runs, in a start-stop fashion.

But in order to further optimize the network performance of the ANN system, a number of test runs need to be implemented so that the LAMSTAR NN will be able fire off the Neurons so that the actual datasets can start being fed into it.

The Issue of Missing Data in the LAMSTAR Neural Network

As it has been mentioned previously, the LAMSTAR NN can run in the absence of missing data that may be present in the datasets. This can be accomplished by statistically summing up the overall values of "k" that are present.

The Decision-Making Process of the LAMSTAR Neural Network

Overall, the network structure of both the LAMSTAR-1 NN and the LAMSTAR-2 NN are very similar in nature. Also, these two types of Neural Networks even share the same kind of decision-making processes when it comes to how the inputs and their associated datasets will be used to compute the outputs from the ANN system. The decision-making algorithm can be mathematically represented as follows:

$$M\Sigma k(w) \ I,nL \ k(w) > M\Sigma k(w) \ I,jL \ k(w) \ Vi, \ j, \ k, \ n, \ j=/n$$

Where:
- I = the It h output module;
- N = the Winning Neuron;
- K(w) = the output module;
- M = the link weight that has been established between the Winning Neuron in the input module (denoted as "k"), and the Neuron (denoted as "j") in the "Ith" output layer.

The Data Analysis Functionality in the LAMSTAR Neural Network

As it was mentioned in the first chapter of this book, data and their corresponding datasets are the "fuel" that make the ANN system go, and that make it produce the desired outputs. But one key aspect of this is that the data must be cleansed and optimized at all times. This even holds true for the LAMSTAR Neural Network. In fact, most of the information and data that is present in this kind of Neural Network actually resides in the statistical weights that have been assigned to the various links, or interconnections, as it has been extensively thus far.

Because of this, the LAMSTAR can also even be utilized as Data Analysis for the ANN system. In this regard, it is the input data that can be further analyzed, in terms of the analysis of the various input layers and the corresponding datasets that are being used. Also, the degree of statistical correlation amongst these datasets can be examined as well. In most cases, the analysis that can be conducted by the LAMSTAR NN is a two-step process which is as follows:

1) The actual establishment of the configuration of the analysis that is to take place;
2) Once the above has been accomplished, then the further analysis can then take the place of the statistical weights and the datasets that are correlated with the links, or interconnections, in the LAMSTAR NN.

The term "analysis" can be a broad one, depending upon the type of applications that the ANN system is being used for, and the desired outputs that are to be achieved from it. For the purposes of the LAMSTAR NN, analysis simply means providing further insight into the actual problem that the application in question is attempting to solve. It should also be noted that that any information/data that is further gleaned from this analysis phase could be further optimized in terms of performance and speed if it is decided at a later point in time that extra Neurons or Input and/or Output Layers need to be added or removed.

From here, the statistical clusters that are associated with the links that have the highest numerical value associated with them will then further determine the anticipated trends of the datasets that are being used as the inputs into the ANN system. From here, it will then "collaborate" to yield the desired outputs that will be computed by the ANN system.

It should be noted that the analysis, which can be conducted by the LAMSTAR NN, can be done at any point when the actual ANN system is learning from the inputs and the datasets that have fed into it, and producing the desired outputs. Especially during the training phase for the ANN system, the LAMSTAR NN will locate those links, or interconnections, with the highest statistical values that have been assigned to them, and from there, retrieve any sort of relevant information/data from the SOM modules that have any further associations with the links or connections, as described previously.

The above-mentioned process can be accomplished via two separate and distinct approaches, which are as follows:

1) Selecting and deploying those links that have a numerical value which far exceeds any sort of predefined threshold;
2) Selecting and deploying a predefined number of links or interconnections that have the highest statistical values that are associated with them.

Another key component of the analysis component of the LAMSTAR NN is its ability to extract unique features that are present in the ANN system. Also, these features can be removed if deemed necessary as well. There are certain properties to this, and they are as follows:

1) The most significant memory and/or input/output layers:
   This can be actually extracted by using a mathematical matrix that is denoted as "$A(I,j)$,"

Where:

I = the Winning Neuron in the SOM storage model that is present in the LAMSTAR NN.

2) The least significant memory and/or input/output layers:
In this particular case, the Winning Neuron is ascertained by this mathematical formula:

$$[i*, s* /dk]: L(I, s/dk) > L(j, p/dk)$$

Where:

P is not equal to "S";

L(I, s/dk) = the statistical weight link between the Winning Neuron (denoted as "j"), in any layer (denoted as "p"), as well as output layer of the Neuron denoted as "dk."

3) The most significant SOM Module:
This is computed by the following mathematical equation:

$$S**(dk): \Sigma i(\{L(I, s/dk)\} > \Sigma j (\{L(j, p/dk)\}$$

4) The least significant SOM Module:
This is computed by the following mathematical equation:

$$L(I, s/dk) > L(j, s/dk)$$

NOTE: The above equation can be applied for any Neuron (denoted as "j") for the same SOM Module that is present in the LAMSTAR NN.

5) Redundancy:
This can be further extrapolated as follows:
Whenever a certain Neuron (denoted as "I" in this particular case) in the SOM input layer is considered to be the winning one, it is also considered to have the winning inputs that should be used as well in that very SOM input layer. This is known as "Redundancy."

6) Zero Information Redundancy:
In this particular case, if there is only one Neuron that is always deemed to be the winner in a certain SOM layer (denoted as "k" for these purposes), then this certain layer will contain absolutely no relevant information/data.

Also as mentioned previously, LAMSTAR NNs contain two more distinct properties, which are as follows:

1) The Correlation Feature:
This is where the most significant SOM layers (whether input- or output-based) contain the most statistically significant Neurons for the various factors that are associated with them (denoted as "m"), assuming that they are correlated

with the same outputs that have been computed by the ANN system. This is all achieved with what is known technically as the "Correlation-Layer Set-Up Rule," and this mathematically represented as follows:

$$m\text{-}1 \sum i{=}1 \; i(\text{per output decision "DK"}).$$

Also, at this particular juncture, the statistical concepts of both Auto Correlation and Cross Correlation can be used at any time-based iteration in the LAMSTAR NN as deemed to be necessary.

2) The Interpolation/Extrapolation Feature:
In this case, the particular Neuron [(denoted as "N(I, p)"] is considered to be either "interpolated" or "extrapolated" if it meets the conditions as set forth by this mathematical equation:

$$\sum q \; \{L(I, p/w, q - dk)\} > \sum \{L(v, p/w, q - dk)\}$$

Where:
I = the various Neurons in a specific SOM Module;
{L(v, p/w, q – dk)} = denotes the links, or the interconnections, that reside within the Correlation Layer in the LAMSTAR NN (which is denoted as "V (p/q)").

It is also important to note that there is only one Winning Neuron for any input that is used (which is denoted as "N(w,q)").

So far in this chapter, we have reviewed extensively the theoretical concepts that are associated with Neural Networks. The rest of this chapter is now devoted to the applications of this theory.

Deep Learning Neural Networks—The Autoencoder

An autoencoder is a type of deep learning neural network used to learn an efficient encoding for a set of data in an unsupervised manner. Basically, an autoencoder attempts to copy its Input to its Output through a constrained coding layer, creating the desired encoding. Autoencoders have been effectively used to solve many problems such as the semantic meaning of words, facial recognition, and predictive maintenance (which will be described in the application section of this chapter).

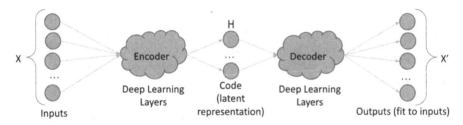

Source: Randy Groves

The basic architecture of the autoencoder is shown in the figure above. The input and output layers have the same number of nodes (*x*) as the set of data to be encoded. In the middle is a hidden layer with fewer than *x* nodes where the coded (or latent) representation (H) will be learned. The deep learning neural network on the left learns to encode X into H while the deep learning neural network on the right learns to decode H into X' with the goal of minimizing the difference between X and X' (known as reconstruction error). Since an autoencoder is learning to produce X' from X, the data itself provides the labels for the model to train against making this an unsupervised learning approach (learning from any dataset without having to label the desired output).

The usual deep learning techniques like back propagation are used to reduce reconstruction error by optimizing the encoder to generate better codes that the decoder can use to reconstruct X. With a small reconstruction error, the middle layer represents the essential (or latent) information in X with all of the noise and redundancy removed. This is similar to compressing a computer file to a smaller representation using something like Zip. One difference is that Zip is a lossless encoding such that the Zip decoder can perfectly reconstruct the original file whereas autoencoders reconstruct X with some intrinsic error.

By selecting the smallest value for *h* with an acceptable reconstruction error, the autoencoder can be used to reduce the dimensions of the input date from *x* to *h* without losing signification information from the original X (known as dimensionality reduction). The code layer can also be used to determine relationships in the input data. For example, the encoded value for a word like "London" should be close to the words "England" and "Paris." Or, the encoding of a new image of your face should be close to previous encodings of your face.

Another use for autoencoders is anomaly detection. By having an autoencoder attempt to reconstruct new data not used in training, a poorly reconstructed input set is an indicator that this new data is different from the original data or that it is anomalous. The input that is most poorly reconstructed is the one that is most different from the training data in relation to the other inputs. These individual input reconstruction errors provide information that can be used to explain what is anomalous about the new data. An example of using an autoencoder for predictive maintenance is provided in the application section of this chapter.

The Applications of Neural Networks

Overall thus far, this chapter has examined the concept of Neural Networks, primarily from a theoretical perspective. It is important to note that all of the theory that has just been detailed has one primary purpose: to lay the foundations for the modern day applications that we see and use on a daily basis. For example, in the world of Cybersecurity, many Neural Network-based applications are now being used for Cyber threat triaging, especially for filtering false positives, so that the IT Security teams can quickly discern and act upon the threat vectors that are real.

But Neural Networks are also being used in the world of what is known as the "Internet of Things," or "IoT" for short. This is where all of the objects that we interact with on a daily basis in both the virtual world and the physical world are interconnected with one another through various network-based lines of communication.

Because Neural Networks are now starting to be deployed in various types of applications, there is the notion that many of these applications are very expensive to procure and complex to deploy. But the truth is that they are not. For example, many of these Neural Network-based applications are now available through many of the largest Cloud-based Providers. With this, of course, comes many advantages, such as fixed and affordable monthly pricing, and above all scalability, so that you can ramp up or ramp down your needs in just a matter of a few seconds. In the next subsection of this chapter, we detail some of these major Cloud Providers.

The Major Cloud Providers for Neural Networks

In this regard, some of the juggernauts in this area are Amazon Web Services (AWS) and Microsoft Azure. There are others as well, and they will also be examined.

1) The Amazon Web Services (AWS):
   It should be noted that the AWS is the oldest of Cloud-based Providers, having been first launched back in 2006. Since then, they have been consistently ranked as one of the top Cloud Platforms to be used, according to "Gartner's Magic Quadrant." But they have been known to be more expensive, and offer more complex solutions that are not well-suited for SMBs as they attempt to deploy Neural Network-based applications.
2) Microsoft Azure:
   Microsoft Azure (aka "Azure") has been holding very steady second place, right after the AWS also according to "Gartner's Magic Quadrant." Azure is especially appealing to those businesses that have legacy-based workloads and for those that are looking to deploy and implement brand new Neural Network applications on a Cloud-based Platform. More importantly, they also offer very specialized platforms for what are known as "Platform as a Service" (aka "PaaS") applications, Data Storage, Machine Learning (which was the main topic of Chapter 2), as well as even the Internet of Things (IoT), with services based around all of these particular services. Also, software developers that are keen on deploying NET-based applications in the Cloud will probably find Azure the best platform to be used in this regard as well. Also, Microsoft has adopted the usage of other software-based platforms into Azure, most notably that of Linux and even Oracle. In fact, 50 percent of the Cloud-based workloads in Azure are Linux-based. In fact, as also noted by Gartner:

   "Microsoft has a unique vision for the future that involves bringing in technology partners through native, first party offerings such as those of from VMware, NetApp, Red Hat, Cray, and Databricks" (Artasanchez & Joshi, 2020).

3) The Google Cloud Platform (GCP):
The Google Cloud Platform, aka the "GCP," was first launched in 2018. When compared to the AWS and Azure, it is ranked in third place in terms of the Cloud-based Providers. The GCP is primarily known for its Big Data Cloud-based offerings, and will soon be leveraging their platform in order to service both SAP- and CRM-based systems. The GCP is also known for Automation, Containers, and Kubernetes and even Tensor Flow. The GCP is primarily focused around making use of Open Sourced Platforms, such as that of Linux.

4) The Alibaba Cloud:
This was first launched in 2017, and they primarily serve the Chinese market, from both a private sector and government standpoint, especially for building Hybrid Cloud platforms.

5) The Oracle Cloud Infrastructure (OSI):
The Oracle Cloud Infrastructure, also known as the "OCI" was first launched back in 2017. They primarily offer Virtualized Machines (aka "VMs") that support primarily Oracle Database Workloads and other basic Infrastructure as a Service (aka "IaaS") Cloud-based services.

6) The IBM Cloud:
Traditionally, IBM has been known for its sheer market dominance for both the Mainframe and Personal Computing market segments. But as they started to erode from view, they tried to embrace a Cloud-based Platform in a manner similar that of both the AWS and Axure. In this regard, their Cloud-based offerings include Container Platforms and other forms of PaaS offerings. The IBM Cloud is primarily geared toward markets that still make use of IBM mainframes as well as other traditional IBM workloads. IBM is also well-known for its AI package known as "Watson."

The Neural Network Components of the Amazon Web Services & Microsoft Azure

In this part of the chapter, we now focus on the various components that relate Artificial Intelligence to the major platforms of the AWS and Azure.

The Amazon Web Services (AWS)

As it has been noted, the AWS has many components that an end user can utilize, not just for Artificial Intelligence. However, when it comes to deploying Artificial Intelligence, here are some of the components that any business can use:

The Amazon SageMaker

This package was initially launched in 2017. This is a specific type of Artificial Intelligence platform in which both software developers and data scientists alike can create, train, and implement AI models on a Cloud-based Infrastructure. In this regard, a very important subset of the Amazon SageMaker is known as the "Jupyter Notebook." These notebooks use certain kinds of source code, namely that of Python, and AI algorithms can be contained within their infrastructure. It is important to note that with the "Jupyter Notebook," .EXE files can be compiled very easily and quickly onto just about any kind of wireless device, especially iOS and Android devices. Also, the Amazon SageMaker consists of the following advantages:

- It is a fully managed service, so there are no worries with regards to security or applying any sort of software patches or upgrades;
- Some of the most commonly used AI tools automatically come with the Amazon SageMaker, and these have been extremely optimized so that any kind or type of application that you can create will run ten times faster than other kinds of AI deployments. Also, you can even deploy your own customized AI algorithms into Amazon SageMaker;
- Amazon SageMaker provides just the right amount of optimization for any type of workload that your AI application demands. In this regard, you can use either the lower end "ml.t2.medium" virtual machine, or the ultra-sophisticated "ml.p3dn.24xlarge" virtual machine.

Also, the Amazon SageMaker allows for the data scientist and any software development team to run smoothly and quickly with other AWS services which include the following:

From the Standpoint of Data Preparation

- S3;
- RDS;
- DynamoDB;
- Lambda.

From the Standpoint of Algorithm Selection, Optimization, and Training

As mentioned, the Amazon SageMaker has a number of very powerful mathematical algorithms that are both extremely fast and extremely accurate. These kinds of algorithms can handle datasets of the size of petabytes, and further increase performance by up to ten times of other traditional AI mathematical algorithms. Here is a sampling of what is currently available in terms of AI algorithms as it relates to the Amazon SageMaker:

- The Blazing Text;
- The DeepAR Forecasting;
- The Factorization Machines;
- The K-Means;
- The Random Cut Forest;
- The Object Detection;
- The Image Classification;
- The Neural Topic Model (NTM);
- The IP Insights;
- The K-Nearest Neighbors (aka "k-NN");
- The Latent Dirichlet Allocation;
- The Linear Learner;
- The Object2Vec;
- The Principal Component Analysis;
- The Semantic Segmentation;
- The Sequence to Sequence;
- The XGBoost.

From the Standpoint of AI Mathematical Algorithm and Optimizing

The Amazon SageMaker also comes with automatic AI Model Tuning, and in technical terms, this is known as "Hyperparameter Tuning." With this process in hand, the best, statistical patterns for your particular AI application are run through a series of several mathematical iterations which make use of the datasets that your AI application will be using. In terms of the metrics of the training, a "scorecard" is also kept of the AI algorithms that are deemed to be running the best, so you can see what will work best for your AI application.

To further illustrate this, imagine that you are trying to implement a Binary Classification type of application. In terms of mathematics, at all possible levels, you want to maximize what is known as the "Area Under the Curve," or "AUC" for short. This will be done by specifically training a mathematical model known as the "XGBoost." The following are the stipulations that will be utilized:

- Alpha;
- ETA;
- Min_Child_Weight;
- Max_Depth.

From here, you can then command a certain range of permutations for the "Hyperparameter Tuning" (Artasanchez & Joshi, 2020).

From the Standpoint of Algorithm Deployment

From the perspective of the software development team and the data scientist, deploying an AI-based model is actually a very easy, two-phased approach, which is as follows:

1) You need to first configure the specific endpoints of your Cloud-based AI application so that multiple instances can be used in the same Virtual Machine (VM);
2) From here, you can then launch more AI-based instances of your application in order for various predictions to be made about the desired outputs. It is also important to note at this point that the Amazon SageMaker APIs can also work seamlessly with other types of AI instances, and because of this, you can make your AI application even more robust.

Also, the Amazon SageMaker can work with the kinds of predictions that are deemed to be both "batched" and "one-offs" in nature. With regards to the former, these kinds of predictions can be made on datasets that are contained and stored in the Amazon S3.

From the Standpoint of Integration and Invocation

The Amazon SageMaker provides the following kinds of tools:

1) The Web-based API:
   This specialized kind of API can be made use of in order to further control and literally "invoke" a Virtual Server instance of the Amazon SageMaker.
2) The SageMaker API:
   This kind of specialized API can make use of the following source code languages:
   ■ Go;
   ■ C++;
   ■ Java;
   ■ Java Script;
   ■ Python;
   ■ PHP;
   ■ Ruby;
   ■ Ruby On Rails.
3) The Web Interface:
   This is a direct interface to the Jupyter Notebooks.
4) The AWS CLI:
   This is the Command Line Interface (CLI) for the AWS.

The Amazon Comprehend

One of the key components of any Artificial Intelligence application is that of Natural Language Processing, also known as "NLP" for short. It can be defined specifically as follows:

> Natural language processing (NLP) is a branch of artificial intelligence that helps computers understand, interpret, and manipulate human language. NLP draws from many disciplines, including computer science and computational linguistics, in its pursuit to fill the gap between human communication and computer understanding.
>
> **(SAS, n.d.)**

In this regard, the AWS makes it easy for you to implement Natural Language Processing for AI application, especially when it comes to human language, and from there, it can ascertain any sort of implicit as well as explicit content in the human languages that are spoken. In this regard, this can also be considered "Big Data," but on a qualitative level. For example, this can include customer support emails, any form of feedback that is provided by the customer, especially when it comes to product/service reviews, any type of call center conversations, as well as those that take place on the various social media sites, especially those of Facebook, LinkedIn, and Twitter.

The name of the Natural Language Processing tool that is used by the AWS is called "Amazon Comprehend." It has the following functionalities:

1) <u>Analyzing Use Cases</u>:
   This tool can very quickly and easily scan just about any type of document, in an effort to find any statistical correlations or hidden patterns that reside from within them. This includes such things as Sentiment Analysis, Entity Extraction, and even Document organization, depending upon the specific type of category that they belong in.
2) <u>The Console Access</u>:
   Amazon Comprehend can be accessed very quickly and easily from within the AWS Management Console. If you have large amounts of quantitative data stored in the S3, you can easily integrate it with Amazon Comprehend. From here, you can use a specialized API to find any correlations or any hidden trends that are not noticeable at first. A key advantage here is that you can even batch up various datasets from S3 in order for it to be further processed by Amazon Comprehend. Also, Amazon Comprehend has six different APIs that you can use, which are as follows:
   ■ The Key Phrase Extraction API: This can be used to identify certain phrases and/or terms from within the qualitative dataset that is provided;

- The Sentiment Analysis API: This will compute the overall level of the feeling of the text that is typed and/or entered in by the individual and rank it either as positive, negative, or neutral.
- The Syntax API: This allows you to differentiate between spoken words, such as nouns, verbs, adjectives, pronouns, etc.
- The Entity Recognition API: This can be used to further identify the actual entities in a text, such as those of places, people, etc.
- The Language Detection API: This can be used to specifically identify the language in which the text is conveyed in.
- The Custom Classification API: With this powerful API, you can even create and deploy a customized classification model for your AI application.

Amazon Rekognition

Amazon Rekognition is a tool in the AWS that has been built specifically for the processing of any sort of images and/or videos that you might be using for your AI application. This is a very powerful tool to use in the sense that it has been literally pretrained with billions of images that it can easily recognize. Although it may sound very complex, on the contrary, it is quite easy to use, because it makes use of Deep Learning mathematical algorithms that are already stored in the AWS via just one API.

The following is just a sampling of how it can be used for AI applications:

- Object and Scene Detection;
- Gender Recognition;
- Facial Recognition: This is where a specific individual's identity is confirmed by the unique features that are found on their face. When used with the AWS, it makes use of Deep Learning techniques and algorithms.

Amazon Translate

As its name implies, this tool in AWS can literally translate any form of written text quickly and easily into another language. The foreign languages that Amazon Translate supports are demonstrated in the following matrix, along with its specific code that is used to identify in it both the AWS and Amazon Translate:

Language	The AWS Language Code
Arabic	ar
Chinese (simplified)	zh
Chinese (traditional)	zh-TW
Czech	cs

Language	*The AWS Language Code*
Danish	da
Dutch	nl
English	en
Finnish	fi
French	fr
German	de
Greek	el
Hebrew	he
Hindi	hi
Hungarian	hu
Indonesian	id
Italian	it
Japanese	ja
Korean	ko
Malay	ms
Norwegian	no
Persian	fa
Polish	pl
Portuguese	pt
Romanian	ro
Russian	ru
Spanish	es
Swedish	sv
Thai	th
Turkish	Tr
Ukrainian	uk
Urdu	ur
Vietnamese	vi

The Amazon Translate can be accessed from three different methods:

- From the AWS Management Console;
- Using a specially crafted AWS API;
  Supported source code languages include the following:
  *Go;
  *C++;
  *Java;
  *Java Script;
  *Python;
  *PHP;
  *Ruby;
  *Ruby On Rails.
- From the AWS CLI.

Amazon Transcribe

This tool in the AWS makes use of what is known as "Automatic Speech Recognition," or "ASR" for short. With this, your software development team can easily and quickly incorporate speech to text functionalities to your AI application. It can also analyze and transcribe audio MP3 files, which can also be used in real time as well. For example, it can take a live audio stream and provide the text in real time. It can even provide a time stamp for each and every word that has been transcribed.

Amazon Textract

One of the most difficult obstacles for any kind of AI application is to recognize the specific handwriting of a particular individual. In other words, it can take garbled handwriting, convert into an image, and from there extract it into a text-based format. Amazon Textract can even ascertain the layout of any form of document and the elements that are associated with it. It can even extract data that are present in embedded forms and/or tables.

Microsoft Azure

In the world of Microsoft Azure, it is the "Azure Machine Learning Studio" that consists of all of the tools you have ever dreamed of in order to create and build an Artificial Intelligence (AI) application. It makes use of a GUI-based approach in order to do this, and it can even integrate with other Microsoft tools, most notably that of Power BI.

The Azure Machine Learning Studio Interactive Workspace

As its name implies, this is an interactive workspace of sorts in which you can feed in gargantuan datasets into your AI application, manipulate it, and then complete an exhaustive analysis of it with many ultra-sophisticated statistical functions and formulas, and even get a glimpse of what the outputs will look like from the AI system that you have just built. This entire process is also technically referred to as the "Machine Learning Pipeline." The main advantage of this is that everything in this process is visually displayed.

It should be noted that the above process can be repeated over and over again as a so-called "Training Experiment" until the results you are seeking have been achieved. Once this has been done, this exercise can then be converted over into the production environment, which is known as the "Predictive Experiment."

The Machine Learning Studio consists of the following functionalities:

- <u>Projects</u>:
  These are a collection of both the Training Experiment and the Predictive Experiment.
- <u>Experiments</u>:
  These are where specific experiments are actually created, revised, launched, and executed.
- <u>Web Services</u>:
  Your production-based experiments can also be converted to specific Web-based services.
- <u>Notebooks</u>:
  The Machine Learning Studio also supports the Jupyter Networks, which is an exclusive service from the AWS.
- <u>Datasets</u>:
  This is where you upload and store your respective datasets that are to be fed into your AI application.
- <u>Trained Models</u>:
  These are the specific AI models that have you have created and thus have been in trained in the Training Experiment or the Predictive Experiment.

It should be noted at this point that there are certain conditions that must be met first before you can start creating and launching AI models and applications. These are as follows:

- You must have at least one dataset and one module already established;
- The datasets that you are planning to feed into your AI models/applications can only be connected to their respective modules;
- Modules can be quickly and easily connected to other models;

- There must be at least one connection to the datasets that you are planning to feed into the AI models/applications;
- You must already have preestablished the needed permutations before you can begin any work.

It should be noted at this point that a module is simply an algorithm that can be used to further analyze your datasets. Some of the ones that are already included in the Machine Learning Studio include the following:

1) <u>The ARFF Conversion Module</u>:
   This converts a .NET dataset into an Attribute-Relation File Format (aka "ARFF").
2) <u>The Compute Elementary Statistics Module</u>:
   This computes basic statistics, such as R^2, Adjusted R^2, Mean, Mode, Median, Standard Deviation, etc.
3) <u>Various Multiple Regression Models</u>:
   You have a wide range of statistical models that you can already choose from, without creating anything from scratch.
4) <u>The Scoring Model</u>:
   This can quantitatively score your Multiple Regression Model that you plan to use for your AI application.

The Azure Machine Learning Service

This is another large platform of Azure which allows your AI applications to be much more scalable. It supports the Python source code, which is the programming language of choice for most typical AI applications. It also makes use of Docker Containers as well. It can be accessed from two different avenues, which are as follows:

- The Software Development Kit (SDK);
- Any other type of visual-based interface, primarily that of the Microsoft Visual Studio.

The primary differences between the Azure Machine Learning Services and the Azure Machine Learning Studio are outlined in the following matrix:

Azure Machine Learning Services	Azure Machine Learning Studio
It supports a Hybrid Environment of the Cloud and On Premises	Only standard experiments can be created, launched, and executed
You can make use of different frameworks and instances of Virtual Machines	It is a fully managed by Azure

Azure Machine Learning Services	Azure Machine Learning Studio
It supports Automated Hyperparameter Tuning	It is only available in the Cloud, not as an On Premises solution

The Azure Cognitive Services

This specific service has the following components to it:

1) <u>The Decision Service</u>:
   As you deploy your various AI applications, certain recommendations will be provided by this system so that to you can make better decisions as to how to further improve the efficiency and optimization of your AI application.
2) <u>The Vision Service</u>:
   This can auto-enable your AI application so that it can analyze and manipulate images and videos.
3) <u>The Search Service</u>:
   You can incorporate the Bing Search Engine into your AI application.
4) <u>The Speech Service</u>:
   This can convert any spoken words into text format. It also fully supports the Biometric modality of Speech Recognition.
5) <u>The Language Service</u>:
   This is the Natural Language Processing (NLP) component of Azure, and it can quickly and easily analyze the sentiment of anything that has been communicated, especially those used in chatbots.

The Google Cloud Platform

When compared to the AWS and Azure, the Google Cloud Platform comes in at a rather distant third place. The biggest component of the GCP is what is known as the "AI Hub." This is a huge interface that consists of plug and play components, sophisticated AI algorithms, instant collaboration features, as well as the ability to import a large amount of datasets that have been stored with other Cloud Providers. Here are some of the key features of the AI Hub:

1) <u>Component and Code Discovery</u>:
   Through this, you can access the following components:
   - Google AI;
   - Google Cloud AI;
   - Google Cloud Partners.

2) Collaboration:

This component helps to avoid duplication, especially if you are building a large scale AI project as part of a massive team effort. It possesses very granular types of controls, and even comes with a set of AI algorithms that you can use right out of the box.

3) Deployment:

This particular functionality allows for the full modification and customization of the AI algorithms that you are either planning to use or are in the process of using for your AI application. Once you have built your application, you can even host them on the platforms of other Cloud Providers as well.

The Google Cloud AI Building Blocks

The Google Cloud Platform (GCP) comes with many other tools as well, which are as follows:

1) The Google Cloud AutoML Custom Models:

The AutoML makes use of a very sophisticated Learning and Neural Network Architecture so that you can create a very specific AI application in a particular subdomain of Artificial Intelligence.

2) The Google Cloud Pre-Trained APIs:

With this, you can literally use specially trained APIs without first having your AI application learn to go through the entire training process. A great feature of these is that these specific APIs are constantly being upgraded to keep them optimized and refined for powerful levels of processing and speed.

3) The Vision AI and AutoML Vision:

With this kind of service, you can gain timely insights from the AutoML Vision or the Vision API models, which are actually all pretrained. It can actually be used to detect the emotion of an individual, especially if you are using your AI application for a sophisticated chatbot tool. Further, with the Google Vision API, you can even make use of both "RESTful" and "RPC API" calls. With these respective APIs, you can quickly and easily classify any sort of image that you may upload into your AI application. This is actually a service that has already been pretrained, and it consists of well over a million category types. It can be used to convert speech to text, and for incorporating Facial Recognition technology into your AI system.

4) The AutoML Intelligence and Video Intelligence API:

This is a service with which you can track and classify objects in a video, using various kinds of AI models. You can use this service to track for objects in streaming video as well.

5) The AutoML Natural Language and Natural Language API:
   Through an easy to use API, you can determine all sorts of "sentiment," which include the following:
   - Entity Analysis;
   Sentiment Analysis;
   - Content Classification;
   - Entity Sentiment Analysis;
   - Syntax Analysis.
   You can even feed datasets into it in order to determine which ones are best suited for your AI application.

6) Dialogflow:
   This is actually a software development service, in which a software development team can create an agent that can engage in a conversation with a real person, such as, once again, a chatbot. Once this has been done, you can launch your chatbot instantly across these platforms:
   - Google Assistant;
   - Facebook Messenger;
   - Slack;
   - The Alexa Voice Services.

7) Text to Speech:
   With this, you can quickly and easily convert any human speech into over 30 different foreign languages and their corresponding dialects. In order to do this, it makes use of a Speech Synthesis tool called "WaveNet" in order to deliver an enterprise grade MP3 audio file.

8) Speech to Text:
   This is simply the reverse of the above. With this, you can also quickly and easily convert the audio files into text by using the Neural Network algorithms that are already built into the Google Cloud Platform. Although these algorithms are quite complex in nature, they can be invoked quite easily and quickly via the usage of a specialized API. In this regard, over 120 separate languages are supported, as well as their dialects. Speech to Text can be used for the following purposes:
   - It can enable any kind of voice command in any sort of application;
   - It can transcribe call center conversations;
   - It can easily co-minge with other non-Google services that are AI related;
   - It can process audio in real time and convert speech to text from prerecorded conversations as well.

9) The AutoML Tables:
   With this type of functionality, you can deploy your AI models on purely structured datasets. Although no specific coding is required, if it needs to be done, then you make use of "Colab Notebooks." It works in a manner that is very similar to the Jupyter in the AWS.

10) Recommendations AI:
This is a unique service in that can deliver any type of product recommendations for a customer-related AI application, once again, like that of a chatbot.

We have now reviewed what the major Cloud Providers, the Amazon Web Services, Microsoft Azure, and Google offer in terms of AI-related services. We now examine some AI applications that you can build, making use of the Python source code.

Building an Application That Can Create Various Income Classes

In this example, we look at how to use the Python source in order to create an application that can create different classifications for various income levels for an entire population as a whole. This can work very well for the Federal Government, especially when it comes to tax purposes and/or giving out entitlements and benefits.

This example makes use of a dataset that consists of a population of 25,000 people:

```
# Input file containing
Data input_file = 'income_data.txt'
# Read the data
X=[]
Y = []
Count_Class1 = 0
Count_Class2 = 0
Max_datapoints = 25000
With open (input_file, 'r') as f:
    For line in f. readiness ():
        If count_Class >=max_datapoints and Count_Class2 >=max_
    datapoints
        Break
If '?' in line:
    Continue
    Data = line [:-1].split (',')
    If data [-1] =="<=50K" and Count_Class1 < max_datapoints;
        X.append(data)
        Count_Class1 ==1
    If data [-1] ====">50K" and Count_Class2 < max_datapoints;
        X.append(data)
```

```
        Count_Class2 +-1
    # Convert to numpy array
    X = np.array
    #Convert string data to numerical data
    Label_encoder = []
    X_encoded = np.empty (X.shape)
    For I, item in enumerate (X[0]);
        If item.isdigit ();
            X_Encoded [;, i] = X [:, 1]
        Else:
            Label_encoder.append(preprocessing.LabelEncoder ())
            X_Encoded [:, i] = label_enocder [-1].fit.tranform (X[:, 1])
        X = X_encoded [:, :-1], astype (int)
        Y = X_encoded [:, :-1], astype (int)
#Create SVM classifier
Classifier = OneVaOneClassifier (LinearSVC (random_state=0);
#Train the Classifier
Classifier.fit (X, y)
#Cross Validation
X_train, X_test, y_train, y_test = train_test_split.train_test_
Split (X, y, test_size=0.2, random_state=5)
Classifier = OneVaOneClassifier (LinearSVC (random_state=0);
Classifier.fit (X_train, y_train)
Y_test_pred = classifier.predict (X_test)
#Compute the F1 score of the SVM Classifier
F1 = train_test_split.cross_val_score (classifier, X, y, scoring='f1_weighted',
    cv=3)
Print ("F1 score: + str(round(100*f1.mean(), 2)} + "%"
#Predict output for a test datapoint
Input_data = ['32', 'Public' or 'Private', '34456', 'College Graduate', 'Married',
    'Physician' 'Has Family', 'Caucasian', 'Female', 23', 'United States']
#Encode test datapoint
Input_Data_Encoded = [-1] * len(input_data)
Count = 0
For I, item in enumerate (input_data);
    If item.isdigit ():
        Input_data_encoded [i] = int (input_data [i])
    Else:
        Input_data_encoded[i] = int (label_encoder[count].
    Transform(input_data[i]))
    Input_data_encoded = np.array(input_data_encoded)
#Run classifier on encoded datapoint and print output
```

```
Predicted_class = classifier.predict (input_data_encoded)
Print (label_encoder [-1].inverse_transform (predicted_class) [0])
```

(Artasanchez & Joshi, 2020).

Building an Application That Can Predict Housing Prices

In good economic times, one of the markets that tends to really get a lot of attention and become "red hot" is that of real estate. This is especially true if you are trying to "flip" a house for a higher value, or just want to sell your existing home. This application can even be used to predict the market value for a house that you wish to purchase. The opposite of this is also true. The model developed here can also be used with other financial-based models in the case of an economic downturn, in which real estate prices can greatly fluctuate.

Here is the Python source code to create this kind of application:

```
#Load housing data
Data = datasets.load_boston()
#Shuffle the data
X, y = Shuffle(data.data, data.target, random_state=32)
#Split the data into training and testing datasets
Num_training = int (0.8 * len (X))
X_trai, Y_train = X[:num_training], y[:num_training]
X_test, Y_test = X(num_training;), y[num_training:]
#Create Support Vector Regression model
Sv_regressor = SVR(kernel = 'linear', C=1.0 epsilon=0.1)
#Train Support Vector Regressor
Sv_regressor.fit (X_train, Y_train)
#Evaluate performance of Support Vector Regressor
Y_test_pred = sv_regressor.predict (X_test)
MSE=mean_squared_error (y_test, y_test_pred)
EVS = explained variance score (y_test, y_test_pred)
Print ("\n### Performance ###")
Print ("Mean squared error =", round (mse, 2))
Print ("Explained variance score =", round (evs, 2))
#Test the regressor on test datapoint
Test_data = (Iterations of housing pricing datasets)
Print ("\nPredicted Proce:", sv_regressor.predict ([test_data]) [0])
```

(Artasanchez & Joshi, 2020).

Building an Application That Can Predict Vehicle Traffic Patterns in Large Cities

Although many people are working from home because of the COVID-19 pandemic, traffic still exists. It may not be so much in the rural areas, but in the much larger metropolitan areas, there are still large amounts of traffic. Given this and the fact that just about anything can disrupt the smooth flow of vehicle traffic, whether it is due to weather, a large accident, or even a Cyberattack, government officials need to have a way in which they can predict what traffic will look like based upon certain outcomes, such as using the permutations just described. Also, the drivers of vehicles need to be constantly updated via their mobile app (especially that of Google Maps), if there is a new route to be taken, in the case of a large scale traffic jam.

Here is the Python source code to help create such an application:

```
#Load input data
Input_file = 'traffic data.txt'
Data = []
With open (input_file, 'r') as f:
     For line in f.readiness ();
          Items = line [:-1], split (',')
          Data.append (items)
Data=np.array(data)
#Convert string data to numerical data
Label_Encoder = []
X_encoded = np.empty (data.shape)
For I, item in enumerate (data[0]):
     If item.isdigit ():
     X_encoded (:, i) = data [:, i]
     Else:
          Label_encoder.append (preprocessing.LabelEncoder(;)
          X_encoded [;, i] = label_encoder [-1].fit_transform(data[I, 1])
     X = X_encoded [:, :-1].astype(int)
     Y = X_encoded [:, -1].astype(int)
#Split data into training and testing datasets
X_train, X_test, y_train, y_test = train_test_split(
     X, y, test_size=0.25, random_state=5)
#Extremely Random Forests Regressor
Params = {'n_estimators': 100, 'max_depth': 4, 'random_state':0)
Regressor = ExtraTreesRegressor (**params)
Regressor.fit (X_train, y_train)
#Compute the regressor performance on test data
Y_pred = regressor.predict (X_test)
```

Print ("Mean absolute error:", round (mean_absolute_error (y_test, y_pred), 2))

#Testing encoding on single data instance

Test_datapoint = ['Friday', '6 PM CST', 'Chicago', 'no']

Test_datapoint_encoded = [-1] * len(test_datapoint)

#Predict the output for the test datapoint

Print ('Predicted Traffic:", int (regressor.predict ([test_datapoint_encoded]) [0]))

(Artasanchez & Joshi, 2020).

Building an Application That Can Predict E-Commerce Buying Patterns

As the COVID-19 pandemic is expected to go on for quite some time, many consumers are now opting to shop online straight from their wireless devices for the products and services that they need to procure, rather than visiting the traditional brick and mortar stores for these kinds of activities. Thus, it will become very important for E-Commerce merchants to have an application that can help to predict buying patterns on a real-time basis, and to even gauge what future buying patterns will look like, so that they can appropriately store the needed inventory levels.

Here is the Python source code to help create such an application:

```
#Load data from input file
Input_file = 'sales.csv"
File_reader = csv.reader (open(inout_file, 'r'), delimeters=', '
X = []
For count, row in enumerate (file_reader):
If not count:
    Names = row[1:]
    Continue
X.append ([float(x) for x in row [1:]])
#Convert to numpy array
X= np.array(X)
#Estimating the bandwidth of input data
Bandwidth = estimate_bandwidth (X, quantile=0.8, n_samples=len(x))
#Compute clustering with MeanShift
Meanshift_model = Meanshift (bandwidth=bandwidth, bin_seeding=True)
Meanshift_model.fit (X)
Labels = meanshift_model.labels_
Cluster_centers = meanshift_model.cluster_centers_
Num_clusters = len (np.unique(labels))
```

```
Print ("\nNumber of clusters in input data =" num_clusters)
Print ("\nCenters of clusters:"
Print ('\t.join([name[:3] for in names]))
For cluster_center in cluster_centers:
        Print('\t'.join([str(int(X)} for X in cluster_center]))
#Extract two features for visualization
Cluster_centers_2d = cluster_centers[:, 1:3]
#Plot the cluster centers
Plt.figure()
Plt.scatter (cluster_centers_2d{:, 0], cluster_centers_2d[:1,1],
        S=120, edgecolors='blue', facecolors='none']
Offset=0.25
Plt.xlim (cluster_centers_2d[:, 0].max() + offset * cluster_
Centers_2d[:, 0].ptp,
        Cluster_centers_2d[:,0], max() + offset *cluster
Centers_2d[:, 0].ptp(),
Plt.ylim (cluster_centers_2d[:, 1].max() + offset * cluster_
Centers_2d[:, 1].ptp(),
        Cluster_centers_2d[:,1], max() + offset *cluster_
Centers_2d[:, 1].ptp())
Plt.title ('Centersof 2D Clusters')
Plt.show()
```

(Artasanchez & Joshi, 2020).

Building an Application That Can Recommend Top Movie Picks

As it has been described throughout this book, the use of chatbots is probably one of the biggest applications of not just Artificial Intelligence, but of Neural Networks as well. The idea behind all of this is that the conversation with either the prospect or the customer should be a seamless one, in which he or she is feeling that they are engaging with a real human being. One of the basic thrusts of this is to also to try to predict in advance what the questions, concerns, or queries might be based upon previous conversations and interactions with the chatbot. In this application, we examine how to embed such a conversation when it comes to recommending movies for an individual. In a way, this is a primitive version of what Virtual Personal Assistants (VPAs) like Siri and Cortana can do as well.

Here is the Python source code:

```
Import argparse
Import json
```

```
Import numpy as np
From compute_scores import pearson_score
From collaborative_filtering import find_similar_users
Def build_arg_parser ():
    Parser = argparse.ArgumentParser (description='Find recommendations
For the given user')
    Parser.add_argument ('—user', dest='user', required=True,
        Help='Input user')
    Return parser
#Get movie recommendations for the input user
Def get_recommendations (dataset, input_user):
    If input_user no in dataset
        Raise TypeError ('Cannot find ' = input_user + ' in the
    Dataset')
    Overall_scores = {}
    Similarity_scores = {}
    For user in [x for x in dataset if x [= input_user]:
            Similarity_score = pearson_score (dataset, input_user, user)
            If similarity_score <=0:
                Continue
        Filtered_list = [x for x in dataset[user] if x not in \
            Dataset[input_user] or dataset [input_user] [x] ==0]
        For item in filtered_list:
            Overall_scores.update ({item: dataset[user] [item] *
        Similarity_score})
                Similarity_scores.update ({item: similarity_score})
        If len (overall_scores) == 0:
                Return ['No movie recommendations are possible'}
#Generate movie selection rankings by normalization
Movie_scores = np.array {[(score/similarity_scores(item), item]
    For item, score in overall_scores.items())]}
#Sort in decreasing order
Movie_scores = movie_scores [np.argsort (movie_scores [:, 0]) [::-1]]
#Extract the movie selection recommendations
Movie_recommendations = [movie for_, movie in movie_scores]
Return movie_recommendations
If___name___ = = ____main____':
    Args = build_arg_parser().parse_args()
    User = args.user
    Ratings_file = 'ratings.json'
    With open (ratings_file, 'r') as f:
        Data = json.loads (f.read())
    Print ("\nMovie recommendations for" + user +":")
```

```
Movies = get_recommendations (data,user)
For I, movie in enumerate (movies):
        Print (str(i+1) + '- ' + movie)
```

(Artasanchez & Joshi, 2020).

Building a Sentiment Analyzer Application

So far in this chapter, one of the subjects that has been discussed is what is called as "Sentiment Analysis." With this, the AI application is trying to gauge what the literal mood is of the end user when any communication is received in a written text format. Even when the message is spoken, given the sheer levels of sophistication of both the AWS and Azure, the Biometric modality of Voice Recognition can be used to gauge the particular mood of the individual as well. This kind of concept is typically deployed in real-time market research, especially when it comes to test marketing a brand new product or service before it is launched to the mass public. In this application, we make use of hypothetical movie review files illustrated in the last application.

Here is the Python source code:

```
From nltk.classify import NaiveBayesClassifier
From nltk.classify.util import accuracy as nltk_accuracy
#Extract features from the input list of words
Def extract_features (words):
        Return dict([word, True) for word in words])
If____name____=='____main____':
        #Load the data from the corpus
        Fields_pos = movie_reviews.fields ('pos')
        Fields_neg = movie_reviews.fields ('neg')
#Extract the features form the movie reviews
Features_pos = [(extract_features (movie_reviews.words(
        Fileside=[f])), 'Positive') for f in fields_pos]
Features_neg = [(extract_features (movie_reviews.words(
        Fileside=[f])), 'Negat') for f in fields_pos]
#Define the train and test split (80% and 20%)
Threshold = 0.8
Num_pos = int (threshold = len (features_pos))
Num_neg = int (threshold = len (features_neg))
#Create training and training datasets
Features_train = features_pos [:num_pos] + features_neg [:num_neg]
Features_test = features_pos [:num_pos] + features_neg [:num_neg]
#Print the number of datapoints that are used
```

```
Print ('\nNumber of training datapoints:', len (features_train))
Print ('Number of test datapoints: ', len (features_test))
#Train a Naïve Bayes classifier
    Classifier = NaiveBayesClassifier.train (features_train)
Print ('\nAccuracy of the classifier:', nltk_accuracy(
Classifer, features_test))
N=15
Print ('\nTop ' + str(N) + ' most informative words:')
For I, item in enumerate (classifier.most_informative_features()]:
    Print (str (i+1) + ', ' + item[0])
    If I == N -1
        Break
    #Test input movie reviews
    Input_reviews = [
            'Movie was great',
            'Movie was good',
            'Movie was OK',
            'Movie was bad',
            'Movie was horrible',
            'I would not recommend this movie',
            'I would recommend this movie',
            ]
    Print("\nMovie review predictions:")
    For review in input_reviews:
            Print("\nReview:", review)
    #Compute the statistical probabilities
    Probabilities = classifier.prob_classify (extract_
Features (review.split()))
#Pick the maximum value
Predicted_sentiment = probabilities.max ()
#Print outputs
Print ("Predicted sentiment:", predicted_sentiment)
Print ("Probability:", round (probabilities.prob (predicted_sentiment),))
```

(Artasanchez & Joshi, 2020).

Application of Neural Networks to Predictive Maintenance

Preventing equipment failures and accidents is critical for companies and governments. Unnecessary downtime can reduce revenues and increase costs significantly, negatively impacting profitability. In military and defense, not only is this expensive, but critical missions can be impacted or canceled. These can also result in significant human injury or death. Thus, significant value is attached to predicting and avoiding these failures and accidents. Predictive maintenance can be a key to avoiding such events.

Physics-based models have typically been used to identify when a complex machine or process is trending toward failure. Completely accurate physics modeling of all of the complex interactions between subsystems is not currently possible. Furthermore, as the assets age, undergo maintenance, and have parts replaced, the behavior of the system begins to drift from the original physics models. What is required are models that can learn how the system is changing over time. Machine Learning models using Neural Networks are capable of doing just that.

As has been emphasized before, Machine Learning models require lots of training data, and that is even more true for Neural Networks. Fortunately, modern machinery and processes have a large number of sensors measuring temperature, pressure, vibration, fluid flow, etc. which are collected and stored in data historians. So, more than enough data is generally available for training Neural Network models.

However, as described in the previous chapters, Machine Learning techniques use supervised learning which requires that the training data be labeled with the expected results. In this case, this means labeled examples of equipment or process failures. Labeled training data of this type could be generated by running a collection of these industrial assets to failure in all of the possible failure modes. Obviously, this is impractical given the complexity and expense of these industrial systems. Furthermore, these systems are inherently highly reliable, which further complicates collecting data of actual failures. Thus, what is available is a large quantity of historical data with a very limited subset of past failure modes. This limited amount of labeled training data usually makes supervised Machine Learning techniques ineffective.

Normal Behavior Model Using Autoencoders

One approach to tackling this problem is to create a model of normal behavior of the asset by training a model using only historical sensor data from all of the normal modes of operation of the asset. If an asset has never failed, this would include all of the past data. Any data from periods of abnormal or failure events will need to be excluded. A model that has learned the normal operation of an asset will be able to indicate when it is beginning to act abnormally which is often a sign of impending failure or suboptimal operation.

A Neural Network Autoencoder described on pages xx-yy is well suited to learn the normal behavior of an asset from historical sensor values from the asset. Remember that an autoencoder attempts to copy its Input to its Output through a constrained coding or latent layer that creates the desired encoding. The diagram of an autoencoder is repeated below. Since the autoencoder is learning X' from X, the training data is self-labeled. All that is required is to remove any abnormal data from the training set.

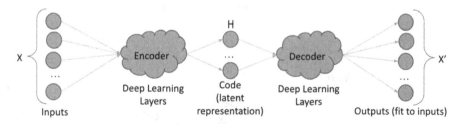

The relevant sensors for the asset are the inputs X. The Encoder learns how to compress the input data into normal operating states encoded in the latent space H. The Decoder also learns how to decode the latent space H to reconstruct the inputs as X'. The latent space, H, needs to be as small as possible, but still large enough to represent all the important normal operating states. Statistical analysis of the data (e.g. Principle Component Analysis or PCA) can determine an appropriate value for H. The model is then trained to minimize the differences between X and X' for all of the training data.

Once trained, live operational data can be fed to the model to predict a new X'. If the error between the predicted X' and X is small, the asset is most likely operating in a normal operating state that is close to one of the states in the training data. As this prediction error increases, the likelihood that the asset is operating in a state not seen during the training data increases since the model is having difficulty reconstructing the input data. The X' values with the largest prediction errors also provide important clues to human operators as indicators to what is abnormal about the current operating state which is critical for explainability and for identification of the actions that need to be taken to correct the abnormality.

Wind Turbine Example

Wind Turbines have become an important source of renewable energy and can be seen on the horizon in many places around the world. They also provide a relatively straightforward example for the application of Neural Network Autoencoders to predict pending failure events. When a Wind Turbine fails, it can take weeks to schedule the necessary crane and other equipment required to make the repairs. During that time, all the electricity (and revenue) that Wind Turbine could have produced is lost forever. Thus, predicting pending failure with sufficient warning is critical to maximizing the revenue from a farm of Wind Turbines.

A simple diagram of a Wind Turbine is shown below. They typically consist of three large rotor blades which are pointed into the prevailing wind. The rotors have airfoils similar to the wings on an airplane. The Bernoulli effect across the rotors pulls them around in a circle. This rotates a shaft within the Main Bearing. The Gear

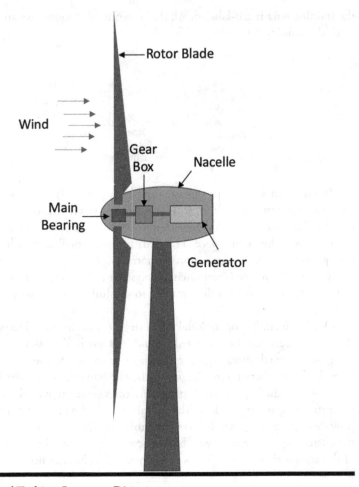

Figure 3.1 Wind Turbine Generator Diagram.

Box translates the slower rotation (RPM) of the rotors to the higher RPM required for efficient electricity generation in the generator. Each of these components within the Wind Turbine can be a source of failure and need to be modeled to predict pending failure. Modeling normal behavior for the main bearing will be used as an example.

For this example, the main bearing temperature sensor will be the primary sensor used to indicate a pending problem with the main bearing. Below are graphs of the air temperature and wind speed near Oakley, Kansas for 2019 from publicly available NOAA weather data and is not from an actual wind farm (though wind farms are plentiful in western Kansas). The air temperature plot shows the annual seasonality trend of winter in January, through summer, and then back to winter in

December. The daily temperature cycle from cooler in the morning to warmer in the afternoon is also visible in this plot.

The wind speed is variable, but not obviously seasonal. A simple spreadsheet simulation of a wind turbine shows that the rotation speed of the turbine (RPM) follows the wind speed except when the wind speed exceeds the upper bound of the rotational capability of the turbine. The RPM is normalized between 0 and 10 for these graphs. The main bearing temperature follows the air temperature but is generally higher due to frictional heating when the turbine is spinning.

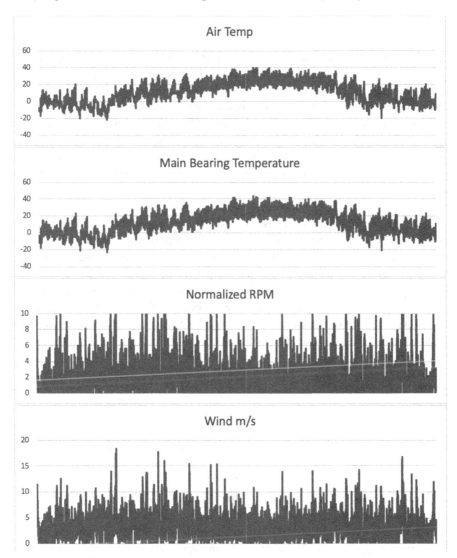

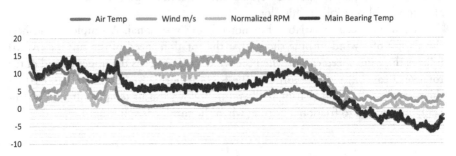

This graph plots all four inputs starting in late October 2019. The green and yellow lines show how the RPM tracks the wind speed until the maximum RPM capabilities of the Turbine is reached. The main bearing temperature in red tracks the air temperature but drifts higher when the RPM of the rotor increases the main bearing temperature due to frictional heating. When the high winds of a cold front come in, the main bearing temperature stays noticeably above the air temperature until after the front has passed and the wind speed returns to a more normal range. From there, the RPM decreases and the main bearing temperature again tracks the air temperature.

A Neural Network Autoencoder can be trained to learn all of these relationships simply from learning how to reconstruct these four inputs plus other relevant sensors on the wind turbine such as blade angles, nacelle temperature, vibration sensors, etc. Once the autoencoder has been trained, it can be used to predict these inputs using live data from the wind turbine. If the main bearing begins to suffer mechanical damage, which increases frictional heating, the model will continue to predict the blue line below, but the actual temperature will begin to deviate to the orange values, indicating the need for maintenance activity. Once repaired, the main bearing temperature returns to matching the predicted values.

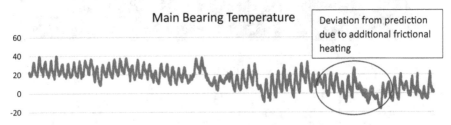

Autoencoders, by definition, have the same inputs X as outputs X'. However, for normal behavior models of physical assets, some modifications are often useful in industrial applications. For example, in this wind turbine case, accurately predicting the air temperature and wind speed are not relevant to detecting pending issues with the turbine as the operator has no control over the wind or temperature. These important, but exogenous inputs can be provided as a set of inputs Y to the encoder that are not included in the outputs X' that the decoder is attempting to reconstruct.

Likewise, time-delayed versions of some of the X inputs can be included in Y, allowing the model to learn time-dependencies in the data. For example, the change in RPM is not instantaneous with a change in wind speed due to the momentum of the large rotors. Likewise, the frictional temperature changes also lag behind the changes in RPM or changes in the air temperature and at different rates. Thus, the neural network encoder may have some subset of X_n, X_{n-1}, X_{n-2}, ... X_{n-m} as well as Y all being fed to the encoder and then used by the decoder to predict X'. This diagram illustrates this concept.

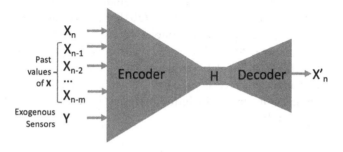

The Wind Turbine example is much simpler than most normal behavior models that would be created for predictive maintenance. A more typical asset would have tens of sensors in X'. In these cases, the signal of abnormal behavior may be contained in the reconstruction error of more than one sensor. Thus, some form of aggregate score using something like Mean Squared Error (MSE) or Hoteling score is used to create a single "abnormality" score. In all cases, the reconstruction error for each sensor is generally a good indicator to the operator of what action to take (e.g. the vibration or temperature is too high).

Given a reasonable set of normal training data, normal behavior models built from neural network autoencoders can be very good at detecting when an asset is behaving differently than it has in the past. However, these models cannot distinguish between abnormal behavior that requires maintenance and an asset that is now operating in a "new normal" state. The latter can happen after repair or maintenance in which new parts or lubrication have changed the relationships between the inputs. If the operator determines that the model is detecting a "new normal," the model will need to be retrained with samples of this new data before it can become effective again. Periodic retraining is also useful to address the inevitable drift as mechanical parts wear and age.

This Wind Turbine example has shown how a normal behavior model can be developed for an industrial asset using historical sensor data and a Neural Network

Autoencoder (or variants). This model can be used with live sensor data to identify when the asset is deviating from its past normal operation and provide important clues about which sensors are deviating from normal. This information can be used to diagnose and take action on an asset that is in a suboptimal state or trending toward failure before the failure occurs. These types of normal behavior models are an important part of a preventive maintenance system.

Resources

Artasanchez A, Joshi P: *Artificial Intelligence with Python,* 2nd Edition, United Kingdon: Packt Publication; 2020.

Forbes: What is Deep Learning AI? A Simple Guide with 8 Practical Examples; n.d. <www.forbes.com/sites/bernardmarr/2018/10/01/what-is-deep-learning-ai-a-simple-guide-with-8-practical-examples/#25cc15d08d4b>

Graupe D: *Principles of Artificial Neural Networks: Basic Designs to Deep Learning,* Singapore: World Scientific Publishing Company; 2019.

SAS: "Natural Language Processing (NLP): What It Is and Why It Matters;" n.d. <www.sas.com/en_us/insights/analytics/what-is-natural-language-processing-nlp.html>

Chapter 4

Typical Applications for Computer Vision

So far in this book, we have covered three main topics: Artificial Intelligence, Machine Learning, and Neural Networks. There is yet one more field in Artificial Intelligence that is gaining very serious traction—that is the field of Computer Vision. This field will be the focal point of this chapter. As the name implies, with Computer Vision, we are trying to replicate how human vision works, but at the level of the computer or machine. In a way, this is very analogous to Artificial Intelligence, in which the primary purpose is to replicate the thought, behavioral, and decision-making process of the human brain.

In this chapter, we will start by giving a high level overview of Computer Vision, and from there, we will do a much deeper dive into the theories and the applications that drive this emerging area of Artificial Intelligence. But before we start delving deeper into this subject, it is first very important to give a technical definition as to what Computer Vision is all about. Here it is:

> Computer vision (CV) is a subcategory of Computer Science & Artificial Intelligence. It is a set of methods and technologies that make it possible to automate a specific task from an image. In fact, a machine is capable of detecting, analyzing, and interpreting one or more elements of an image in order to make a decision and perform an action.
>
> **(Deepomatic, n.d.)**

Put in simpler terms, the field of Computer Vision from within the constructs of Artificial Intelligence examines certain kinds of images that are fed into the system, and from there, based upon the types of mathematical and statistical algorithms that are being used, the output is generated from the decision-making process that takes place. In this regard, there are two very broad types of Image Recognition, and they are as follows:

1) <u>Object Detection</u>:
   In terms of mathematics, this is technically known as "Polygon Segmentation." In this regard, the ANN system is specifically looking for the element from within a certain image by isolating it into a particular box. This is deemed to be far more superior and sophisticated rather than using the pixelated approach, which is still used most widely.

2) <u>Image Classification</u>:
   This is the process that determines into which category an image belongs based specifically upon its composition, which is primarily used to identify the main subject in the image.

Typical Applications for Computer Vision

Although Computer Vision is still in its infancy, when used with an ANN system, as mentioned, it is being used in a wide variety of applications, some which are as follows:

■ Optical Character Recognition: This is the analysis of, for example, various pieces of handwriting, and even automatic plate recognition (aka ANPR);

■ Machine Inspection: This is primarily used for Quality Assurance Testing Purposes, in which specialized lights can be shone onto different kinds of manufacturing processes, such as that of producing separate parts for an aircraft and even looking into them for any defects that are otherwise difficult to detect with the human eye. In these particular cases, X-Ray vision (which would actually be a subcomponent of the ANN system) can also be used;

■ 3-D Model Building: This is also known as "Photogrammetry," and it is the process in which 3-Dimensional Models from aerial survey photographs, or even those images captured by satellites, can be automatically recreated by the ANN system;

■ Medical Imaging: Computer Vision in this regard can be used to create preoperative as well as postoperative images of the patient just before and after surgery, respectively;

■ Match Move: This process makes use of what is known as "Computer Generated Imager" (aka "CGI"), in which various feature points can be tracked down in a source-based video. This can also be used to further estimate the level of the 3-Dimensional Camera motion, as well as the other shapes that can be ascertained from the source video;

■ Motion Capture: The concepts here are used primarily for Computer Animation, in which various Retro-Reflective Markers can be captured;

- Surveillance: This is probably one of the most widely used aspects of Computer Vision. In this regard, it can be used in conjunction with CCTV technology as well as Facial Recognition technology in order to provide the proof positive for any apprehended suspect.

It is important to note at this point that Computer Vision can also be used very well for still types of photographs and images, as opposed to the dynamic ones just previously described. Thus, in this regard, some typical applications include the following:

- Stitching: This technique can be used to convert overlapping types of images into one "stitched panorama" that looks virtually seamless;
- Exposure Bracketing: This can take multiple exposures from a sophisticated camera under very difficult lighting conditions by merging all of them together;
- Morphing: Using the mathematics of "Morphing," you can turn one picture into another of the same type;
- Video Match Move/Stabilization: With this particular process, one can take 2-Dimensional and 3-Dimensional images and literally insert them into videos to automatically locate the nearest mathematical-based reference points;
- Photo-based Analysis: With this specific technique, you can circumnavigate a series of very different pictures, to determine where the main features are located;
- Visual Authentication: This can also be used as a form of authentication, very much in the same way that a password or your fingerprint can 100 percent confirm identity, for example, when you gain access to shared resources.

A Historical Review into Computer Vision

When compared to Artificial Intelligence, Machine Learning, and the Neural Networks, Computer Vision has not been around nearly as long, just because the advancements made in it have taken longer than the others. But it, too, has had a rather rich history, and in this section, we will review some of the major highlights of it.

- The 1970s:
  This is deemed to be the very first starting point for Computer Vision. The main thought here was that Machine Learning would merely mimic the visual component and aspect of the human brain. But, it was not realized back then just how complicated this process would actually be. So instead, the primary focus was on building Computer Vision (CV) systems as part of the

overall ANN system that could analyze just about any kind of visual input, and use that to help produce the desired outputs. In fact, the first known major efforts in CV took place when a well-known MIT researcher known as Marvin Minsky asked one of his research associates to merely link up a camera to a computer and get that to deliver outputs as to what it literally saw. At this time, a strong distinction was made between CV and the field of Digital Image Processing. In this regard, various 3-Dimensional images were extrapolated from the 2-Dimensional images themselves. Other key breakthroughs that occurred in this time period also include the following:

*The development Line Labeling Algorithms;

*The development of Edge Detection formulas to be used in static images;

*The implementation of 3-Dimensional modeling of non-Polyhedral Objects, making use of Generalized Cylinders;

*The creation of Elastic Patterns to create automated Pictorial Structures;

*The first qualitative approaches to Computer Vision started with the use of Intrinsic Images;

*More quantitative approaches to Computer Vision were created such as Stereo Correspondence Algorithms and Intensity-based Optical Flow Algorithms.

*Three key theories of Computer Vision were also formulated, which are:

The Computational Theory:

This questions the purpose of what a specific Computer Vision task is, and from there, ascertains what the mathematical permutations would be to get to the desired outputs from the ANN system.

The Image Representation and the Corresponding Algorithms Theory:

This theory aims to answer the fundamental questions as to how the input, output, and the intermediate datasets are used to calculate the desired outputs.

The Hardware Implementation Theory:

This particular theory tries to determine how the hardware of the Computer Vision system can be associated with the hardware of the ANN system in order to compute the desired outputs. The reverse of this is also true, in that it tries to determine how the hardware can be associated with the CV algorithms in the most efficient manner.

■ The 1980s:

In this specific time frame, much more work was being done on refining and advancing the mathematical aspects of Computer Vision, whose groundwork was already established in the 1970s. The key developments in this era include the following:

*The development of Image Pyramids for use in what is known as "Image Blending";

*The development of Space Scale Processing, in which created pyramids can be displaced into CV applications other than those they were originally intended for;

*The creation of the stereo-based Quantitative Shape Cue to be used in many types of X-Ray applications;

*The refinement of both Edge and Contour Detection-based mathematical algorithms (this also led to the creation of "Contour Trackers");

*The development of various types of 3-Dimensional-based Physical Models;

*The development of the discrete Markov Random Field Model, in which stereo, flow, and edge detection mathematical algorithms could be unified and optimized as one cohesive set to be used by the ANN system;

*Other, further refinements were also made to the Markov Random Field Model, which include the following:

*The mapping of the "Kalman Vision Filter";

*The automated mapping of the Markov Random Field Model so that it can be used as a precursor to parallel processing to take place from within ANN systems;

*The development of 3-Dimensional Range Data Processing techniques, to be used for the acquisition, merging, mathematical modeling, and recognition of various images to be inputted into the ANN system.

■ The 1990s:

This time era in Computer Vision also witnessed the following key developments:

*The development of what are known as "Projective Reconstruction" algorithms which have been primarily used for exacting the calibrations of the camera for it to take the necessary images to be used by the ANN system;

*The creation and implementation of "Factorization Techniques" in order to accurately calculate the needed approximations for Orthographic based cameras;

*The development of the "Bundle Adjustment Techniques" to be used in just about all types of Photogrammetry techniques;

*The development of using color and intensity in specific images, which made use of what is known as "Radiance Transport" and "Color Image Formation" that could be directly applied to a new subset of Computer Vision at that time known as "Physics based Vision";

*The continued refinement of a majority of the Optical Flow Methods that are used by the Computer Vision component that come from within the ANN system;

*The refinement of the Dense Stereo Correspondence Algorithms;

*Much more active and dynamic research started to take place in the implementation of Multi-View Stereo Algorithms that could be applied to replicate and easily produce 3-Dimensional pictures;

*The development of mathematical algorithms that could be used to record and produce various 3-Dimensional Volumetric Descriptions from upon various Binary-type silhouettes;

*Techniques were also established for the development of the construction of what are known as "Smooth Occluding Contours";

*Image Tracking algorithms were greatly improved upon in which various Contour Tracking algorithms such as "Snakes," "Particle Filters," and "Level Sets" were primarily established;

*Much more active research also started to precipitate a subset field of Computer Vision known as "Image Segmentation." Such techniques that were developed in this area included Minimum Energy, the Minimum Description Length, Normalized Cuts, and Mean Shifts that could be applied to image analysis from within the ANN system;

*This specific time period also saw the birth of the first statistical-based algorithms that were used in Computer Vision. These were first applied to such ANN system applications such as Principle Component Analysis (aka "PCA"), which relies upon the heavy usage of Eigenfaces, and the development of the Linear-Based Dynamical Systems, which were used in Curve Tracking;

*Probably the most lasting development in Computer Vision that occurred during this time period was the increased interaction with Computer Graphics, which could also be used in the subfields of Image-based Modeling and even Rendering;

*Various kinds of Image Morphing algorithms were also created, in order to create computer animation from both static and dynamic images. These specific algorithms could also be applied to Image Photo Stitching, and Full Light Field Rendering;

*Other kinds of both mathematical and statistical algorithms were developed so that 3-Dimensional Image Models could be automatically created from a series of static images.

■ The 2000s and Beyond:

This specific time period witnessed probably the biggest interactions between Computer Vision and Computer Graphics. Here is what has transpired thus far:

*The subfields of Computer Vision, which include Image Stitching, Light Field Capturing, and Rendering, as well as High Dynamic Range (aka HDR) techniques were combined into one specific field of Computer Vision, which became known as "Computational Photography." From its emergence, various kinds of "Tone Mapping" algorithms were developed;

*Various other kinds of both statistical- and mathematical-based algorithms were also created so that Flash-based Images could be easily combined with Non-Flash-based Images, as well as to segregate overlapping segments in both static and dynamic images into their own unique entities;

*The techniques of Texture Synthesis and Inpainting were developed in order to create new images from sample images;

*Numerous principles, which became known as "Feature-based Techniques" also evolved, which can used for Object Recognition by the ANN system. This included the development of the Constellation Model and the Pictorial Structures Techniques, as well as Interest Point-based Techniques, which make use of contours and region segmentation in both static and dynamic images;

*The "Looping Belief Propagation" theory was also established in which both static and dynamic images can be embedded and further analyzed onto a Cartesian Geometric Plane and other complex graphing planes;

*Finally, this time period has also witnessed the combination of the techniques of Machine Learning into Computer Vision that can be used by the ANN system in order to derive the generated outputs.

So far in this chapter, we have provided a technical definition for Computer Vision and some of the various applications it serves, as well as given a historical background as to how it became the field it is today, and explored its sheer dominance in the field of Artificial Intelligence. The remainder of this chapter is now devoted to doing a deeper dive into the theoretical constructs of Computer Vision.

The Creation of Static and Dynamic Images in Computer Vision (Image Creation)

Now that we have covered to a great degree what Computer Vision is, there are a lot of theoretical constructs, processes, and procedures that go along with it. The first place to start with in this regard is Image Creation, whether it be static or dynamic in nature. The following subsections will delve into this in much more detail.

The Geometric Constructs — 2-Dimensional Facets

Any kind of image, once again whether it be static or dynamic, is pretty much created using the principles of Geometry. The concepts here are used heavily in order to create robust 3-Dimensional images. The building blocks for these are the simple lines, points, and planes. But keep in mind that these can become very complex in nature as well, depending upon how rich the 3-Dimensional image actually is.

We first start with what are known as 2-Dimensional Points. This can be mathematically represented as follows:

$$X = (x,y) \ E \ R^{\wedge}2.$$

If these 2-Dimensional Points make use of what are known as "Heterogenous Coordinates," these can then be implemented back into their geometric plane, which is technically known as a "2-Dimensional Projective Space." Various kinds of Homogenous Vectors are thus used, and they be mathematically represented as follows:

$$X = (\underline{X}, \underline{Y}, \underline{W}) = \underline{W}(X, y, 1) = W\underline{X}i$$

Where:

$\underline{W}(X, y, 1)$ = The Augmented Vector.

With the 2-Dimensional Points, come along the 2-Dimensional Lines. A single line in this regard can be mathematically represented as follows:

$$\underline{X} * \underline{I} = ax + by + c = 0.$$

The intersection of two 2-Dimensional Lines is represented mathematically as follows:

$$\underline{X} = \underline{I}1 \; X \; \underline{I}2.$$

Now, if these two 2-Dimensional Lines can be joined together, it is represented mathematically also as follows:

$$\underline{I} = \; = \underline{X}1 \; X \; \underline{X}2.$$

Now that we have 2-Dimensional Lines and 2-Dimensional Points, the next thing that can be created in an image that is static or dynamic are what are known as "Conics," or simply, Cones. These make use of Polynomial Homogenous equations, and this can be represented by using a semi-quadratic formula which is as follows:

$$\underline{X}^{\wedge}T \; X \; Q\underline{x} = 0.$$

In fact, Quadratic equations play a huge role in the calibration of the camera from which the image is captured.

The Geometric Constructs — 3-Dimensional Facets

Now we move on to cover the important 3-Dimensional features for images that are either static or dynamic. For example, a 3-Dimensional Point is mathematically represented as follows:

$$X = (\underline{X}, \underline{Y}, \underline{Z}, \underline{W}) \; E \; P^{\wedge}3.$$

From the 3-Dimensional Points come the 3-Dimensional Planes. The mathematical equation that is used to further represent this is as follows:

$$\underline{X} * \underline{M} = ax + by + cz + d = 0.$$

The various angles in this kind of geometric plane can be seen as follows:

$$N = (COS\ 0,\ COS\ 0/,\ SIN\ 0/\ COS0/,\ SIN\ 0/).$$

It should be further noted that in these geometric planes, spherical coordinates are used, but the usage of polar coordinates is much more commonplace for today's Computer Vision applications in the ANN system.

Probably the most basic building block in the creation of the 3-Dimensional angles is that of the 3-Dimensional line. At its most primitive level, two linear points on one single line can be mathematically represented as follows:

$$(p,\ q).$$

In terms of linear-based mathematics, the combination of these two points can be seen as follows:

$$R = (1 - Y)p + Yq.$$

If homogenous coordinates are used, the 3-Dimensional Line can then be represented mathematically as follows:

$$\underline{R} = u\underline{p} + Y\underline{q}.$$

It should be noted at this point that a primary disadvantage of 3-Dimensional Lines is that there are way too many statistical degrees of freedom at the endpoints of this kind of line. In this typical instance, there are three degrees of freedom for the two endpoints of one single 3-Dimensional Line. In order to mitigate this shortcoming, with the end result being that a 3-Dimensional Line can be angled at virtually any orientation, the concepts of the "Plucker Coordinates Theorem" is used. This is represented mathematically as follows:

$$L = \underline{p}q^{\wedge}T - \underline{q}p^{\wedge}T$$

Where:

$\underline{P},\ \underline{Q}$ = Any two linear points that lie along a 3-Dimensional Line.

Just as in the case of the 2-Dimensional Cones, 3-Dimensional Cones can be created, also making use of the semi-quadratic equation. This is mathematically represented as follows:

$$\underline{X}^{\wedge}TQ\underline{x} = 0.$$

The Geometric Constructs — 2-Dimensional Transformations

It is important to keep in mind that any lines, points, or cones (it does not matter if they are 2-Dimensional or 3-Dimensional) can be manipulated in such a way that the particular image they form can be transformed into a related image. The mathematical constructs to do this are known as "Transformations." From the standpoint of two 2-Dimensional transformations, this can be mathematically represented as follows:

$$X' = x + t$$

Where:
   I = a 2 X 2 Identity based Matrix.

This particular kind of matrix is also mathematically represented as follows:

$$X' [1\ t] * [0^{\wedge}T\ 1] * X.$$

Once the above has been completely established, the transformation can be rotated in varying degrees as is required by the ANN system. This is technically known as "2-Dimensional Rigid Body Motion," or is also known as "2-Dimensional Euclidean Transformations." There are two separate and distinct mathematical ways in which this can be represented, and these are as follows:

$$\text{Representation \#1: } X' = [R\ t] * \underline{x}$$

$$\text{Representation \#2: } X' = Rx + t$$

Where:
   R = [COS 0/, SIN 0/] * [-SIN 0/, COS 0/].

It is important to note that both of the above representation cases make use of what are known as "Orthonormal Rotation Matrices."

   But, this is not the only transformations that exist for 2-Dimensional images that are either static or dynamic. There are others as well, and they are as follows:

■ The Scaled Rotation:
This is also known technically as a "Similarity Transformation," and this can mathematically represented as follows:

$$X' = [sR\ t] * \underline{x} = [a, b] * [-b, a] * [Tx, Ty] * \underline{X}1.$$

■ The Affine Transformation:
This is mathematically represented as follows:

$$X' = [a00, a10] * [a01, a1I] * [a02, a12]] * \underline{X.}$$

■ The Projective Transformation:
This kind of 2-Dimensional transformation makes use of Homogenous Coordinates (as previously reviewed earlier in this chapter), and this is mathematically represented as follows:

$$X' = [h00 + h01y + h02] * [h20x + h21y + h22]$$
$$Y' = [h10x + h11y + h12] * [h20x + h21y + h22].$$

It is also important to make note that the 2-Dimensional Lines in this kind of transformation can also be transformed one by one, and not as one, cohesive unit. This can be accomplished with the following mathematical formula:

$$\underline{L} * \underline{x} = \underline{l}^\wedge T * H\underline{x} = (\underline{H}^\wedge Ti)^\wedge T\underline{x} = \underline{l} * \underline{x} = 0.$$

■ The Stretch and Squash Transformation:
This kind of transformation can literally change the mathematical ratio of the image. This can be represented as follows:

$$X' = SxX + tX$$
$$Y' = syY + Ty1.$$

■ The Planar Surface Flow Transformation:
This type of transformation technique is used in particular instances where the image, whether it is static or dynamic, goes through a series of specific rotations, but only at small, incremental levels so that these changes can be captured by the ANN system. This technique can be accomplished with the following two mathematical equations:

$$X' = a0 + a1x + a2y + a6x^\wedge 2 + a7xy$$
$$Y' = a3 + a4x + a5y + a7x^\wedge 2 + a6xy.$$

■ The Bilinear Interpolant Transformation:
This particular kind of technique can be used to correct any deformities in the image, whether it is static or dynamic, if it is more or less a square image. The following mathematical equations can be used to accomplish this particular task:

$$X' = a0 + a1x + a2y + a6xy$$
$$Y' = a3 + a4x + a5y + a7xy.$$

The Geometric Constructs — 3-Dimensional Transformations

The total number of transformation techniques that are available for 3-Dimensional images that are static and/or dynamic are not as numerous as for 2-Dimensional images. But they are still quite important in their use specific uses and functionalities, and they are as follows:

■ The Basic Transformation Technique:
The mathematical equation that is used for this instance is represented as follows:

$$X' = [I \ t] * x$$

Where:
I = A 3 X 3 mathematical-based Identity Matrix.

■ The Rotation and Translation Transformation:

This is a special kind of transformation technique that is exclusive for those 3-Dimensional images that are either static or dynamic in nature. It is also referred to technically as the "3-Dimensional Rigid Body Motion," and the following mathematical formula can be used to accomplish this particular kind of task:

$$X' = R(x- c) = Rx - Rc.$$

■ The Scaled Rotation Transformation:
This kind of technique can be represented as following, mathematically:

$$X' = [sR \ t] * \underline{x.}$$

■ The Affine Transformation:
This technique is used where either a static or dynamic image assumes a three-by-four mathematical matrix. It is represented as follows:

X' [a00, a10, a20] * [a01, a11, a21] * [a02, a12, a22] * [a03, a13, a23] * x.

■ The Projective Transformation:
This technique also makes use of Homogenous Coordinates, and in more technical terms, it is also known as the "3-Dimensional Perspective Transformation." It is mathematically represented as follows:

$$\underline{X} = \underline{Hx.}$$

The Geometric Constructs — 3-Dimensional Rotations

Unlike 2-Dimensional images, 3-Dimensional images (whether static or dynamic) can be rotated to varying amounts in various directions. These rotations can be as small as just a few degrees, or much larger than that, at the other extreme. There are a number of mathematical techniques that can be used to accomplish this kind of task for the ANN system to process, and they are as follows:

■ The Euler Angles:
This is where a specific degree of rotation is accomplished when the mathematical product of three independent movements takes place around the axis points of the image, whether it is static or dynamic. But this technique is not used very much these days because there is no established set of permutations to follow in which to rotate the 3-Dimensional image in question.

■ The Exponential Twist Technique:
This technique is used when a 3-Dimensional image (whether it is static or dynamic) is rotated around in various degrees by a 3-Dimensional mathematical vector. This kind of rotation is computed by the following mathematical formula:

$$V|| = n^{\wedge}(n * v) = (n^{\wedge}n^{\wedge}) * v.$$

In order to make 3-Dimensional image rotations optimized as much as possible, various kinds of mathematical vectors are used. One such popular vector technique is represented as follows:

$$U = uT + v|| = (I + SIN\ 0/[n^{\wedge}]x + (1 - COS0)[n^{\wedge}]\ 2/x) * v.$$

■ The Unit Quaternions Technique:
This specific technique makes use of a four-vector mathematical matrix. This can be mathematically represented as follows:

$$Q = (qx, qy, qz, qw).$$

It is important to note at this point that this technique assumes that the rotational nature of a 3-Dimensional image is always continuous in nature, and will not be stopped by the ANN system until the specific permutations have been inputted into it. This technique is widely used for the kinds of applications that make use of poses. It is important to note that the "Quaternion" can be computed by the following mathematical formula:

$$Q = (v, w) = (SIN0/2 \text{ } n^{\wedge}, COS0/2).$$

The opposite of a Quaternion is known as the "Antipodal" Quaternion, and it is computed by the following mathematical formula:

$$Q2 = q0/q1 = q0q1^{\wedge}\text{-}1 = (v0 \text{ X } v1 + w0v1 - w1v0 - w0w1 - v0 * v1).$$

Incremental rotations in this regard are also technically known as "Spherical Linear Interpolation," and they are computed by the following two mathematical formulas:

$$Q2 = q^{\wedge}ar * q0$$

$$Q2 = [SIN(1 - A)^{\wedge}0/SIN0] * q0 + [SINA0/SIN0] * q1.$$

Ascertaining Which 3-Dimensional Technique Is the Most Optimized to Use for the ANN System

When it comes to specific rotations of the 3-Dimensional image, which of the techniques to be used (as reviewed in the last subsection) is primarily dependent upon the application in question and what the desired outputs from the ANN system are. It should be further noted that the mathematical representation of any sort of angles or axes in the 3-Dimensional image (whether it is static or dynamic) does not require any extra processing power or overhead on the part of the ANN system.

In order to determine any sort of technique as the most effective, it is very important to express it as a condition of geometric degrees. This can also be expressed as a function of what are known as "Radians." In this regard, the ANN system can also make use of Quaternions (also examined earlier in this chapter). But, this technique, from the standpoint of optimization, should only be used when the camera that is taking the snapshots of the image is actually in motion, whether it is linear or curvilinear in nature.

How to Implement 3-Dimensional Images onto a Geometric Plane

Now that we have established a very firm foundation of the principles that go along with either 2-Dimensional or 3-Dimensional images (whether they are static or dynamic), the next step in this process is determining how to project the 3-Dimensional image so that the ANN system can actually process it. In terms of mathematics, this task can be specifically accomplished by making use of either a 3-Dimensional or 2-Dimensional projection matrix. In this particular instance, probably the most efficient and simplest mathematical matrix to use is that of the "Orthographic Matrix."

This can be mathematically represented as follows:

$$X= [I2x2|0] * p.$$

However, if Homogenous Coordinates are being used in this instance, then the above algorithm can be stated as follows:

$$\underline{X} = [1, 0, 0] * [0, 1, 0] * [0, 0, 0] * [0, 0, 1] * \underline{P}1.$$

This kind of mathematical matrix can be applied specifically to cameras that make use of lenses that are "Telecentric" in nature, for example, if this lens makes use of a very long focal point and the reference point of the image to be captured is shallow relative to the overall foreground of it. Scaling is a very important concept here, and thus, "Scaled Orthography" is widely utilized in this regard. It can be mathematically represented as follows:

$$X = [sI2x2|0] * P.$$

This kind of scaling can be typically used in various image frames, in a rapid, successive fashion. This is also referred to as "Structure In Motion." It should also be noted that this technique is widely used to recreate a 3-Dimensional image that has been captured from a very far distance. The variable of "Pose" is very important here, and statistically, it can be represented onto the geometric plane as the Sum of Least Squares. The mathematical properties of "Factorization" can also be used as a substitute.

Another technique that is used to deploy a 3-Dimensional image (whether it is static or dynamic) onto the geometric plane is known as the "Para Perspective" concept. In this regard, all reference points in the 3-Dimensional image are first projected onto a subset of the actual geometric plane that will be used. But once this particular subset is ready, it will not be projected onto the geometric plane in an orthogonal fashion, rather, it will be in a parallel fashion. In terms of mathematics, this parallel projection onto the geometric plane can be represented as follows:

$$X = [a00, a10, 0] * [a01, a11, 00 * [a02, a12, 0] * [a03, a13, 1] * P.$$

The 3-Dimensional Perspective Technique

As the title of this subsection implies, the 3-Dimensional image in question is projected onto the geometric plane by actually dividing up the reference points that are in the 3-Dimensional image itself. This makes heavy usage of homogenous coordinates, and this is mathematically represented as follows:

$$X = Pz (P) = [X/Z] * [Y/Z] * [1].$$

The representation of the homogenous coordinates is given by the following mathematical matrix:

$$\underline{X} = [1, 0, 0] * [0, 1, 0] * [0, 0, 1] * [0, 0, 0] * \underline{P}1.$$

A subset of this technique actually makes use of a two-phased approach:

1) The coordinates from the 3-Dimensional image are converted over into what is known as "Normalized Device Coordinates," which are mathematically represented as follows:

$$(x, y, z) \, E \, [-1, -1] \, X \, [-1, 1] \, X \, [0, 1].$$

2) These coordinates are then re-scaled and even re-projected into the geometric plane by making use of another technique called "Viewport Transformation." This is represented as follows:

$$\underline{X} = [1, 0, 0, 0] * [0, 1, 0, 0] * [0,0, -zFAR/zRANGE, 1] * \\ [0, 0, zNEARzFAR/zRANGE, 0] * Pr$$

Where:
zNEAR and zFAR = the Z Clipping Planes.

2-Dimensional images can also be projected onto a geometric plane, but are not done nearly as commonly for the 3-Dimensional images, just because of the sheer lack of mathematical algorithms. But if the application requires a 2-Dimensional image, the technique of "Range Sensors" is used, in which a four-by-four mathematical matrix is used.

The Mechanics of the Camera

Once the above steps have been accomplished, the reference points in the 3-Dimensional image in question (whether it is static or dynamic), still must be pixelated into the geometric plane relative to its point of origin (if quadrants are used, this would be represented as [0,0]). In order to complete this specific task, the following mathematical algorithm is most typically used:

P = [Rs|Cs] * [Sx, 0, 0, 0] * [0, Sy, 0, 0,] * [0, 0, 0, 1] * [Xs, Ys, 1] = Ms$\underline{X}$s.

Now, the specific relationship of the reference points from the 3-Dimensional image and its projection onto the geometric plane can be defined mathematically as follows:

$$Xs = aM^{-1}s * Pc = KPc.$$

The result of this projection becomes a three-by-three mathematical matrix, which is denoted as "K." This is also called the "Calibration Matrix," and it provides an overview into the mechanics of the camera that is taking the snapshot of the 3-Dimensional image in relation to its vector orientation on the geometric plane. The latter is known as the "Extrinsics" of the camera.

Once the 3-Dimensional image has been embedded into the geometric plane by using the concepts of Pixelation, the camera then needs to be calibrated so that a seamless picture of the image can be taken so it can be processed quickly and efficiently by the ANN system to obtain the desired outputs. This specific calibration can be accomplished with the following mathematical algorithm:

$$Xs = K [R|t] * Pw = Pps^t$$

Where:
  Pw = the 3-Dimensional "World Coordinates";
  K [R|t] = the mathematical matrix that is used by the camera in question.

Determining the Focal Length of the Camera

One of the biggest hurdles that still has yet to be overcome in the field of Computer Vision is determining and ascertaining how the focal lengths from the camera to the 3-Dimensional image need to be represented. The primary reason for this lack of understanding is the fact that the focal length is extremely dependent upon the specific units that are used to actually gauge the measurement of the pixels. One method to overcoming this dilemma is to determine the mathematical relationship between the Focal Length (denoted as "f") of the camera and the numerical width of the sensor (denoted as "W") that has been implanted into the camera with its overall field of photographic capture (which is denoted as "0/").

This is mathematically represented as follows, in two different formats:

Format 1: TAN 0/2 = W/2f;

Format 2: f = W/2 [tan)/2] ^ -1.

If a common camera is used to capture a snapshot of the 3-Dimensional image, then the standard metric unit of millimeters is often the best choice to be used from the standpoint of optimization purposes. Another common metric that can be substituted for this millimeters are pixels. Yet another solution to the above-stated dilemma is to express the pixel coordinates as a set of mathematical ranges, which can go anywhere from -1 all the way to 1. This is also known as "Scaling Up."

But if a longer range has to be used, this can be mathematically represented as follows:

$$[-a^{-1}, a^{-1}].$$

This is also known as the "Image Aspect Ratio Formula," and this can be mathematically represented as follows:

$$X's = (2Xs - W)/S;$$

$$Y's = (2Ys - H)/S$$

Where:
$$S = max(W, H).$$

The "Scaling Up" technique has a number of key advantages to it, which are as follows:

- The Focal Length (denoted as "f") and the Optical Center (denoted as "Cx, Cy") actually become independent of one another. Because of this, images such as cones and pyramids can be easily captured by the camera, and because of that, they can be further manipulated so that it can be processed quickly by the ANN system to get to the desired outputs;
- The focal length can also be used in a landscape or portrait setting quickly and efficiently;
- Converting between the different focal measurement units can be done quickly.

Determining the Mathematical Matrix of the Camera

For today's Computer Vision applications, many types of mathematical matrices can be used, but the most common that is used by the ANN system is that of the "3 X 4 Camera Matrix," and this is represented as follows, in terms of mathematics:

$$P = K [R|t].$$

Also, a mathematical four-by-four matrix can be used as well, and this can be mathematically represented as follows:

$$P = [K, 0^{\wedge}T; 0\ 1] * [R, 0^{\wedge}T; t, 1] = \underline{K}e1$$

Where:

E = the 3 Dimensional Euclidean Geometric transformation;
$\underline{K}$ = the "Calibration Matrix."

If this mathematical four-by-four matrix is actually used, it can automatically map, in a direct fashion, the 3-Dimensional "World Coordinates" (which is denoted as Pw = [Xw, Yw, Zw, 1]) to the "Real World" Coordinates (which is denoted as Xs = [Xs, Ys, 1, d]).

Determining the Projective Depth of the Camera

In this particular instance, if a four-by-four mathematical matrix is being used, the last row (and even column) of it can be automatically re-mapped in order to fit what is known as the "Projective Depth" of the camera in question. The last row and column of the four-by-four mathematical matrix can transformed in this regard by using the following mathematical formula:

$$D = S3/z\ (n0 * Pw + c0)$$

Where:

Z = the numerical distance from the center of the camera (denoted as "C") in conjunction to its Optical Axis (denoted as "Z");
Pw = the Reference Plane.

It should also be noted at this point that the term "Projective Depth" can also be referred to as the "Paralax" or even the "Plane Plus the Paralax."

The inverse of the above-mentioned mapping can also happen if need be, and this can be mathematically represented as follows:

$$\underline{Pw} = \underline{P}^{\wedge}\text{-}1 * Xs.$$

This above-mentioned inverse technique is not used very often for applications in the ANN system. The primary reason for this is that more than one geometric plane has to be used in this regard, thus consuming more processing power from within the ANN system.

How a 3-Dimensional Image Can Be Transformed between Two or More Cameras

One of the key questions that has been addressed in the field of Computer Vision is whether a 3-Dimensional image taken from a certain position in one camera can be transposed over to yet another camera (or maybe even more than two of them) without losing the full integrity of the 3-Dimensional image (it is does not matter if it is static or dynamic). This has been more or less addressed by using, once again, a four-by-four mathematical matrix, which in this particular case is denoted as "$\underline{P} = \underline{K}\,E$."

The transposition to this can be done from one camera to the next quite easily by making use of this mathematical algorithm:

$$\underline{X}0 = \underline{k}0E0p = \underline{P}0p.$$

Also, if multiple 3-Dimensional images have to be transposed to two or more cameras in a parallel fashion, then the following mathematical algorithm must be used:

$$\underline{X}1 = \underline{k}1E1p = \underline{K}1E1E0^{\wedge}\text{-}1K0^{\wedge}\text{-}1\underline{x}0 = \underline{P}1\underline{P}0^{\wedge}\text{-}1\underline{x}0 = M10\underline{x}0.$$

In many cases, the variable of "Perception Depth" does not need to be ascertained by the ANN system in order to produce the desired results. Thus, yet another method in which 3-Dimensional images can be moved from one camera to another is by making use of the following mathematical algorithm:

$$\underline{X}1 = K1R1R0^{\wedge}\text{-}1K0^{\wedge}\text{-}1\underline{x}0 = K1R10K0^{\wedge}\text{-}1\underline{x}0.$$

In this particular instance, a 3-Dimensional image can easily be transposed between two or more cameras by making use of a three-by-three mathematical matrix that is "Homographic." But in order to accomplish this specific task, the following variables have to ascertained:

- The known "Aspect Ratios";
- The Centers of Projection;
- The Rotation Degree or Level;
- The Parameterization properties of the mathematical three-by-three matrix.

How a 3-Dimensional Image Can Be Projected into an Object-Centered Format

It may be the case many times that the camera that is being used to capture the 3-Dimensional image could very well be using a lens that has a very long focal length.

While this certainly can be advantageous for the ANN system, in terms of statistics, it can become quite cumbersome to properly estimate what this specific focal length should be. The primary reason for this is that the focal length of the camera in question and the actual, numerical distance of the image that is being captured are extremely correlated amongst one another, and as a result, it can become quite difficult to ferret the two out of each other.

But, this can be worked out to a certain degree with use of mathematical algorithms, and the two which have been proven to be useful in scientific research are as follows:

$$Xs = f [Rx * p + Tz]/[Rz * p +Tz] + Cz;$$

$$Ys = f [Ry * p + Ty]/[Rz * p +Tz] + Cy1.$$

The above two algorithms can also be further optimized so that it is formulated as follows:

$$Xs = f [Rx * p + Tz]/[1 + N2R2 * P] + Cz;$$

$$Ys = f [Ry * p + Ty]/ [1 + N2R2 * P] + Cy.$$

The above two equations thus permit for the focal length of the projection to be measured much more accurately than ever before. In technical terms, this is also known specifically as "Foreshortening."

How to Take into Account the Distortions in the Lens of the Camera

It should be noted that all of the theories and mathematical algorithms presented up to this point in this chapter have pretty much assumed that a linear approach has been taken to capture a snapshot of the image in question. In other words, there is one straight line that can be visualized from the lens of the camera to the image in question, whether it is static or dynamic. However, many of the sophisticated cameras of today that are used by the ANN system often will take a snapshot of the image via a "Curvilinear" approach. This is also technically known as "Radial Distortion."

As a result, the projection, as described previously in the last subsection, becomes curved. Because of this, there can be resultant distortions which occur in the snapshot of the particular image that is captured. This can lead to blurring, and because of that, the outputs that are produced by the ANN system could become highly skewed. But once again, the use of mathematics, especially when it comes to the semi-quadratic equation, can be used to help mitigate this error from occurring in the first place. These two algorithms can be represented as follows:

$$Xc = [Rx * p + Tx]/[Rz * P + Tz];$$

$$Yc = [Ry * p + Ty]/[Rz * P + Tz].$$

The above two algorithms can also be referred to as technically the "Radial Distortion Model." The basic postulate of it states that the images which are to be captured by the ANN system are technically "displaced" either away (known as the "Barrel Distortion Effect") or closer (known as the "Pincushion Distortion Effect"). Both of these effects are highly statistically correlated by an equal amount from their so-called "Radial Distance." To take both of these effects into further consideration, Polynomial Equations can be used, and they are as follows:

$$Xc = Xc * (1 + k1r^2c + k2r^4c);$$

$$Yc = Yc * (1 + k1r^2c + k2r^4c)$$

Where:
    K1 and K2 = the Radial Distance Parameters.

Once these distortions have been countered (especially that of blurring, as just reviewed), the final, geometric coordinates of the pixels of the image can be computed as follows:

$$Xs = fX^rc + Cx;$$

$$Ys = fY^rc + Cy.$$

But at times, depending upon how the ANN system is capturing the snapshot of the image in question, these two mathematical algorithms may not be suitable enough to be applied. Therefore, much more sophisticated analytical theories, which are known as the "Tangential Distortions" and the "Decentering Distortions" can be used to some degree.

Also, the use of a special lens called the "Fisheye Lens" can be used as well to counter the effect of the above-mentioned distortions. To accomplish this specific task, an "Equi-Distance" projector can be used from a certain distance away from the Optical Axis of the snapshot of the image that is to be taken. To do this, a full-blown quadratic equation must be used. But all of these 3-Dimensional images (whether they are static or dynamic) are actually deemed to be rather small in nature.

The primary reason for this is that the image must be able to be easily and quickly processed by the ANN system, in rapid succession.

However, even larger images can be used, even though it could slow down the processing time in order to produce the desired of results of the ANN system. For these types of 3-Dimensional images, the use of both a "Parametric Distortion Model" and "Splines" will be needed. In this particular instance, it can be quite difficult to come up with the appropriate center point of projection along the geometric plane that is being used. One may have to mathematically construct what is known as the "3-Dimensional Line" that must be statistically correlated to each and every pixel point that is represented in the 3-Dimensional image in question.

How to Create Photometric, 3-Dimensional Images

At this point in this chapter, we have assumed that both the 2-Dimensional and 3-Dimensional images (whether they are static or dynamic) are made up just one band of mathematical values. In other words, we have also assumed that these 2-Dimensional and 3-Dimensional images are typically black and white. But, it is very important to keep mind that while these colors are extremely suitable for the ANN system because they do not require as much processing power, both 2-Dimensional and 3-Dimensional images of full color can be applied and used as well.

Thus, they will possess what are known as different "Intensity Values." But, it is also very important to make sure that these various "Intensity Values" are statistically correlated with one another in some fashion. In this section, we examine some of the major variables that can affect the statistical correlation of these many types of "Intensity Values."

The Lighting Variable

Truth be told, and it is quite obvious, unless there is a good amount of lighting from the external environment, a good quality 2-Dimensional or 3-Dimensional image cannot be captured. Thus, there must be light that can be shone onto the image from at least two sources, preferably even more. Thus, lighting sources can be further subdivided into both Point and Area Light Sources, which are examined in greater detail here.

1) The Point Light Source:
   This kind of lighting stems typically from just one source at just one point in time. These types of lighting sources also have specific levels of intensity and utilize a color spectrum that can be distributed over differing wavelengths. This can be specially denoted as "L(Y)."

2) <u>The Area Light Source</u>:
In this kind of environment, the intensity of the light that stems from this particular source actually diminishes over time when the mathematical square of the distance from the specific source of light for the image in question has started to become illuminated. The primary reason for this is that light being projected from the source point is actually distributed over the surface of either the 2-Dimensional or 3-Dimensional image in a parabolic fashion, either up or down. This is can be mathematically represented as either $Y=X^2$ or $Y=-X^2$, respectively. Although the "Point Light Source" may sound simple to understand in theory, it can actually be difficult to accomplish in the real world, typically when the ANN system is being used. A typical example of this is known specifically as "Incident Illumination," and it can be represented by the following mathematical equation:

$$L * (0/Y).$$

The above algorithm makes the scientific assumption that light that is originating from its source point can travel in an infinite fashion.

The Effects of Light Reflectance and Shading

We typically don't think of this too often, but when a specific beam of light hits either a 2-Dimensional or 3-Dimensional image, the light beam actually becomes scattered in nature, and is often reflected back into space yet again. There are many theories that have been established to explain this particular phenomenon, and they are reviewed in more detail in this subsection.

1) <u>The Bidirectional Reflectance Distribution Theorem</u>:
This is actually the most widely accepted light theory today. Essentially, it states that a 4-Dimensional Mathematical Function can statistically describe the intensity of each and every wavelength that enters into what is known as the "Incident Direction" (denoted as "$\underline{V}$") is actually bounced back off again into what is known as the "Reflected Light Direction" (denoted as "$\underline{Vr}$"). This kind of function can be mathematically represented as follows:

$$fR \ (0/z1, \ 0/r, \ 0/r, \ Y).$$

It is very interesting to note that this theorem can actually be considered a mathematical reciprocal, in which the specific roles of "$\underline{Vi}$" and "$\underline{Vr}$" can be interchanged amongst one another. Also, equally important is the fact that the surfaces in either the 2-Dimensional or 3-Dimensional image (whether they are static or dynamic) are considered to be what is known as "Isotropic" in nature. In other words, there is no specific direction from where the light has to be transmitted. This "Isotopic" nature can be represented mathematically as follows:

$$Fr \ (o/I, \ 0/r \ |0/r - 0/I;Y);$$

Or also as:

$$Fr \ (\underline{V}1, \ \underline{V}r, \ N, \ \underline{Y}).$$

Finally, in order to specifically calculate the amount of light which is being bounced off of either the 2-Dimensional or 3-Dimensional image, the following mathematical algorithm is used:

$$Lr \ (\underline{V}r; \ Y) = F \ (Li(\underline{V}i; \ Y) \ Fr(\underline{V}i, \ \underline{V}r, \ \underline{N}, \ Y) \ COS^\wedge + 0/I, \ d\underline{V}i.$$

2) The Diffuse Component of the Bidirectional Reflectance Distribution Theorem:
   This is actually a specific subcomponent of the above-mentioned theorem, and it can also be referred to as the "Lambertian" or "Matte" Reflection Property. This component actually assumes that the light source and the light that is emitted from it is statistically distributed in a uniform pattern throughout the 2-Dimensional image or 3-Dimensional image in question. This is the component that leads to what is known as "Shading." Essentially, this is the non-shiny light that is being transmitted onto the object (which is either the 2-Dimensional image or 3-Dimensional image). In these instances, the light is actually absorbed and bounced off yet again. It is important that when the light stemming from its source point is spread out in a uniform fashion, the above-mentioned theorem actually becomes constant in nature, and can be represented by the following mathematical algorithm:

$$Fd \ (\underline{V}i, \ \underline{V}r, \ \underline{N}, \ Y) = Fd(Y).$$

In order to take into account the "Shading Effect" as just described, the following mathematical algorithm is also utilized:

$$Ld \ (Vr; \ Y) = \Sigma \ Li(Y)Fd(Y) \ COS^\wedge + 0/I = \Sigma \ Li(Y)Fd(Y) * [\underline{V}i * \underline{n}]^\wedge +.$$

3) The Diffuse Component of the Bidirectional Reflectance Distribution Theorem:
   This is deemed to be the second major component of the above-mentioned theory, and it actually takes into specific account the reflection of light that is "Specular" in nature. In other words, it is "Glossy"-looking when it is transmitted onto either the 2-Dimensional or 3-Dimensional image in question.

This is technically known as "Incident Lighting," and it can be rotated in a 180-degree fashion upon the object in question. This is mathematically computed as follows:

$$\underline{Si} = v\| \ 0 \ vT = (2\underline{nn}^{\wedge}T - I) * Vi.$$

Thus, the amount of light transmitted in this regard is primarily dependent upon the following variables:

■ The Angle of Incidence (denoted as $0/ = COS^{\wedge}-1 * (\underline{Vr} * \underline{Si})$);
■ The View Direction (denoted as "$\underline{Vr}$");
■ The Specular Direction (denoted as "$\underline{Si}$").

4) The Phong Shading Theory:

This specific theory states that both the Diffusement and Specular aspects of reflected light can be referred to technically as "Ambient Illumination." This refers to the fact that the light that is shone onto either the 2-Dimensional image or the 3-Dimensional image can be spread out in an even distribution, but that it is "diffused" in nature. In this theory, the color of the light becomes a very important factor, which takes into further account the specific degree of what is known as "Ambient Illumination." This can be mathematically represented as follows:

$$Fa(Y) = Ka * [(Y) \ La(Y)].$$

The Phong Theory can be mathematically stated as follows as well:

$$Lr(Vr;Y) = Ka(Y)La(Y) + Kd(Y) \ \Sigma Li(Y) *[\underline{Vi} * \underline{n}]^{\wedge}+ \\ + Kz(Y) \ \Sigma Li(Y) * (\underline{Vr} * Si)^{\wedge}k.$$

It is important to note that both the Ambient and the Diffused Colors, which are distributed throughout the 2-Dimensional or 3-Dimensional image (denoted as "Ka(Y)" and "Kd(Y)") are considered to be literally the same in feature design. Also, the typical Ambient Illumination which is present has a different type of color shading from the light sources in which it is projected. In addition, the "Diffuse Component" of this particular theory is heavily dependent upon the Angle of Incident of the incoming bands of light rays (which is specifically denoted as "Vi"). But, this is not the only particular theory that is used in this regard. In fact, other sophisticated models that are currently being used in Computer Graphics typically supersede this theory.

5) The Dichromatic Refection Model:

This is also known as the "Torrance and Sparrow Model of Reflection." This theory merely states that all of the colored lighting that is used to further illuminate either the 2-Dimensional or the 3-Dimensional image (which can either be static or dynamic) is uniformly spread, and typically comes from just one source of light, and it is comprised of two mathematical algorithms, which are as follows:

$$Lr(Vr; Y) = Li\ (\underline{V}r, \underline{V}i, \underline{N}, Y) + Lb\ (\underline{V}r, \underline{V}i, \underline{N}, Y) = Ci(Y)m1$$
$$(\underline{V}r, \underline{V}i, \underline{N},) + Cb(Y)Mb\ (\underline{V}r, \underline{V}i, \underline{N},)$$

It should be noted that this specific theory has been used in Computer Vision to segregate colored objects that are located in either the 2-Dimensional or 3-Dimensional images where there is a tremendous of mathematical variation in the amount of shading that is shone onto them.

6) The Global Illumination Theory:

As a review, the theories above assume that the flow of light is projected form its original source point, and will bounce off either the 2-Dimensional or 3-Dimensional image with changing intensities, and will thus be projected back to the camera in a mathematical, inverse trajectory. But these theories reviewed assume that this only happens once. The truth of the matter is that this sequence can happen many times, over many iterations, in a sequential cycle. In this regard, there have been two specific methodologies that have attempted to address this unique phenomenon. They are as follows:

■ Ray Tracing:

This is also technically known as "Path Tracing." This methodology makes the assumption that the separate rays from the camera will bounce back numerous times from either the 2-Dimensional or the 3-Dimensional image to the sources of light. Further, the algorithms that constitute this particular methodology assume that the "Primary Contribution" can be mathematically computed by using various forms of Light Shading equations. Additional light rays that are deemed to be supplementary in nature can be used here as well.

■ Radiosity:

The same principles hold true here as well, but instead of colored lights being used, another specialized type of lighting is used, which is called a "Uniform Albedo Simple Geometry Illuminator." Also, the mathematical values that are associated with either the 2-Dimensional or 3-Dimensional images are statistically correlated amongst one another. Thus, among the light that is physically captured is what is known as the "Form Factor," which is just a function of the vector orientation and other sorts of reflected properties. With regards to this methodology, this can be denoted as "$1/r^2$." But, one of the main disadvantages of this specific methodology is that it does not take into consideration what are known as "Near Field Effects," such as the lack of light entering into the small shadows within either the 2-Dimensional or 3-Dimensional image, or even the sheer lack of ambient lighting.

In fact, various attempts have been made to combine the above-mentioned methodologies into one cohesive one. The primary advantage of this is that additional types of lighting sources can be used.

The Importance of Optics

One of the key aspects in Computer Vision as it used by the ANN system is what is known as "Optics." What exactly is Optics? It can be defined technically as follows:

> Classical optics is divided into two main branches: geometrical (or ray) optics and physical (or wave) optics. In geometrical optics, light is considered to travel in straight lines, while in physical optics, light is considered as an electromagnetic wave.

As it is stated in the above definition, there are two main types of optics that can be used in Computer Vision, which are as follows:

- Geometrical Optics;
- Physical Optics.

Put in simpler terms for purposes of this chapter, Optics can be considered as the light that must pass through the lens of the camera before it reaches the camera's sensor. Or even simpler, it can be thought of as the small pinhole that will project all of the rays of light from all of the sources of origin into one main center, which can then be shone onto either the 2-Dimensional or 3-Dimensional image (which is either static or dynamic in nature).

But of course, the above scenario as just depicted can get much more complex; a lot depends of the requirements that are set forth by the ANN system. For example, some of the extra variables to consider are the following:

- The focus properties of the camera;
- The exposure rates of the camera;
- Vignetting;
- Aberation.

In this regard, the typical setup for the usage of Optics will ensure that there is also what is known as a "Thin Lens" which is basically made up of just one piece of glass which possesses a very low parabolic feature on either side of it. There is a special theorem for this, which is technically known as the "Lens Law." This specific-ally stipulates that the mathematical relationship between the distance of either the

2-Dimensional or the 3-Dimensional image (which can be denoted as "Zo"), as well as the specific distance from behind the lens from which either the 2-Dimensional or 3-Dimensional image is captured. This can be mathematically represented as follows:

$$(1/z0) + (1/Zt) = (1/f)$$

Where:

F = the Focal Length.

There is also another important concept related to Optics, and this is specifically known as the "Depth of Field." This is a mathematical function of the Focal Distance that is present on the "Aperture Diameter," which is denoted as "d." This can be mathematically represented as follows:

$$f/\# = N = f/d$$

Where:

f = the Focal Length;
d = the Geometric Diameter of the Aperture of the camera.

It should be noted at this point that the above-mentioned "f" value is represented as a series of integers, such as the following:

$$f/1.0, f/2.0/, f/3.2, f/4.8, \ldots$$

The above-described numerical representations are actually a progression of iterations, which are based on "Full Stops." For example, as f/1.0 is fully processed by the ANN system, it stops for a brief second or two so it can process the next "f" value, which in this case would be f/2.0. But, one of the key disadvantages of using optics in this regard is that the lens can be typically very thin, and this can lead to a phenomenon that is known as "Chromatic Aberration," which is examined in more detail in the next section.

The Effects of Chromatic Aberration

Chromatic Aberration deals with what is known as the "Index of Refraction." This is when the colored lights that come from their various sources actually end up focusing at distances that are just minutely different from the intended target values. These variances can be measured by a metric that is known as the "Transverse Chromatic Aberration," and this can be modeled by a per color basis, depending upon which ones are being transmitted to illuminate either the 2-Dimensional or 3-Dimensional image.

Any blurs that can be created in this illumination are technically known as the "Longitudinal Chromatic Aberrations." They pose a major disadvantage in that these types of blurs typically cannot be undone once they are projected onto either a 2-Dimensional or 3-Dimensional image. In order to mitigate these kinds of effects as much as possible, the camera lens makes use of a technology that is known as the "Compound Lens." These are made up of different glass-based elements.

Rather than just having what is known as a "Single Nodal Point" (which can be denoted as "P"), these kinds of lenses make use of what is known as a "Front Nodal Pane." This is where all of the light beams that are being used to illuminate either the 2-Dimensional or 3-Dimensional image come into one central location from within the camera, and then leave through the "Rear Nodal Point" on its way to the sensor. It should be noted that when trying to calibrate the camera, it is only this specific Point that is of main interest.

However, not all camera lenses have these kinds of specialized "Nodal Points." A typical example of this would be the Fisheye Lens, as was reviewed earlier in this chapter. In order to counter this kind of setback, a specialized mathematical function is often created so that the various pixel coordinates and any 3-Dimensional effects can be statistically correlated amongst one another.

The Properties of Vignetting

Another property of Chromatic Aberration is that of "Vignetting." In terms of its scientific principle, this is where the brightness of the light rays that are shone onto either the 2-Dimensional or 3-Dimensional image makes its way, for some reason or another, toward the outer ends of the image in question. In this regard, there are two types of Vignetting, and they are reviewed as follows:

1) Natural Vignetting:
   This is occurs when "Foreshortening" occurs on the surface of either the 2-Dimensional or 3-Dimensional image, or any of the pixels that are contained within it. This can be mathematically represented as follows:

$$00COSY/r^20 \; TT * (d/2)^2 \; COS \; A = 00 * (TT/4)$$
$$* (d^2)/z^2 COS^4 \; A.$$

Any light that is transmitted onto the image in question can also be mathematically represented as follows:

$$00/0i = (z^2/z^2i).$$

Finally, the mathematical relationship between the sheer amount of light that is transmitted onto the pixels of either the 2-Dimensional or 3-Dimensional image (denoted as "i"), the geometric diameter of the Aperture of the camera (denoted as "d"), and the focusing distance (denoted as Zi-f), and any off angles (denoted as "A") can be mathematically represented as follows:

$$Oo*(TT/4) * (d^2/z^2o)COS^4A = Oo*(TT/4) * (d^2/z^2o)COS^4A = (diTT/4) * (d/f)^2 COS^4A.$$

Also, the "Fundamental Radiometric Relation" that exists from the "Radiance Light" (denoted as "L") and the "Irradiance Light" (denoted as "E") can also be mathematically represented as follows:

$$E = L(TT/4) * (d/f) COS^4 A1.$$

2) <u>Mechanical Vignetting</u>:
This is also technically referred to as "Internal Occlusion," and this occurs when the elements of the camera lens cannot absorb all of the light rays that are transmitted from the light sources. However, this can be more or less be easily fixed as the length of the Camera Aperture can be decreased.

The Properties of the Digital Camera

This section provides the basic constructs of how a digital camera can be used in conjunction with an ANN system in order to produce the desired results. First, any light that is triggered from the various lighting sources is typically gathered by what is known as an "Active Sensing Area," which can last throughout the time period of exposure of the 2-Dimensional or 3-Dimensional image. This usually is all done within a fraction seconds, and then from there, the light is then transmitted over to what are known as "Sense Amplifiers." The technologies behind this are the "Charged Couple Device" (also known as the CCD"), and the metal oxide that exists within it, which is very often Silicon-based (also known as the "CMOS").

From this point, the photons are then actually stacked up against one another during the time frame of the exposure period of the 2-Dimensional or 3-Dimensional image in question. Then, in what is known as the "Transfer Phase," these photonic charges are transferred yet again to what are known as the "Sense Amplifiers." As its name implies, these signals are amplified and, from there, are sent off to what is known as the "Analog to Digital Converter," also known as the "ADC."

It should be noted here that in older generations of the CCDs, images were very often subject to a phenomenon called "Blooming." This occurs when the pixels in either the 2-Dimensional or 3-Dimensional images transfer into other pixels that are either adjacent or parallel to it. But with the newer versions of the CCDs, this phenomenon is greatly mitigated by using "Troughs." This is where the extra photonic charges can be transferred safely into another area of the digital camera that is being used by the ANN system.

There are other factors as well that can greatly impact both the processing power and the performance of the CCD, and these are as follows:

- The shutter speed;
- The sampling pitch;
- The fill factor;
- The size of the Central Processing Unit (CPU) within the digital camera;
- The resolution from the analog to digital converter;
- The analog gain;
- The sensor noise.

The above are all reviewed in the next subsections.

Shutter Speed

This particular functionality of the digital camera has direct control over the amount of light that enters into the digital camera, and also has an immediate impact on whether the 2-Dimensional or 3-Dimensional images will either be under-exposed or even over-exposed. For 2-Dimensional or 3-Dimensional images that are dynamic, the shutter speed can also be a huge factor in deciding how much "Motion Blur" will be in the resultant image. A general rule of thumb here is that a proportionately higher shutter speed can make later forensic analysis of either the 2-Dimensional or 3-Dimensional image feasible.

Sampling Pitch

This metric is deemed to be the actual, physical spacing between the sensor cells and the imaging chip that is located within the digital camera itself. A good rule of thumb here is that a higher level of sampling pitch will usually yield a much better resolution of either the 2-Dimensional or 3-Dimensional image. The converse of this is also true, in that a smaller pitch rate means that only a smaller area of the image will be captured, and thus, they could have extraneous objects on them.

Fill Factor

This can be deemed to be the actual "Sensing Area" of the digital camera. This metric is represented as numerical fractions, and the higher the fill rate, there will be more light shone, with the end result being that a much more robust snapshot of either the 2-Dimensional or 3-Dimensional image will be captured.

Size of the Central Processing Unit (CPU)

There are many miniature-sized CPUs that are available for the digital camera that are being used by the ANN system, ranging in a fraction of inches. But for the most robust outcomes, it is highly recommended that a larger-sized CPU be utilized. The main disadvantage with this is that the larger the CPU is, the statistical probability of it being a more defective chip also rises.

Analog Gain

In older digital cameras, the analog gain was amplified by what is known as a "Sense Amplifier." But in the digital cameras of today that are used by the ANN system, the "Sense Amplifier" has been replaced by the "ISO Setting." This is an automated process, in that a higher level of analog gain will permit the digital camera to yield much better quality snapshots of either the 2-Dimensional or 3-Dimensional images under very poor or substandard lighting conditions that may be present in the external environment.

Sensor Noise

During the entire lifecycle of the digital camera capturing a snapshots of either a 2-Dimensional or 3-Dimensional image, there can be a lot of "extraneous" noise that can be added during this whole process. These types of "noises" can be further broken into the following categories:

- Fixed pattern noise;
- Dark current noise;
- Shot noise;
- Amplifier noise;
- Quantization noise.

It is important to note at this point that with all of the above five factors, the lighting sources that are used can typically impact the 2-Dimensional or 3-Dimensional image that is being currently used by the ANN system. But this problem of "noise" can be alleviated by making use of Poisson Distribution Models that are statistical based in nature.

The ADC Resolution

This is an acronym that stands for "Analog to Digital Conversion." This can be deemed to be amongst the final steps in the processing of the 2-Dimensional or 3-Dimensional image before it is transmitted over to the ANN system to compute the desired outputs. There are two other factors that are of prime concern here, and they are as follows:

- The Resolution: This is a metric that reflects the total byte size of the 2-Dimensional or 3-Dimensional image;
- The overall "Noise" level of these particular images, as it was just reviewed in the last subsection.

For the first one, it is recommended that the 2-Dimensional or 3-Dimensional image be no greater than 16 bits so that the processing power of the ANN system is thus optimized and is not being overtaxed beyond its design limits.

The Digital Post-Processing

Once all of the steps in the last subsections have been accomplished, the digital camera can then take the snapshot of the 2-Dimensional or 3-Dimensional image, further enhance it, and compress it down further so that the image can be easily used by the ANN system. Some of the techniques that can be used here include the following:

- The Color Filter Array Demosaicing (also known as "CFA");
- The setting of various White Points;
- Calculating the Gamma Function of 2-Dimensional or 3-Dimensional images that are only dynamic in nature.

The Sampling of the 2-Dimensional or 3-Dimensional Images

As the tile of this section implies, the 2-Dimensional or 3-Dimensional images that are going to be processed by the ANN system must first be sampled to see which of the snapshots taken will be the most effective in terms of computing the desired outputs. This concept can also be referred to as what is known as "Aliasing." There is a direct mathematical algorithm to help out in this process, and this can be referred to as "Shannon's Sampling Theorem." This theory computes the minimum amount of sampling that is needed in order to reconstitute a rather robust light signal. The term "robust" can be defined as being at least twice as high (2X) as the highest frequency that is actually yielded by the digital camera.

This can be mathematically represented as follows:

$$Fs > 2Fmax.$$

Thus, in this regard, the highest level of frequency can also be referred to as what is known as the "Nyquist Frequency." The "Nyquist Rate" can also be defined as the minimum of the inverse of the frequency in question, and can be mathematically represented as follows:

$$Rs = 1/Fn.$$

At this point, one could simply ask the question, what is the point of even engaging in the sampling process to begin with? Well, the primary objective of this is to reduce the amount of frequency levels that are transmitted to the 2-Dimensional or 3-Dimensional images, so that they can be much easier processed by the ANN system. In this regard, another key metric that can be used is what is known as the "Point Spread Function." This postulates that the response levels of the pixels that are embedded within the image of the 2-Dimensional or 3-Dimensional snapshots can actually be used to point to the optimized light source that should be used.

The "Point Spread Function" (also known as the "PSF") is a mathematical summation of the blurs that are present, and the "Integration Areas" which can actually be created by the chip sensor of the digital camera that is being used for the ANN system. In other words, if the fill factor is known (as previously described), the PSF can also be computed. Also, the "Modular Transfer Function" can be computed in order to statistically ascertain how much sampling is truly needed before the snapshots of the 2-Dimensional or 3-Dimensional images are thus fed into the ANN system.

It should be noted at this point that the sampling technique just described can be used for purposes other than determining which of the 2-Dimensional or 3-Dimensional images are best suited for the ANN system. These include the following:

■ Resampling;
■ Unsampling;
■ Downsampling;
■ Other types of Image Processing applications.

The Importance of Color in the 2-Dimensional or 3-Dimensional Image

So far in this chapter, the concepts of how the various lighting functions and the surfaces that are used to capture the snapshots of both 2-Dimensional and 3-Dimensional images have been reviewed in good detail. For example, when the light is coming inbound from its various projection source points, these various ray are actually broken down into the various colors of the spectrum: red, green, and the blue colors, also known as "RGB." There are other colors as well, such as cyan, magenta, and yellow, or "CYMK." These are also known as the "Subtractive Colors." The other colors previously described are known as the "Additive Primary Colors." These are actually added together to produce the CYMK color regime. Also, these various colors can be combined in order to produce other types of colors as well. But, it is important to keep in mind that these colors are not intermixed or combined automatically on their own. Rather, they appear to be mixed together because of the way our Visual Cortex in the human brain has been created.

All of this is a result of what is known as the "Tri-Stimulus" nature of our vision system, as just described. But when all of this is applied to the field of Computer Vision, you will want to use as many different and various wavelength colors as you possibly can in order to create the most robust snapshots of either the 2-Dimensional or 3-Dimensional images.

The CIE, RGB, and XYZ Theorem

These three separate acronyms are also technically known as the "Tri Chromatic Theory of Perception." In this regard, an attempt is made in order to come up with all of the monochromatic colors as just three primary colors for the ANN system to use both efficiently and optimally as well. This specific theory can be mathematically represented as follows:

$$[X, Y, Z] = 1/0.17697 \ [(0.49, 0.17697, 0.000) * (0.31, 0.81240, 0.01) * (0.20, 0.01063, 0.99)] * [R, G, B].$$

The specific color coordinates of this theorem can be mathematically represented as follows:

$$X = (X/X+Y+Z), y = (Y/X + Y + Z), z = (Z/X + Y + Z)$$

This all comes up to the value of 1.

The Importance of the L*a*b Color Regime for 2-Dimensional and 3-Dimensional Images

While the last subsection of this stressed the importance of how the human visual cortex can literally separate the luminance-based colors from the chromatic-based colors, the theories just outlined typically do not cover the fundamental question of how the visual cortex can actually examine the subtle and minute differences in the various color regimes just examined in the last subsection of this chapter.

To counter this effect (because Computer Vision tries to replicate the entire human visual system), a concept known as the "L*a*b Color Regime" has been formulated. This is also referred to as "CIELAB." This can be mathematically be represented as follows:

$$L* = 116f * (Y/Yn).$$

The above computes the "L*" component. The following mathematical algorithms thus compute the "a*" and the "b*" components:

$$A* = 500 [f(X/Xn) – f(Y/Yn)]; b* = 200[f(Y/Yn - f(Z/Zn].$$

The Importance of Color-Based Cameras in Computer Vision

So far, we have reviewed in this chapter, particularly in the last few subsections, how the various colors can be applied. But, despite all of this, there is still one color regime that has not been examined yet—"RGB." These specific colors are that of red, blue, and green. The mathematical representations for each of these colors of the spectrum can be further defined as follows:

$$R (Red) = \Sigma L(Y)Sr(Y)dYr;$$

$$G (Green) = \Sigma L(Y)Sg(Y)dYr;$$

$$B (Blue) = \Sigma L(Y) Sb(Y)dYr.$$

Where:
  $L(Y)$ = The incoming spectrum of any of the above-mentioned colors at any specific location of the 2-Dimensional or 3-Dimensional image;
  $\{Sr(Y), Sg(Y), Sb(Y)\}$ = The red, blue, and green "Spectral Sensitivities" of the correlated sensor of the digital camera that is being used by the ANN system.

Although we know now the colors that will be used, the one item that cannot be ascertained is the sensitivities of these three light colors. But, all that is needed by the ANN system is what is known as the "Tri Stimulus Values."

The Use of the Color Filter Arrays

The digital cameras that collect and make use of the RGB color spectrum also have a special sensing chip as well, and this is known as the "Color Filter Array," also called the "CFA" for short. In this regard, and in specific relation to this type of chip structure, we have what is known as the "Bayer Pattern." In this specific instance, there are at least twice as many (2X) green types of filters as there are red and blue filters. The primary reason for this is that there are various luminance signals going to the digital camera, and from there the 2-Dimensional or 3-Dimensional image is deemed to be much more sensitive to higher frequency values than the other color and chromatic regimes,.

It should be noted also that the green color regime is also much more suscep-tible to what is known as "Interpolation," or "Demosaicing." Also, it is not only the digital cameras that are used by the ANN system which make typical usage of the RGB color regime, the standard LCD Monitors make use of them as well. A key advantage that the RGB color regimes have over the others is that they can be digit-ally pre-filtered in order to add more robustness to the snapshots that are taken of either the 2-Dimensional or 3-Dimensional image in question.

The Importance of Color Balance

It is important to note that in the RGB color regime, what is known as "Color Balancing" is used in order to move any chromatic color regimes (typically that of the white color) in a corresponding shade of color that resides from within either the 2-Dimensional or 3-Dimensional image. In order to perform this kind of pro-cedure, a specialized kind of "Color Correction" is performed, in which each of the multiplicative powers of the specific RGB value is actually in turn multiplied by a different numerical factor. In this specific instance, a diagonal matrix transformation can be conducted.

Much more advanced techniques can also be applied here, such as the "Color Twist," in which a three-by-three mathematical transformation matrix is used.

The Role of Gamma in the RGB Color Regime

In the RGB color regime, which is used by the digital camera for the ANN system, the specific mathematical relationship between the voltage of the digital camera and its corresponding can be referred to at times as "Gamma," and it can be represented in one of two ways, which are as follows:

$$\text{Representation 1: } B = V^1;$$

$$\text{Representation 2: } Y' = Y^{1/z}.$$

This is actually a nonlinear approach, but it should be noted that it has one primary advantage to it: any sort of "noise" that arises from taking the snapshots of either the 2-Dimensional or 3-Dimensional image to be processed by the ANN system can be automatically diminished where the colors are exposed to it. Also, to provide further optimization to the ANN system that will be processing the various snapshots, they are also further compressed down by making use of what is known as an "Inverse Gamma" technique.

However, another specific drawback of the above-mentioned technique is that any presence of Gamma features in the snapshots that are taken of either the 2-Dimensional or 3-Dimensional image can lead to further shading. This can be alleviated if the corresponding value of the Gamma can be calculated, but many of the digital cameras that are being used by the ANN systems of today are not capable of doing so. There are also other issues in this regard as well, such as determining what a normal surface typically is on either a 2-Dimensional or 3-Dimensional image. To help combat this level of uncertainty, another sophisticated technique is also used, and using what is known as the "Photometric Stereo." This will help to reverse any Gamma-based computations that have been done and even to further re-balance any "splotched" colors that may exist in either the 2-Dimensional or 3-Dimensional image.

If the "Inverse Gamma" technique is to be utilized directly by the ANN system, a "Linearization Technique" then is very often needed as well.

The Role of the Other Color Regimes in 2-Dimensional and 3-Dimensional Images

As it has been stated before, although it is both the RGB and the XYZ color regimes that are mostly used in digital cameras today, there are a few other types of color regimes that have been established as well, and these can also be used by the ANN system for producing desired outputs. Two such color regimes are known as "YIQ" and the "YUV." It is interesting to note that both of them, respectively, make further use of what is known as a "Y Channel." This can actually be mathematically represented as follows:

$$Y'601 = 0.299R' + 0.587G' + 0.144B'$$

Where:

R', G', and B' are actually the Red, Green, and Blue compressed color regimes that are embedded minutely in the other two color regimes just previously described. From this, Ultraviolet parts can be filtered out by making use of the following mathematical algorithm:

$$U = 0.42111 * (B' - Y');$$

$$V = 0.877283 * (R' - Y').$$

By using these mathematical algorithms, "Backward Compatibility" can even ferret out for the "High Frequency Chroma"-based signals that can still persist on the digital camera that is used by the ANN system.

With the "YIQ" and the "YUV" color regimes, .JPEG images can be created as well. But, it is important to keep in mind that these are not the standard .JPEG format file extensions, these are the ones that have to be specially created in order for the ANN system to process them in order to compute the desired outputs. This can be computed by the following mathematical algorithm:

$$[Y', Cb, Ct] = [0.299, -0.168736, 0.5] * [0.587, -.331264, -0.418688] *$$
$$[0.144, 0.5, -0.081312] * [R', G', B'] + [0, 128, 128]$$

Where:
R', G', B' = the 8 bit Gamma color components in either the 2-Dimensional or 3-Dimensional image that has been further compressed down.

Also, the above mathematical algorithm can be used for other "Deblocking" purposes as well.

There is also yet another color regime that has come about, and which can also be used by the ANN system as well. This is known specifically as the "Hue, Saturation, Value" color regime, and is also known as the "HSV" for short. This is also a subset of the RGB color regime. The HSV color regime has the following properties as well:

- Maximum Color Value;
- Saturation:
  A scaled distance from the pixels in either the 2-Dimensional or 3-Dimensional image.
- Hue:
  The vector orientations of this specific color scheme in either the 2-Dimensional or 3-Dimensional image.

The above-mentioned properties can be represented mathematically as follows:

$$R = (R/R+G+B); G = (R/R+G+B); B = (R/R+G+B).$$

The Role of Compression in 2-Dimensional and 3-Dimensional Images

This particular phase, which is known as "Compression," is the last step in processing of snapshots of 2-Dimensional or 3-Dimensional images that are taken by the digital camera. There are specific mathematical algorithms in order to accomplish this task, but in general terms, the "Luminance Signal" is further compressed down with a much higher fidelity frequency/signal. After this first phase is done, the next stage is known as the "Block Transformation." This is where a specific mathematical algorithm, referred to as the "Discrete Cosine Transformation," is a factored product of the "Fourier Transform."

After this is done, in the third step in this process, the values of the coefficients that have been computed are converted over to a smaller set of integer-based values. It is important to keep in mind that it is not just the 2-Dimensional or 3-Dimensional images that are used by the ANN system in order to calculate the required outputs. Video streams can also be used, but these, of course, will require much more processing and computational power on the part of the ANN system.

If video is used in lieu of the 2-Dimensional or 3-Dimensional images, then another mathematical approach called "Motion Compensation" is used. This is used specifically to encode the variances that exist between each and every block of video, and to come up with a statistical matrix of the blocks that have been encoded in the previous iterations. The more modern variations of this particular mathematical algorithm can automatically size up the blocks that are used in the video segments by the ANN system, create sub-pixel coordinates, and create the required mechanism for the ANN system to actually tag previous blocks in the video stream that have already been compressed.

Finally, the effectiveness and the robustness of the mathematical formulas and equations that are used in this compression sequence as detailed in this subsection can be measured by using what is known as the "Peak Signal to Noise Ratio," or the "PSNR" for short. This is a statistical-based derivation of the "Average Mean Square Error," which is mathematically represented as follows:

$$MSE = 1/n\sum x * [I(x) - \underline{I}(x)]^2$$

Where:

    $I(x)$ = The Original Uncompressed Image;
    $\underline{I}(x)$ = The Compressed Counterpart.

From here, the PSNR can be mathematically computed as follows:

$$PSNR = 10LOG10 * (I^2max/MSE) = 20LOG10 * (Imax/RMS)$$

Where:

    Imax = The absolute extent to which signals can be transmitted from the digital camera to the 2-Dimensional and 3-Dimensional images.

Image Processing Techniques

Now that we have reviewed in great detail how 2-Dimensional and 3-Dimensional images can be created, we turn our attention to how they can be further processed so that the ANN system can use these images (whether they are static or dynamic) in the most efficient and optimal manner so that the desired outputs can be produced. In this part of the chapter, we review such processing techniques, also referred to as "Transformation." In this instance, "Point Operators" can be used, as well as "Neighborhood Operators."

Both of these concepts make use of a specialized technique which is known as the "Fourier Transform." Further, the "Operator"-based techniques just described can also be used to create what are known as "Image Pyramids" and "Wavelets" that can be used by the ANN system to further analyze the 2-Dimensional or 3-Dimensional images. Finally, "Geometric Transformations" can be used to create certain rotational aspects in the 2-Dimensional and 3-Dimensional images as well.

The Importance of the Point Operators

Point operators are deemed to be the least complex, and probably the easiest transformation techniques that are out there. For example, to demonstrate its sheer level of simplicity, each pixel-based value that is computed relies upon the previous value that has been reached, from the preceding pixels. These kinds of point operators can be used for the following characteristics of the 2-Dimensional and 3-Dimensional images:

- Level of brightness;
- Level of contrast;
- Degree of color correction;
- Geometric degree of transformation.

In terms of the mathematical algorithms that are involved with "Pixel Transformation," some the most important ones are as follows:

$G(X) = h[f(x)]$, which can also be represented as $g(x) = h *[Fo(x)], ... Fn(x)]$.

The above represents the most basic pixel transformation technique that is most widely used by the ANN systems of today. In this regard:

X = the Dimensional Domain;
F, g = the specific statistical ranges of the pixels that are being examined.

But, if discrete, or static 2-Dimensional or 3-Dimensional images are going to be used by the ANN system, there can be considered what is known as a definite, or finite set of pixel-based locations with these kinds of images. This can be mathematically represented as follows:

$G(I,j) = h[f(I, j0)]$.

Also, the other two other types of point operator that are used with pixel-based transformations use both multiplicative and addition-based mathematical properties, and can be represented as follows:

$$G(x) = a\ f(X) + b.$$

Two mathematical variables that are important in point (or pixel) transformations are those of the "Gain" and "Brightness." They are represented as follows:

$$G(x) = a(x) * f(x) + b(x).$$

It should be noted that the multiplicative property just described can also be used as a linear approach as well, and this is mathematically represented as follows:

$$H(f0 + f1) = h(f0) + h(f1).$$

Also, dual point operators can be used quite easily and effectively as well, and they can be mathematically represented as follows:

$$G(x) = (1-A) * f0(x) + Af1(x).$$

It should also be noted that this specific mathematical algorithm can be used to conduct what is known as "Cross Dissolvation" between two or more 2-Dimensional or 3-Dimensional images and/or video segments. Also, a technique known as "Gamma Correction" can also be conducted, in which any type of linear relationship between the pixel coordinates can be eliminated as is deemed necessary by the ANN system. This can be accomplished with the mathematical algorithm below:

$$G(x) = [f(x)]^\wedge{-1}/A.$$

The Importance of Color Transformations

We have touched upon the different color regimes that are available for 2-Dimensional and/or 3-Dimensional images in quite a bit of detail in the previous subsections of this chapter. But when it comes to Image Processing, these types of distinct color regimes should be thought of as ultra-correlated signals that can be associated with the pixels that are located in these images. The ANN system can further enhance the mathematical values of these kinds of signals by simply adding the same numerical iterations to them over and over again, in an iterative fashion. But, the drawback here is that the levels of Hue and Saturation can also be greatly increased as well.

The question now arises as to how the above can all be resolved. In this regard, it is very important to use the concepts of "Color Balancing" (as also previously reviewed in this chapter) to multiply and find the numerical product that works best so that the pixel coordinates in either the 2-Dimensional or 3-Dimensional images (whether they are static or dynamic) can be associated with one another in some sort of linear-based format.

The Impacts of Image Matting

Another very important key aspect in Computer Vision as it relates to 2-Dimensional and 3-Dimensional images is known as "Matting." This is a specific technique where an object in the "Foreground" of one these images can be put into the background of a totally different 2-Dimensional or 3-Dimensional image in a seamless fashion. It should be noted that the latter process, in which the object is placed into an entirely new image is known as "Compositing." The steps that are required in the middle for all of this to happen are known as the "Alpha Matted Color Image."

But in the above-mentioned process, there is yet another channel that is created, and this is known as the "Alpha Channel." This metric reflects the relative degree of "Fractional Coverage" of light that is beamed at each of the pixel coordinates of the 2-Dimensional or 3-Dimensional image. It should be noted at this point that any of the pixel coordinates that are deployed from within the object that are displaced on the newer 2-Dimensional or 3-Dimensional image are opaque in color, whereas any pixel coordinates that lie outside this specific object are transparent in nature.

To further achieve the "Compositing" technique as just described, the following mathematical algorithm is typically used:

$$C = (1-A)^\wedge B + aF.$$

Finally, when the light source is bounced back from a very plain background to the 2-Dimensional or 3-Dimensional image, the mathematical values of the light that passes through them are numerically added together. This is also known as "Transparent Motion."

The Impacts of the Equalization of the Histogram

One of the key questions that is often asked in Computer Vision today is, how can the mathematical values be ascertained for the brightness and gain characteristics of 2-Dimensional and 3-Dimensional images? Or in other words, how can they be further optimized to be best-suited for the ANN system? A simpler methodology to address these key questions is to locate the darkest and the lightest pixel coordinates in these specific images, and contrast them with a black and white Cartesian Geometric Plane.

Of course, a much more statistical approach to this would be to find the average value of all of these pixel coordinates, and from there further expand the mathematical range that they are currently in. In this specific instance, one will need to construct a "Histogram" of all of the color regimes that are present in the 2-Dimensional or 3-Dimensional image, and from there, once again use statistics to compute the following properties:

■ The Minimum Value;
■ The Maximum Value;
■ The Average Intensity Values.

A technique that is known as "Histogram Equalization" can be used here. With this technique, the goal is to strike a certain balance between the darker and brighter pixel coordinates that are present in the 2-Dimensional image or the 3-Dimensional image. From here, the ANN system can take random samples of these pixel coordinates in order to determine which ones of them will work best to compute the desired outputs. This can be done via the "Probability Density Function," which is also sometimes referred to as the "Cumulative Distribution Function," and this can be mathematically represented as follows:

$$c(I) = 1/NI \sum i{=}0h(i) = c(I{-}1) + 1/Ng(T)$$

Where:

N= the total number of pixels in either the 2-Dimensional or 3-Dimensional image.

But despite the advantages that "Histogram Equalization" can bring, one of its key disadvantages is that in the darker pixel coordinates in the 2-Dimensional or 3-Dimensional image, any miniscule, extraneous objects can be greatly magnified, thus distorting the overall quality of the image in question.

Making Use of the Local-Based Histogram Equalization

It should be noted that the technique just reviewed in the last subsection is deemed to be "Global" in nature. This simply means that the entire 2-Dimensional or 3-Dimensional image is analyzed as a whole. But at times, it may not be necessary to do this. In other words, it may just be enough to further analyze only certain segments, or regions, of either the 2-Dimensional or 3-Dimensional images. Thus, in this regard, a mathematical matrix (denoted as "MxM") can be used to apply the mathematical algorithm for the "Histogram Equalization," and be used for only certain pixel coordinates in the images.

But, this process can actually be somewhat automated in the sense that a statistical-based "Moving Window" can be applied to all of the pixel coordinates to the 2-Dimensional or 3-Dimensional image in question. But this will need some coding to be done, and this can actually be accomplished with the Python Source Code.

There is also yet another methodology that can be used in this regard, and this can be technically referred to as "Adaptive Histogram Equalization." With this, the mathematical values of the non-overlapping pixel coordinates in the 2-Dimensional or 3-Dimensional image can be calculated. This is mathematically represented as follows:

$$F_{s,x}(I) = (1-s) * (1-t) f00(I) + s(1-t)f10(I) + (1-s)^t f01(I) + stf11(I).$$

But, a much more streamlined version of this is to conduct a statistical-based lookup at each of the four corners of the generic, mathematical-based MxM matrix. From here, the pixel coordinates of these four corners can be thus combined into one entire summation, which can be further statistically distributed; the mathematical equation to do this is as follows:

$$H_{k,j}[I(I,j0] += w(I, j, k)$$

Where:

$w(I, j, k)$ = the Bilinear Weighting Function between the various pixel coordinates.

The Concepts of Linear Filtering

The technique that was reviewed in the last subsection, which is called "Local Adaptive Histogram Equalization," is also a perfect replication of what is known in statistics as the "Neighborhood Operator." In this particular instance, this specialized technique can be used to ascertain the mathematical summation of the values of the pixel coordinates just based upon one of them that is deemed to be close by in either the 2-Dimensional or 3-Dimensional image in question.

This technique can also be used for specific subsets of the pixel coordinates, in order to compute its final value. Also, it can be used to enhance the following characteristics of the image in question:

■ Setting the Color Regime tonality adjustments;
■ Adding subtle blurred objects for enhancement purposes;
■ Add more details;
■ Make the edges more pronounced in nature;
■ Remove any unneeded or extraneous objects.

To accomplish the above, a specialized "Linear Filter" is used, and the mathematical algorithm for this is as follows:

$$G(I,j) = \sum k,l\ f(i+k,\ j+1) * h(k,L)$$

Where:
  h(k,L) = the Filter Coefficients.

A more filtered version of the above mathematical algorithm is represented as:

$$G = f0/\backslash h.$$

But, it is important to keep in mind that the above mathematical algorithm is only suited for 2-Dimensional or 3-Dimensional images that are quite simple by design. Keep in mind though, that the ANN systems of today, by design, have been programmed to process very complex images, and that doing so does not tax their processing or computational resources to the breaking point. But in order for this to happen, yet another specialized mathematical equation has to be used, and this is as follows:

$$G(I,j) = \sum k,I\ f([-k,\ j-I) * h(k,L) = \sum k,\ I\ f([-k,\ j-I).$$

The Importance of Padding in the 2-Dimensional or 3-Dimensional Image

Yet, another primary disadvantage of the mathematical techniques reviewed in the last subsection is that which is known as "Boundary Effects." This is merely the super darkening of all of the pixel coordinates that are located in all of the four corners of the 2-Dimensional or 3-Dimensional image. In order to alleviate this negative effect, the concepts of what are known as "Padding" can be used, and some of the more important ones (as they relate to the ANN system) are as follows:

■ Zeroing:
  This sets all of the pixel coordinates to a mathematical value of "0" in the 2-Dimensional or 3-Dimensional image.
■ The Constant:
  This is when all of the pixel coordinates are computed and associated with a preset mathematical value.
■ Clamping:
  The above two processes can be repeated in an iterative fashion, in an automatic fashion.

- The Cyclical Wrap:
  This creates various loops around the pixel coordinates in the 2-Dimensional or 3-Dimensional image.
- Mirroring:
  This is a particular mathematical property that is used to further reflect the pixel coordinates in either 2-Dimensional or 3-Dimensional images.
- The Extension:
  This is the mathematical extension of the pixel coordinates in the 2-Dimensional or 3-Dimensional image when it is compared to the signals that are transmitted from the pixel coordinates at the edges of the 2-Dimensional or the 3 Dimensional-image.

In the world of Computer Graphics these "Padding" techniques are also known as "Wrapping or Texture Addressing Mode." This helps to keep the pixel coordinates in the four borders of the 2-Dimensional or 3-Dimensional image from any further effects of darkening. But in the off chance that this does indeed happen, the "RBGA" color regime (as reviewed in detail earlier in this chapter) can have its "Alpha" values statistically computed so that this effect can be immediately terminated.

The Effects of Separable Filtering

There is also a process that is known as "Convolution" in the world of Computer Vision. This makes use of what are known as "K2" mathematical operators (which are simply multiplication and addition) in each of the pixel coordinates of the 2-Dimensional or 3-Dimensional image. In these cases, the value of "K" merely represents both the total height and width of the image in question. This "Convolution" technique can also be applied separately to the height and width, respectively.

If the above is done, then the "K"-based values are deemed to be what is known as "Separable" in nature. Further, this can be mathematically represented as follows:

$$K = vh^{\wedge}T.$$

But, in order to truly ascertain if the "Separable" functionality has indeed been done in the 2-Dimensional or 3-Dimensional image, the following mathematical algorithm must be used:

$$K = \Sigma i O i u 2 v^{\wedge} T i.$$

It is important to keep in mind that the above mathematical algorithm can be used only if the entire 2-Dimensional image or 3-Dimensional image is being further analyzed. In order to ascertain if the "Separation" function has indeed been accomplished to both the height and the width on an individual basis, then the following two Square Root computations must be made:

For the Height: SQUAREROOT o0u0;
For the Width: SQUAREROOT O0v^Tu.

What the Band Pass and Steerable Filters Are

It should be noted that so far, there are other specialized types of "Operators" as well, other than the ones just reviewed in the last subsections. For example, there are what are known as "Sobel" and "Corner" Operators, and these are primarily used to help smooth out any curves that are needed in either the 2-Dimensional image or the 3-Dimensional image. This can be mathematically represented as follows, when a sophisticated statistical tool known as the "Gaussian Filter" is used:

$$G(x,y,O) = (1/2TT0^2) - (x^2 + y^2/2n^2).$$

The above are also referred to as what is known technically as the "Band Pass Filters." This is used to especially filter out for those frequencies that are typically not needed from the light projection sources. There is also another specialized "Operator" that is known as the "Laplacian Operator." This specific technique can be used to reduce any subtle blurring in either the 2-Dimensional or 3-Dimensional image. This is represented via mathematics as follows:

$$^2G(x,y,z) = (x^2+y^2/0^4) - (2/O2) * G(x,y,z).$$

More specifically speaking, the "Sobel Operator" can be used to statistically extrapolate the vector orientation (either from the Directional or Oriented perspectives). But, the above-mentioned mathematical algorithm can be used to accomplish this task as well. From here, a "Directional Directive" can be used, which is statistically represented as follows:

$$V\underline{u} = o/0\underline{u}.$$

There is one more specialized filter that needs to be reviewed in this subsection, and it is that of the "Steering Filter." The mathematical algorithm that drives this concept is illustrated below:

$$G\underline{uu} = u^2Gxx + 2uvGxy + v^2Gyy.$$

This technique is most widely used to create what are known as "Feature Descriptors" around the pixel coordinates in either a 2-Dimensional image or 3-Dimensional image. In these cases, a two-by-two mathematical matrix is used.

The Importance of the Integral Image Filters

If a 2-Dimensional image or 3-Dimensional image is going to be used in sequence, over and over again in an iterative fashion in the ANN system, then the Integral Image Filter needs to be used. In this regard, it is crucial that the ANN system pre-establishes what is known in terms of mathematics as the "Summed Area Table." This is also mathematically demonstrated as follows:

$$S(I,j) = I \sum k=0 * f(k,l)$$

Where:
    S(I,j) = the Integral Image.

Now, the "Summed Area Table" is identified as follows:

$$[i0, i1] X [j0, j1].$$

From here, the four separate corners of the 2-Dimensional image or 3-Dimensional image are summated together in order to speed up the efficiency cycle of the iterations that take place (as just described previously). This is achieved by the following mathematical algorithm:

$$S(i0 \ldots i1, j0 \ldots j1) = i1 \sum i=i0 \, j1 \sum j=j0 *$$
$$S(i1, j1) - s(i1, j0-1) - s(i0-1, j1) + s(i0-1, jo-1).$$

It should be noted at this point that one of the biggest disadvantages of using this kind of specialized technique is that it is also deemed to be a logarithmic approach (denoted as M + logN). Any large gatherings of either 2-Dimensional or 3-Dimensional images will result in a huge bit size, which will further require an enormous amount of both processing and computational power on the part of the ANN system that is being used.

This technique has also been used in earlier versions of Facial Recognition Technology for lower kinds of applications. The images that are taken from here are often modeled as "Eigenfaces," which consist of many, many geometric-based rectangles. Technically speaking, these are known as "Boxets." If high level statistics are thus used here, the "Summation of the Squared Differences" (also known as the "SSD") can also be used, in an effort to compute the total mathematical value of the pixel coordinates in the various Eigenfaces that have been used by the Facial Recognition system.

A Breakdown of the Recursive Filtering Technique

This kind of filtering technique is primarily used for signal processing. This is where the various color regimes that are transmitted onto the 2-Dimensional image or

3-Dimensional image actually gather up and accumulate into one area of the image, and thus, can cause more blurriness or other forms of obstructive objects to be present, thus further degrading the quality of the image. This is also technically known as the "Infinite Impulse Response," or the "IRR" for short. The primary reason why it has been given this name is that some of these color regimes can be projected onto infinity, if there are no other obstructions in its path. The "IRR" method is typically used to statistically compute massive kernels that have smoothened out in either the 2-Dimensional or 3-Dimensional image. But, as it was reviewed in detail previously in this chapter, the "Pyramid" approach can be used as well, in order to reach the same level of goal.

The Remaining Operating Techniques That Can Be Used by the ANN System

Although we have covered a good amount of "Operators" in this chapter thus far, there are still more that remain and that can also be used by the ANN system. Broadly speaking, they can fit into the following categories:

- Edge-Preserving Median Filters;
- Bilateral Filters;
- Morphological Filters;
- Semi-Global Filters.

It should also be kept in mind that the "Operators" and their corresponding filtering techniques have been traditionally linear-based. In this section of this chapter, we now examine the filtering techniques that are nonlinear-based in approach. Actually, the linear-based approaches are the easiest to compute, in the sense that the mathematical value of each pixel coordinate in either the 2-Dimensional or 3-Dimensional image can be considered as a complete, mathematical summation of the surrounding pixel coordinates.

These kinds of linear-based filtering techniques are the most favored to be used for an ANN system, for the sheer fact that they require less overhead, and are easy to deploy in order to compute the desired outputs that are required. But also keep in mind that the ANN systems of today are very sophisticated and powerful in nature; thus they can take into account any nonlinear-based filtering techniques as well. Thus, the intent of this section in this chapter is to examine these kinds of techniques in greater detail.

An Overview of the Median Filtering Technique

With this specialized technique, the statistical median value each of the closest by pixel coordinates surrounding the central ones in the 2-Dimensional image or the

3-Dimensional image is thus calculated. By using this kind of approach, any pixel coordinates that do not further contribute to the 2-Dimensional image or the 3-Dimensional image are automatically eradicated and purged. But despite this key advantage, one of the primary disadvantages of using this kind of approach is that it can only look at one pixel coordinate at a time.

In other words, it cannot look at the overall median summation of groups of pixel coordinates at one time. This can no doubt take a lot of time to process, thus further exacerbating the time that has been allotted to the ANN system to compute the desired outputs. Thus, another alternative for this specific approach is to use what is known as the "Weighted Median Index," in which this grouping functionality can be made use of.

This is mathematically represented as follows:

$$\Sigma k, j * w(k, l) * f(I + k1j + 1) - g(I, j)|^\wedge P$$

Where:

- $g(I, j)$ = the desired output that is to be computed by the ANN system;
- p = a numerical value of "1" for the Weighted Median Index.

Also, another key advantage of making use of the "Weighted Median Index" is that it can be used for "Edge Preserving" in either the 2-Dimensional image or the 3-Dimensional image. This allows for the edges of these kinds of images to appear smoother than they normally are in nature.

A Review of the Bilateral Filtering Technique

As mentioned in the last subsection of this chapter, the "Weighted Median Index" cannot be used in an automatic fashion. But in this specific technique, which is known as the "Bilateral Filtering" concept, this process is not only automated, but it also uses the same principle, in which the statistical median value of each of the closest pixel coordinates surrounding the central ones in the 2-Dimensional image or the 3-Dimensional image is subsequently calculated.

The mathematical formula for this technique is as follows:

$$G(I, j) = [\Sigma k, I * f(k, l) * w(I, j, l)]/[\Sigma w(I, j, l)].$$

Finally, a concept known in mathematics known as "Vector Distancing" is also used to help not only automate the process just described, but to speed it up as well.

The Iterated Adaptive Smoothing/Anisotropic Diffusion Filtering Technique

With this form of specialized technique, the Bilateral Filters (as reviewed earlier in this chapter) can also be used over and over again in an iterative manner. But in these circumstances, only a very small grouping of pixel coordinates are actually needed. This grouping can be depicted as follows, in terms of mathematics:

$$D(I, j, k, l) = EXP [(i-k)^2 + (j-i)^2)]/2O^2d = \{1, V = e^{-1/2o^2d}, |k-i| + |t-j| = 0, |k-i| + |t-j| = 1$$

Where:

R = $\sum(k,j)^r(I, j, k, l)$, (k, l) are the closest by pixel coordinates in the 2-Dimensional image or 3-Dimensional image;

(I,j) = the iterative process just described earlier.

The above mathematical algorithm can also be referred to as the "Anisotropic Diffusion Filtering Technique," and the primary advantage of this is that it can be applied to virtually any type of Computer Vision problem for which an ANN system is required.

But, it should be further noted that that this particular mathematical technique can also be used to a convert a static 2-Dimensional or 3-Dimensional image into a dynamic one. However, it is always best that any smoothing issues to be resolved in this regard are done in a joint, statistical approach.

The Importance of the Morphology Technique

At this point, it should be further reiterated that it is the nonlinear-based filtering techniques that are very often used to further either the 2-Dimensional or 3-Dimensional grayscale images that are used by the ANN system. But this can only occur after a specific "Thresholding Operation" has occurred, and this is done using this statistical technique:

$$0/(f,t) = \{1 \text{ if } f > t; 0 \text{ Else}).$$

Very often, binary techniques are used in this regard, and these are technically referred to as "Morphological Operations." The primary reason they are called this is because that they can literally change the geometric shape of the objects that are deemed to be binary in nature in either the 2-Dimensional image or 3-Dimensional image. In order to carry out this kind of procedure, these specific objects are statistically conjoined together with what is known as the "Structuring Element."

From here, the "Binary Output Value" is then selected, which is a direct function of the permutations that have been set forth in the Conjoining Process. It is important to note that this can take any type of geometric shape, and can also be applied to any three-by-three mathematical matrix. The statistical formula for doing this kind of computation is:

$$C = f \, 0/\!\backslash \, S.$$

This is an integer-based approach to be used. The following are some of the most important properties of the "Morphological Technique":

- The Dilation:
  This is represented as:

  $$\text{Dilate}(f,s) = 0\backslash(c.1).$$

- The Erosion:
  This is represented as:

  $$\text{ERODE}(f,s) = 0\backslash(c,S).$$

- The Majority:
  This is represented as:

  $$\text{MAJ}(f,s) = 0(c, S/2).$$

- The Opening:
  This is represented as:

  $$\text{OPEN}(f,s) = \text{DILATE}[\text{ERODE}(f,s), s)].$$

- The Closing:
  This is represented as:

  $$\text{CLOSE}(f,s) = \text{ERODE}[\text{DILATE}(f,s), s)].$$

In these specific properties, the Dilation actually deepens, or thickens the pixel coordinates in the 2-Dimensional or 3-Dimensional image, and it is Erosion that actually shrinks them down in terms of their mathematical values. Also, the Closing and Openings do not affect any large, one entity-based areas that are present in the 2-Dimensional image or 3-Dimensional image.

The Impacts of the Distance Transformation Technique

This is a concept that is used to mathematically calculate a distance that has been assigned to a parabolic curve in which there are at least two or more points that have been firmly established on it. This technique can do the following:

- The calculation of Level Sets;
- Conducting Fast Transfer Matching;
- The use of Feathering and Image Stitching in the 2-Dimensional or 3-Dimensional image.

The mathematical algorithm that is used to calculate is as follows:

$$D1(k, l) = |k| + |I|.$$

But, the above mathematical algorithm is only "generic" in nature. There are two other specific techniques that can be used which are known as follows:

- The Manhattan Distance;
- The Euclidean Distance.

The Euclidean Distance is mathematically represented as follows:

$$D1(k, l) = SQUAREROOT\ k\char`\^2 + l\char`\^2.$$

The Manhattan Distance is mathematically represented as follows:

$$D(I,j) = MIN\ k,j\ b(k,l)=0 * d(i-k, j-1).$$

Since the two mathematical algorithms mentioned above are deemed to be quite efficient in nature, there is really no need to use the "Euclidean Distance" formula for these types of applications. But in place of this, the "Vector Valued Distancing" mathematical formula can be used as well. This is where the corresponding "x" and "y" values of the pixel coordinates in the 2-Dimensional or 3-Dimensional image are used to calculate the Square Areas, or the "Hypotenuse" of the image in question.

There is also yet another Distancing Formula that exists, and it is specifically known as the "Signed Distance Transformation" technique. This specifically computes the mathematical distances for all of the pixel coordinates in the 2-Dimensional or 3-Dimensional image, and this is done by using it parallel with the other distancing techniques just described above. The fundamental, bottom line is that all of the particular distancing techniques can be quite efficient when it comes to the alignment and the merging of the 2-Dimensional objects that are curvilinear in nature with the 3-Dimensional surfaces that have been created that way by design.

The Effects of the Connected Components

This kind of technique is deemed to be semi-global in nature. In this theorem, the geometric regions that are close by, or adjacent, to the pixel coordinates in the 2-Dimensional or 3-Dimensional image actually possess the same level of input value. The use of the "Connected Component" theorem can be used for the following kinds of applications by the ANN system:

- The finding and locating of specific objects in any type of image that is either 2-Dimensional- or 3-Dimensional-based;
- The finding and locating of any type of "Thresholded Objects" in the 2-Dimensional or 3-Dimensional images, and from there calculating the needed statistics to be used by the ANN system.

To use this specific technique, either the 2-Dimensional image or the 3-Dimensional image must be split apart horizontally. Once this specific task has been accomplished, then the next phase is to merge the various color regimes (as reviewed earlier in this chapter) together, as one cohesive unit, or structure.

The area statistics that can be computed for the 2-Dimensional or 3-Dimensional image by using the "Connected Components" theorem are as follows:

- The geometric area (which is the mathematical summation of all of the pixel coordinates);
- The perimeter (which is the mathematical summation of all of the boundary level pixel coordinates);
- The centroid of the 2-Dimensional or 3-Dimensional image (which is nothing but the statistical average of the "x" and "y" values of the pixel coordinates);
- Computing the "Second Moments" which is done as follows:

$$M = \sum(x,y)Er\ [x\text{-}\underline{x}]\ *\ [y\text{-}\underline{y}]\ *\ [x\text{-}\underline{x},\ y\text{-}\underline{y}].$$

Once the above-mentioned statistics have been calculated, they can then be used to automatically sort for the different regions in the 2-Dimensional or 3-Dimensional image.

The Fourier Transformation Techniques

Fourier Transformation is a specialized statistical technique that can be used specifically to further analyze the various color regimes and the many types of filters that can be used with them. Also, "Fourier Analysis" can be used to further describe and analyze the "qualitative-based content" that is associated with the 2-Dimensional or 3-Dimensional image in question. If these specific images are large enough to be processed, then another, more modern approach is to use what is known as the "Fast Fourier Transform Technique," also known merely as "FTT" for short. Also, the light source frequencies that are associated with the 2-Dimensional or 3-Dimensional image can be studied as well, making use of the FTT techniques, as just described.

The mathematical algorithm for doing all of the above is described below:

$$S(x) = SIN *(2TTFx + 0\backslash) = SIN *(Wx + 0\backslash i)$$

Where:
   F = the Frequency Levels;
   W = 2TTf = the specific Angular Frequencies;
   0\i = the specific Phases;
   X = the Spatial Coordinates of either the 2-Dimensional image or the 3-Dimensional image in question.

The primary reason for using "X" to denote the above is because it can also be considered what is known as an "Imaginary Number." By using this kind of numerical regime, it thus becomes much easier to distinguish amongst the horizontal-based (denoted as "x") and the vertical-based (denoted as "y") in the frequency space of either the 2-Dimensional image or the 3-Dimensional image. If these axis coordinates are used, then the imaginary number plane can also be represented as "j" in this regard.

Also, an extra "Sinusodial Signal" (denoted as "s[x]") can also be incorporated into the above mathematical algorithm, and the resultant equation will look like this:

$$O(x) = h(x) * s(x) = Asin * (wX + o\backslash O)t.$$

Finally in the end, the "FTT" technique can be mathematically represented as follows:

$$H(w) = F\{h(x)\} = Ae^{\wedge}j0\backslash$$

Where:
   W = the statistical response to a complex-based Sinusoid Frequency;
   H(x) = the specialized frequency through which the light filter array is passed through.

For the ease of processing and optimization by the ANN system, the FTT technique can also be mathematically represented as follows:

$$H(x) \Downarrow \lozenge F \Downarrow \lozenge H(w).$$

But, it is important to keep in mind that the above mathematical algorithm cannot be used for all applications for the ANN system. In other words, the filters and the Sinusodial Functions follow a certain iteration, which is as follows: "Phase, Shift, Repeat." This iterative process can go for as many times as needed by the ANN system until the desired outputs have been computed. The primary drawback to this is that doing this for an infinite number of loops can literally drain the processing and computational resources of the ANN system. Thus, yet another mathematical algorithm can be used in order to pre-calculate the total number if iterations that are needed for the ANN system, and this can be mathematically represented as follows:

$$H(w) = S \ (+ \ INFINITE) \ (- \ INFINITE) \ h(x)e^{\wedge}\text{-Jwedx1}.$$

It should be noted that the above mathematical algorithm is only in the "Continuous Domain." If you want to use it for a "Discrete Domain" for the ANN system, then the following mathematical algorithm must be used:

$$H(k) = 1/N * [N\text{-}1 \ \Sigma \ x\text{=}0 * h(x)e^{\wedge}\text{-j2TTke/N}]$$

Where:
> N = the total mathematical length of the Sinusodial signal that is being transmitted to the specific area or region on the 2-Dimensional or 3-Dimensional image that is being studied or analyzed by the ANN system.

It should be noted at this point that the mathematical algorithm just described is also technically referred to as the "Discrete Fourier Transform," or "DFT" for short. But the one disadvantage of using this is that it can only be typically used in the mathematical range as denoted below:

$$K = [\text{-}N/2, +N/2].$$

The reason for this is that the mathematical values in the higher numerical range actually provide for more information and detail about the various frequencies that are bounced back from the 2-Dimensional image or the 3-Dimensional image when the various color regimes are shone onto them.

Now that the FTT technique has been examined in greater detail, it is important at this stage to review some of its more important properties, which can be described as follows:

1) The Superposition:

   This property represents the mathematical summation of all the FTT values that have been generated by both the 2-Dimensional image and the 3-Dimensional image.

2) The Shift:

   It should be noted that the FTT is actually deemed to be a "shifted signal" from the transformation that has been created by the original lighting sources that have been used. This is then actually further multiplied to get a product which is known as the "Linear Phase Shift." It is also referred to technically as the "Complex Sinusoid."

3) The Reversal:

   This is when the FTT has actually become a "reversed signal," and thus becomes a complex mathematical summation (or "Conjugate") of the transformation of the various signals that are generated by the different color regimes.

4) The Convolution:

   This is an FTT that has been transformed via a dual pair of "Convolutional Signals" which is the multiplicative product as described in "The Shift."

5) The Correlation:

   This is an FTT which is just a statistical-based correlation of the multiplicative product of the first transformation that is conducted by the ANN system which is then multiplied again with the second "Complex Conjugate."

6) The Multiplication:

   This is the FTT which is actually a transformation of two separate signals that are transmitted by the different color regimes that have evolved in the "Convolution" of the transformation process.

7) The Differentiation:

   This is the FTT transformation of when the mathematical derivative of the signal from a specific color regime becomes "transformed" when it is individually multiplied by its own frequency level.

8) The Domain Scaling:

   This is the FTT transformation in which an "Elongated" or "Stretched" signal is mathematically equivalent to the "Compressed" or "Scaled" signal from its original derivative, and the opposite is also true.

9) The Real Image:

   This is the FTT transformation in which the mathematical-based absolute values of the signals are generated from the color regimes and are also geometrically symmetrical in nature to their point of origin from the pixel coordinates in either the 2-Dimensional image or the 3-Dimensional image in question. One primary advantage of this property is that is it can help carve out more storage space for both quantitative and qualitative data that are used by the ANN system.

10) Parseval's Theorem:

This involves the specific levels of energy that are generated from the color regimes that are shone onto either the 2-Dimensional image or the 3-Dimensional image. This is represented as the mathematical summation of statistical-based, squared values.

The Importance of the Fourier Transformation-Based Pairs

In this subsection, we examine in closer detail what are known as the "Fourier Transformation Pairs" and how they can be implemented into an ANN system. More specifically, these pairs are derived from the following properties:

1) The Impulse:

This consists of a mathematical constant which is the summation of all the FTT transformations, as it was reviewed in the last subsection.

2) The Shifted Impulse:

This specific property has a shifted level of impulse, either to the right, left, up, or down, if it is placed onto a mathematical quadrant. It also makes use of various types of linear-based phases.

3) The Box Filter:

This is actually a statistical-based Moving Average of all of the filters that have been used, and it is mathematically represented as follows:

$$Box(x) = \{1 \text{ if } |x| < 1, 0 \text{ ELSE}\}.$$

Its FTT transformation is based upon the following mathematical algorithm:

$$SINC(w) = SINw/W.$$

It should be noted that the above two mathematical algorithms can actually possess an infinite number if iterations of what are known as statistical-based "Side Lobes." Also, the SINC component, as it is represented in the second mathematical algorithm, is also actually a statistical-based filter, but the main drawback of this is that it can only be utilized for filters that have a much lower mathematical value.

It is important to note that the Fourier Transformation Pairs also consist of the following properties:

1) The Tent Property:
This is a piecewise, mathematical-based linear function, and is represented as follows:

$$Tent(x) = max(0, 1 - |X|).$$

2) The Gaussian Property:
This is a geometric property, and is mathematically represented as follows:

$$G(x, 0) = (1/SQUAREROOT\ 2TT0 * c) * (e^x{}^2/2TT^2).$$

3) The Laplacian Property:
This is actually based upon the mathematical properties of what are known as the "Gabor Wavelet Theorem." This is the multiplicative product of a specific Frequency Cosine (which is denoted as "w|0") and a Gaussian mathematical function (which is denoted as "0\"). It should be noted that this specific property has the following sub-properties:

■ The Gaussian Width, which is denoted also as "0\";
■ The summation of two separate Gaussian Widths, which is denoted also as "0^-1." This is actually statistically centered at the centroid of the pixel coordinates of either the 2-Dimensional image or the 3-Dimensional image, and this is denoted as "w = +-w0."

4) The Unsharp Mask Property:
This is actually another FTT-based transformation, and it can be used optimally by the ANN system at much higher color regime frequency levels.

5) The Windowed Sinc Property:
This property is most ideal for ANN systems that make use of a specific "Response Function," which attempts to estimate any low-passed filters that are generated by the color regimes. This specific property is mathematically represented as follows:

$$RCOS(x) = \tfrac{1}{2} * (1 + COS\ TT\ x) * BOX(x).$$

The Importance of the 2-Dimensional Fourier Transformations

It should be noted at this point that the FTT techniques that have been reviewed thus far in this chapter can actually only be used for signals that are mathematically 1-Dimensional in nature, which can thus be further translated into a 2-Dimensional image, which is either static or dynamic. With this kind of technique, it is not just the height or width that is taken into consideration. Rather, all vector orientations can be taken into consideration. This can be mathematically represented as follows:

$$S(x,y) = SIN * (W_xX + W_yY).$$

The convoluted version of this is mathematically as follows:

$$H(W2, W_y) = h(x,y) * e^{-j(W_zX + W_zY)} * (D_xD_y).$$

The discrete version of this is mathematically represented as:

$$H(K_x, K_y) = 1/MN * (M-1 \sum_{z=0} * N-1 \sum_{y=0}) * [h(x,y)e^{-j2TT} * K_x + K_yZ/M, N]$$

Where:
  M = the width of the 2-Dimensional image;
  N = the height of the 2-Dimensional image.

The Impacts of the Weiner Filtering Technique

It should be noted at this point that the FTT technique is not only highly advantageous to further study the frequency characteristics of the various color regimes, but it can also be used to help analyze an entire grouping of them. This is where the concept known as the "Wiener Filter" comes into play, and it can be mathematically represented as follows:

$$\{|S(W_z, W_y)]^{\wedge}2]\} = P_s * (W_z, W_y).$$

In order to group all of the color regimes into one broad category (and even one subcategory), the "Gaussian Noise Image" is used, and it is mathematically represented as follows:

$$S * (W_z, W_y).$$

But, there is also a specific mathematical algorithm as well to group the subcategories, and this is also represented as follows:

$$O(x,y) = s(x,y) + (n,y)$$

Where:
  S(x,y) = the various color regimes that are to be broken up into the various subcategories;
  N(x,y) = the Additive Signal;

o(x,y) = the main color regimes that have been grouped into one particular category.

Although the FTT technique is primarily linear in nature, it can also be applied to those color regimes that are also curvilinear when they are shone onto either the 2-Dimensional or 3-Dimensional image, and whether they are static or dynamic in nature. To accommodate for this special provision, the following mathematical algorithm must also be used as well:

$$O(Wx, Wy) = S(Wz, Wy) + N(Wz, Wy).$$

Finally, one group of color regimes can also be superimposed onto another group with the FTT technique by making further use of this mathematical equation:

$$O(Wx, Wy) = b(x, y) + s(x, y) + n(x, y).$$

The Functionalities of the Discrete Cosine Transform

The Discrete Cosine Transform, or the "DCT" for short, is actually deemed to be a subset of the FTT technique as well. In this regard, the pixel coordinates of the 2-Dimensional image or the 3-Dimensional image can be shrunk down into various smaller "Blocks" so that the ANN system can easily and quickly process these kinds of images. There are two different versions of the DCT, depending upon which is most applicable for the outputs that are computed by the ANN system. These are mathematically represented as follows:

For 1-Dimensional Uses: $F(k) = N\text{-}1 \sum i\text{=}0 \; COS \; [(TT/N(I + \frac{1}{2})k)] * f(i).$

The above mathematical algorithm actually further compresses, or encodes the pixel coordinates of the 2-Dimensional image or the 3-Dimensional image into a linear-based fashion.

For 2-Dimensional Uses: $F(k,l) = N\text{-}1 \sum i\text{=}0 \; N\text{-}1 \sum j\text{=}0 \; COS[TTN(I + \frac{1}{2})k]$
$+ COS[TTN(I + \frac{1}{2})l)] * f(I, j).$

It should be noted at this point that the above two mathematical algorithms as just described can also be applied to separate color regimes, but do not have to be applied as an entire group. Also, these two mathematical algorithms are being further supplemented by applying the principles of Gabor Wavelet mathematics on them, as previously described in this chapter. In fact, these new types of optimizations help reduce the total number of "Blocking Artifacts" that can show up on either the 2-Dimensional or the 3-Dimensional image in question.

The Concepts of Pyramids

So far, all of the mathematical algorithms in this chapter which have been reviewed in great extent can only work in conjunction with the ANN system to calculate the inputs that are fed into those that are of the same type of mathematical value. But, depending upon the specific application that is being used for the ANN system, it should also be possible to be able to change the resolution size of either the 2-Dimensional image or the 3-Dimensional image before any further processing can take place by the ANN system in order to compute the desired outputs.

For example, it may be the case that you want to further reduce the size of the datasets that are being fed into the ANN system (it does not matter if they are quantitative-based or qualitative-based) so that the desired output computed by the ANN system will be right on the first attempt, rather than having to keep tweaking the same type of datasets over and over again in order to finally arrive at the optimal outputs that are required.

Also, it can even very well be the case that the overall size of the 2-Dimensional or 3-Dimensional image has to be further reduced in nature (in this regard, you are looking at further cropping down the height and width of them) in order to further optimize the speed and efficiency of the ANN system, or to even simply make more room for storage in either the 2-Dimensional image or the 3-Dimensional image. Also, when it comes to Biometric Technology, especially in using that of Facial Recognition, certain Facial-based images have to found. In this particular instance, Eigenfaces is typically used the most, but also "Pyramid"-based geometric diagrams can be used as well. In actuality, making use of these kinds of diagrams can be more effective, since they are much simpler in design, so the database of the Facial Recognition System can be scanned much quicker. If Eigenfaces are used, this process can take a much longer time, because they are far more sophisticated in nature than the pyramid-based diagrams.

Yet another key advantage of using pyramid-based diagrams is that they can be used to quickly and seamlessly integrate separate 2-Dimensional or 3-Dimensional images into one complete, cohesive unit by nature. Also, it should be noted that a subset of these pyramid-based diagrams are also known as "Wavelets," and as its name implies, this is also based upon the mathematical foundations of Gabor Wavelet Theory. The use of pyramid-based diagrams can also be used to decouple the 2-Dimensional image or the 3-Dimensional image (this is technically known as "Interpolation"), or to compress them down further for the ANN system after they have been decoupled (this is known as "Decimation").

Finally, the concept known as "Multi-Resolution Pyramids" can be used as well, and this is where a specific and established hierarchy can be formulated and created making use of different kinds of pyramid-based diagrams. Since, once again, these tend to be less complex in nature, they can also be used by just about any application for the ANN system in order to compute the desired, or needed, outputs.

The Importance of Interpolation

In the last subsection, we reviewed what "Interpolation" is all about. We further examine it much more detail in this subsection. First, the mathematical algorithm to represent this is as follows:

$$G(I, j) = \Sigma k, I\ f(k, l) * h(I - rk, j\text{-}rl).$$

This algorithm is actually directly applicable to what is known as the "Discrete Convolution Formula," which was also reviewed earlier in this chapter. For some applications that are more ubiquitous in nature, this can also be referred to as the "Polyphase Filter Form." In this particular instance, a specialized form of mathematical values known as "Kernels" are also used. A typical question that gets asked at this point is what makes a good 'Kernel," from a scientific standpoint? A lot of this is heavily dependent upon the specific application that is being used by the ANN system, as well as the processing and computational times that are also incorporated. Here are some important characteristics that need to be taken into further consideration:

1) The Linear Interpolator:
   This is used to produce parabolic shaped curves, either that are positive or negative in nature. Mathematically, this can be represented as follows:

   A Positive Parabola: $Y = X^2$;

   A Negative Parabola: $Y = X^{-2}$.

   But the primary disadvantage of this is that it can actually create unwanted "Creases" in either the 2-Dimensional image or 3-Dimensional image, whether they are static or dynamic in nature.

2) The Approximating Kernel:
   This is also technically referred to as the "Cubic B Spline." These can actually create "softer" 2-Dimensional or 3-Dimensional images, in which the high levels of frequency that are created by the various color regimes are statistically diminished before they are plugged into the ANN system in order to compute the desired levels of outputs.

3) The Bicubic Kernel:
   This is actually a highly specialized type of mathematical algorithm, which has been especially created for 2-Dimensional or 3-Dimensional images that are extremely high intensity in terms of the color regimes that they make specific use of. This specialized kind of algorithm is represented as follows:

   $$H(x) = \{1 - (a+3)x^2 + (a+2)\ |x^3, a(|x|\text{-}1) * (|x|\text{-}2)^2); 0\ \text{if}\ |x| < 1,$$
   $$\text{if} < |x| < 2, \text{otherwise}\}$$

Where:

A = the derivative of where x = 1.

But it should be noted that in terms of the ANN system, the value of a = -0.5 is often typically used, as this has been deemed to be the most optimal. This can also be referred to as a "Quadratic Reproducing Spline," in which both quadratic and linear functionalities can be incorporated as well. As you may have noticed, the term "Spline" has been used quite a bit in this chapter. To provide some more technical insight into this, this is a specific mathematical function that is used primarily for computing both functional- and data-based "Value Interpolations" because they can also compute mathematical-based derivatives as well. They are also heavily used to help to create the geometric-based pyramids. But, as it relates specifically for applications of Computer Vision for use by the ANN system, Splines are typically used for the following kinds of operations:

■ The creation of Elastic 2-Dimensional or 3-Dimensional images;
■ The creation of Motion Estimation (this is especially used for video-based datasets that are fed into the ANN system;
■ The creation of surface-based interpolations.

The Importance of Decimation

It should be noted at this point that both the techniques and concepts of interpolation can be used to increase the particular resolution size of the 2-Dimensional image or the 3-Dimensional image, either of which is used by the ANN system. But, the mathematical opposite of this is known as "Decimation," in which the resolution size of either the 2-Dimensional image or the 3-Dimensional image is actually decreased in both size and scope. There are two separate mathematical components that are associated with "Decimation," and they are as follows:

The First Component: $G(I, j) = \sum k, I = \sum k, l *(k, l) * h(Ri - k, rj - l);$

The Second Component: $G(I, j) = \sum k, I = \sum k, l *(k, l) * h(i - k/r, j - l/r).$

The different types of "Decimation" are also knows as "Filters," and the different kinds of them are as follows:

1) The Linear-based Filter:
   As its name implies, this is linear in nature, based upon the mathematical range from [1, 2, 1].
2) The Binomial Filter:
   This operates upon the mathematical range from [1, 4, 6, 4, 1]. It is primarily used for reducing any extra frequencies that are generated from the color

regimes that are shone onto the 2-Dimensional or 3-Dimensional image, and even when they are also shone onto the pyramid-based diagrams, as discussed at length earlier in this chapter.

3) The Cubic Filters:
   This operates upon the mathematical range from [-1 to -0.5].

4) The QMF Filter:
   There is no specific, mathematical range that has been given for this, but it is quite heavily used for what is known specifically as "Wavelet Denoising" for either the 2-Dimensional image or the 3-Dimensional image in question.

The Importance of Multi-Level Representations

Now that we have extensively laid down the theoretical foundations for the geometric-based pyramids that are used by the ANN systems and Computer Vision today, we will now review in some greater detail how these geometric-based pyramids can be built in this subsection. In this regard, probably one of the most well-known and best-regarded foundations for building such geometric-based pyramids is that of the "Adelson and Laplacian Pyramid."

In order to start constructing this with this specific methodology, either the 2-Dimensional or 3-Dimensional image is first "blurred" by a mathematical exponential factor of nearly two. This is stored and is also used to form and create the foundation. It is very important to note here that this is a completely automated and iterative process, and will only stop until the very top of the geometric-based pyramid has been reached. This is also referred to as to what is known as the "Octave Pyramid."

This can be diagrammatically represented as follows:

$$|C\ |B|A|B|C|$$

Where:
$$B = \frac{1}{4}$$
$$C = \frac{1}{4} - a/2.$$

But, it should be noted at this point that "A" is actually set to the mathematical value of 3/8, which is the optimal point for the ANN system.

This can be diagrammatically represented as follows:

$$1/16\ |1|4|6|4|1|.$$

It is interesting to note that the second mathematical diagram is actually far easier to implement into the ANN system than the first one, as just described. These two diagrams are also known as the "Gaussian Pyramid," because they both, at some point in time in the iterative cycle, converge.

There is also yet another geometric diagram pyramid technique, and this is the "Laplacian Pyramid." When this specific theory was first formulated, the bottom of the pyramid was first constructed utilizing a watered-down version of the first geometric pyramid that was initially created. This lower level was then mathematically subtracted to create what is known as a "Band Pass Laplacian Image." The primary advantage of this was that the ANN system that was using it stored permanently and deleted when necessary.

In fact, the above description also came to be technically known as the "Perfect Reconstruction," depending on the specific application that it is being used for. There is also another variation to this type of geometric-based pyramid, where it can be even be created from the initial snapshots that have been taken of the 2-Dimensional image or the 3-Dimensional image, whether they are static or dynamic. The first Laplacian Geometric Pyramid can be mathematically represented as follows:

$$DoG\{I; 01, 02\} = G01 * I - G02 * I = (G01 - G02) * I.$$

The variant, as just previously described, can also be mathematically represented as follows:

$$V2 = (02/0x^2) + (02/0y^2).$$

The Laplacian Geometric Pyramid technique is actually the favored one to use in most types of ANN systems. For example, this can be used to further analyze in much more granular details the edges of either the 2-Dimensional image or the 3-Dimensional image. There is another mathematical derivative of these techniques, and this is known as the "Half Octave Pyramids." These actually were first created back in 1984, and they were known specifically back then as the "Difference of Low Pass Transformations," or "DOLP" for short. However, this specific technique is not used very much in applications today for the ANN systems.

But when the above-mentioned technique is further combined with a statistical technique that is known as "Checkerboard Sampling," the outputs from the ANN system (which make use of this combined technique) become known as a "Quincux"-based statistical sampling.

The Essentials of Wavelets

It should be noted at this point that while the geometric-based pyramids are actually the most preferred to be used by the ANN systems of today, there is yet another alternative to this. These are known specifically as "Wavelets," and their theoretical foundations come from Gabor Wavelet Mathematics. These are extremely specialized filters that can actually localize the color regimes that are shone onto either the

2-Dimensional image or the 3-Dimensional image (as well as their respective frequencies). They can also be further mathematically defined as a specific hierarchy of various scales that has been designed by certain permutations in order to further smoothen out those frequencies into various types of subcomponents, which can be very closely statistically correlated with the geometric-based pyramids, which have been described in great detail over the last subsections of this chapter. The usage of Gabor Filters, in fact, goes all the way back to the late 1980s, and going into the early 1990s as well.

It should be noted at this point that use of Wavelets can be heavily found in the field of Computer Graphics. In this area, they can be used to perform all sorts of "Multi-Resolution Geometric Processing" for either the 2-Dimensional image or the 3-Dimensional, which will be used by the ANN system. Now, the question that often arises with Computer Vision experts who deal specifically with ANN systems is, what is the primary difference between the geometric-based pyramids and the Wavelets, as just described? With the former, more pixel coordinates are often used than what is deemed to be typically necessary, but with the latter, only the minimum required amount of pixel coordinates are utilized. The primary benefit of this is that the integrity of the 2-Dimensional or 3-Dimensional image is still left intact, despite all of the processing that they go through with the ANN System.

In fact, in order to accomplish this specific task, the Wavelets use what are known as "Tight Frames." They also make more usage of mathematical-based vector orientations in order to help further optimize this specific procedure. Further, at this point, it is only the 2-Dimensional Wavelets that are used by the ANN systems of today, nothing higher than that, although the prospect of using 3-Dimensional Wavelets is currently in its evolvement stages.

The process for creating a specific 2-Dimensional Wavelet is as follows:

- The "High Pass Filter" is first established, in which a ¾ inch space is deployed into the 2-Dimensional image;
- The "Low Pass Filter" is next created, in which lower filters are established, making use of only a ¼ inch space to further segregate them apart;
- The resultant filters from the above two steps are then further divided into two separate and distinct sub-stages;
- The above two sub-stages are then termed the "High-High" (also known as "HH" for short), and the "High-Low" (also known as "HL" for short);
- After the last step has been accomplished, a brand new sub-stage is then created, and this is known specifically as the "High-Low" frequency (also known as "HL" for short);
- It is the "HL" and the "LH" frequencies that are then transmitted over to both the horizontal and vertical axes of the 2-Dimensional image;
- It is then the "HH" frequency level that can, from a mathematical point of view, take the above two (as just described), and summate them together by merely taking their mutual derivatives and adding them up together.

A question that once again that gets asked very often is, how are these three frequencies mathematically calculated amongst one another? This has been issue that has been dealt with for even the last twenty years in the field of Computer Vision. The primary answer to this question is actually dependent upon the type of application that they are being used for by the ANN system, taking into further account these key statistical-based permutations:

■ If the Wavelets will be designed for Compression of the 2-Dimensional image;
■ What kind of Image Analysis will be done upon the 2-Dimensional image in question;
■ If any sort of "Denoising" will be conducted upon the 2-Dimensional image in question.

In fact, even to some Computer Vision professionals, the thought of creating and deploying specific Wavelets into the ANN system can deemed to be a very "tricky" sort of art. In other words, there is no quantitative-based approach to carry out this task; it is all dependent upon the permutations that have to be decided on. But of course, in the end, this will largely hinge once again upon the requirements that are needed in order to create the desired outputs by the ANN system. But, if one is searching for a quick rule of thumb in order to accomplish this task, then it is very important to take the following steps:

■ Split the three different frequency levels (as just previously described) into both even and odd mathematical-based values;
■ Then, use these above-mentioned values to specifically reverse the order of these three frequency levels;
■ Once the above two steps have been accomplished, these then become known as the "Lifted Wavelets." But, this actual procedure just described also becomes known as the "Lifting Scheme for Second Generation Wavelets."

The primary reason why this latter name has been chosen is that the above-mentioned, general technique can also be applied seamlessly to other various types of statistical based "Sampling Topologies" as well, which can also be fed into the ANN system. This actually works quite well for those specific types of applications (that are to be used by the ANN system) for what is known technically as "Multi-Layered Resolution Surface Manipulation." In fact, a derivative is specified as the "Lifted Weighted Wavelets," in that the statistical-based coefficients that are harnessed from it can be used for most types of applications that make use of 2-Dimensional images only.

But, it should be noted that if the three-step methodology (as just detailed previously) cannot be made use of for whatever reason, then there is yet another theorem that can be applied to resolve this situation. This theory is specifically known as the

"Pyramidal Radial Frequency Implementation," but the shortened version of this theory is "Steerable Pyramids." It possesses the following characteristics:

■ The mathematical computations that are derived from using this specific theorem are deemed to be statistically "Overcomplete" in nature and by design;
■ It has numerous types of mathematical-based, vector-based orientations that can be seamlessly and automatically picked up by the ANN system in order to compute the desired outputs;
■ It also possesses what are known as "Synthesis"-based mathematical functions, which can be technically inverted or reversed, depending upon the type of application that the ANN system is being specifically used for;
■ The end result becomes what is known as a "Steerable Pyramid," and these are actually used quite commonly in conducting structural-based analyses.

Finally, "Steerable Pyramids" are best suited for the following types of analysis and studies that can be conducted on a 2-Dimensional image:

■ Texture-based analyses;
■ Synthesis-based analyses;
■ "Image Denoising" (this concept was just mentioned in the last few subsections).

The Importance of Geometric-Based Transformations

These kinds of transformations, when performed in a geometric plane (such as that of a Cartesian-based one) can also be used to either further enhance or even optimize the overall resolution of either the 2-Dimensional image or the 3-Dimensional image, whichever one is planned to deployed into the ANN system in order to calculate the desired outputs. These can also be technically referred to as specific "Image Rotations," or even "General Warps." But, unlike the various Point Processing techniques that have been examined in great detail in the last few subsections, these kinds of procedures can be typically used for an entire range of pixel coordinates, throughout the entire 2-Dimensional or 3-Dimensional image. This particular process can be mathematically represented as follows:

$$G(x) = h[f(x)].$$

The above mathematical algorithm can also be used for a mathematical-based range of numerical values. If it is the desire of the ANN system to focus on a specific "Domain" or grouping of pixel coordinates that reside in either the 2-Dimensional image or the 3-Dimensional image, then the following mathematical algorithm must be utilized:

$$G(X) = f[H(X)].$$

The main method that is most widely used in this regard is that of "Parametric Transformation," and this is discussed further in the next subsection.

The Impacts of Parametric Transformations

This specific technique can literally be applied to the entire pixel coordinate range of either the 2-Dimensional or 3-Dimensional image that is in question. One of the biggest advantages of making use of the "Parametric Transformation" technique is that it only requires a very small and finite set of mathematical-based permutations that need to be formulated and implemented into the ANN system. One of the key questions that arises at this point is, how can the new pixel coordinates be computed from the original 2-Dimensional image or 3-Dimensional image (both can be denoted as "f(x)"), and use that to create an entirely new 2-Dimensional or 3-Dimensional image (both can also be denoted as "g(x)") using just the general parametric transformation model? Keep in mind that the general mathematical algorithm for the parametric transformation technique is represented as follows:

$$X' = h(x).$$

The above is also technically referred to as "Forward Warping," but it possesses a number of serious disadvantages, which are as follows:

■ You cannot simply "Copy and Paste" a pixel coordinate (represented as "f(x)") to a newer location (denoted as "g") into the newly derived 2-Dimensional image or 3-Dimensional image";
■ There are not enough well-defined non-integer-based mathematical values.

There are some workarounds to this, which typically include the following:

1) The mathematical value of "x'" can be rounded up in order to copy and paste the original pixel coordinates into the newly derived 2-Dimensional image and/or 3-Dimensional image;
2) The above can also be statistically distributed to the nearest quadrant-based pixel images in the new 2-Dimensional image or 3-Dimensional image.

It should be noted that the last step is also referred to as "Splatting." But it can at times lead to a fair amount of "Blurring" in either the 2-Dimensional image or the 3-Dimensional image. There is yet another major problem that can occur, and this is that various sorts of "Cracks" can also appear in the newly created 2-Dimensional image or 3-Dimensional image. Yet, there is another workaround to help resolve these two problems, and this is technically known as "Inverse Sampling." As its name implies, it is actually the reverse of "Forward Sampling," and in this particular technique, the pixel coordinates in the newly derived 2-Dimensional image or 3-Dimensional image can actually be "Reverse Sampled" back again to the original 2-Dimensional image or 3-Dimensional image in question. The mathematical algorithm for the "Inverse Sampling" technique is as follows:

$$G(x, y) = \sum f(k, l) * h(x - k, y - l)$$

Where:
    (x,y) = the sub pixel coordinates;
    H(x, y) = the Interpolating or the Smoothing mathematical values.

Also, the Fourier Analysis can be applied to the above mathematical algorithm for further optimization and refinement of it. It can be mathematically represented as follows:

$$G(Ax) \Downarrow \Diamond |A|^{\wedge}\text{-}1 * G(A^{\wedge}\text{-Tf}).$$

Resources

Deepomatic: Different Applications of Computer Vision; n.d. <deepomatic.com/en/computer-vision/>

Szeliski R: *Computer Vision: Algorithms and Applications*, London: Springer, 2011.

Wikipedia. "Camera Lens." <en.wikipedia.org/wiki/Camera_lens#:~:text=A%20camera%20lens%20(also%20known,an%20image%20chemically%20or%20electronically>

Chapter 5

Conclusion

The primary purpose of this book is to serve the CIO and/or CISO a guide that they can use in their specific decision-making process when it comes to procuring and deploying any sort of Artificial Intelligence System. The main thrust behind any kind of Artificial Intelligence (AI) system is to actually mimic the human brain and to try to replicate its thinking and reasoning processes to real world applications. As such, AI can be used by about just about any industry, but this book is geared toward that of Cybersecurity.

In this regard, AI is still finding its permanent home in this industry. While certainly it holds great promise for a whole host of applications well into the future, its main applications fall into two specific branches of Artificial Intelligence:

- Filtering and triaging through all of the alerts and warnings that the Cybersecurity Team receives. This is for the most part an automated process, but the primary advantage of this is that it can be used to help filter for False Positives that appear so many times day in and day out, thus alleviating the problem that is known as "Alert Fatigue." In this regard, the IT Security Team can then focus on responding quickly to only those alerts and threats that are real and legitimate in nature.
- It can also be used to help automate the processes that are involved in both Threat Hunting and Penetration Testing exercises. The primary benefit here is that the Red, Blue, and Purple Teams can then focus on the big picture for their client, while the more routine and mundane processes can be fully automated.
- Artificial Intelligence can also be used to help model the Cybersecurity Threat Landscape. In this regard, there are tons of data that have to be used if this were to be modeled manually. Not only that, but it would take literally hours if not days for the IT Security team to accurately predict with some kind of

certainty what could happen in the future. With this huge time lag, what has been predicted will thus become outdated very quickly, and more efforts will have to be devoted yet again in order to come up with a reasonable prediction of the Cybersecurity Threat Landscape. During this lost time, more threat variants will be emerging, and because of that, less time will be devoted to actually combatting them, putting the business, their customers, as well as their digital assets at grave risk, especially when it comes to theft and/or hijacking of Personal Identifiable Information (PII) datasets. But by using the concepts and principles of Artificial Intelligence, this modeling can be done on a real-time basis, with far greater accuracy than any human being could accomplish. As a result, the IT Security team can thus focus not only on combatting the daily threat variants on a real-time basis, but they can also come up with new lines of defenses in order to combat those threat variants as well as whatever the future holds in stock in for them. Another key advantage of using Artificial Intelligence in this regard as well is that it can consume an enormous amount of data and information, and analyze it within just a matter of a few seconds, at most.

Chapter 1 covered what the basics of what Artificial Intelligence are all about, and a bulk of that chapter discussed the importance of using data for the ANN system. Remember, one of the key tenets of Artificial Intelligence is that of "Garbage In and Garbage Out," meaning whatever kinds of datasets you feed into the ANN system, that is what will be produced in the end by the ANN system. If the data is of poor quality, then the outputs that are computed will be of poor result. Therefore, it is very important to keep the datasets (both quantitative and qualitative in nature) optimized and up-to-date on a real-time basis, so that not only the ANN system will learn properly and accurately, but that the datasets will be of a very robust nature.

Chapter 2 went into great detail about Machine Learning. The first half of the chapter did a deep dive into most of the theoretical algorithms that are involved with it, and the remainder of this chapter looked at how Machine Learning can be applied to other areas of Cybersecurity as well. Also, examples of where the Python source can be applied were examined, as this is the primary programming language that is used the most in Artificial Intelligence.

Chapter 3 of this book took a parallel path as that of Chapter 2, but instead, it focused on Neural Networks. Once again, the key theoretical algorithms were reviewed, and Python source code programming examples were provided. With the major Cloud providers, especially those of the Amazon Web Services (AWS), Microsoft Azure, and Google, which now offer premium level services, Artificial Intelligence systems are now very affordable to even the smallest of businesses. The primary advantages in this regard are elasticity, scalability, and on demand services. The major features and components that are offered by these Cloud Providers in terms of the usage of Artificial Intelligence were closely examined as well.

Chapter 4 reviewed in extensive detail the concepts of Computer Vision. This is yet another area of Artificial Intelligence that is upcoming in terms of its specific applications for Cybersecurity. The primary goal of Computer Vision is to try to mimic the Visual Cortex of the human brain, and to try to emulate that process into the ANN system, especially when it comes to analyzing both 2-Dimensional Images and 3-Dimensional Images, and even those of videos that can produce datasets on a real-time basis. Given the breadth and scope of Computer Vision, only two specific components were examined, which are as follows:

■ Image Formation;
■ Image Processing.

But with the many advantages that come with using Artificial Intelligence in Cybersecurity, there is also the downside as well, in that it can also be used for nefarious purposes by the Cyberattacker. Thus, in this regard, it will be up to the CIO or the CISO to conduct a benefit-cost analysis, and determine if the benefits outweigh the risks in the procurement and deployment of an Artificial Intelligence system.

Index

Printed in the United States
By Bookmasters